D0593114

WHAT COLLEGE PRESIDENTS SAY

WHAT COLLEGE PRESIDENTS SAY

By

EDGAR W. KNIGHT
KENAN PROFESSOR OF EDUCATION
The University of North Carolina

Chapel Hill

THE UNIVERSITY OF NORTH CAROLINA
PRESS
1940

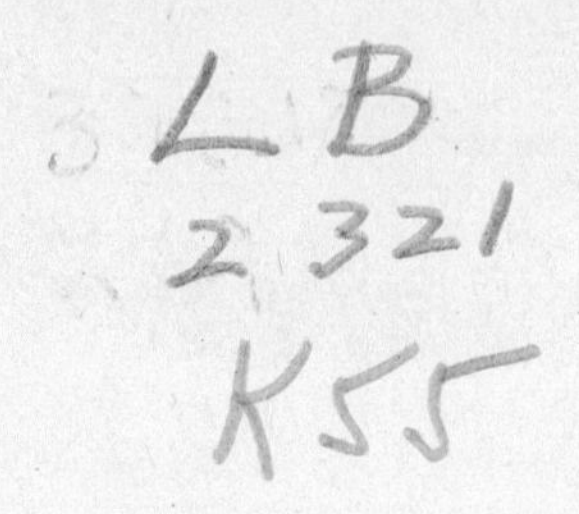

PRINTED IN THE UNITED STATES OF AMERICA
BY EDWARDS & BROUGHTON CO., RALEIGH, N. C.;
BOUND BY L. H. JENKINS, INC., RICHMOND, VA.

PREFACE

EDUCATION is the largest public business of the United States. The value of its property is estimated at ten billion dollars—a sum that ranks second only to that of the national debt. Thirty-two million people, about one-fourth of the population of the United States, are enrolled in more than two hundred seventy-one thousand schools of various types, with about a million teachers. This social enterprise probably costs nearly three billion dollars annually.

Higher education is an important part of this immense social undertaking. In 1895 the United States Bureau of Education reported five hundred and ninety-four institutions of so-called collegiate grade. In 1938 there were more than seventeen hundred, with more than two million students, countless alumni, about twenty thousand members of governing boards, and innumerable presidents, vice-presidents, provosts, deans, assistant deans, and hosts of professors. Capital investments in higher education were valued at about three billions.

These great resources of the higher learning in American democracy have been developed largely during the present generation. All the colleges and universities of the country in 1900 had endowments valued at about 170 million; today the sum is said to be about 1,600 million. A recent study of gifts to forty-nine colleges and universities shows that these institutions received the sum of 780 million dollars between 1920 and 1937.

The presidents are, potentially, the most influential persons connected with these institutions. Their statements on educational and other questions are considered significant, even though it has been said that public interest in the choice of a college or university president today is far less than that exhibited in the choice of a football coach.

Apparently so-called "problems" of higher education for more than two centuries between the founding of Harvard and the Civil War were few and somewhat petty as compared with the problems that have appeared during the past seven or more decades. The purpose of higher education was then mental and cultural discipline and the materials and methods of instruction were largely prescribed and employed to attain that purpose. Higher education was largely moral and religious in management and outlook; presidents and boards of trustees were chiefly clerical.

Presented in the following pages are some statements of presidents of higher educational institutions in the United States, mainly during the past seventy-five years. These statements are taken from the inaugural addresses, reports to trustees, and occasional addresses and articles of these higher educational officers. Also included are statements made by presidents and others at the inaugurations of college and university presidents and on other academic occasions.

The period selected for the study is easy to explain. F. A. P. Barnard became president of Columbia College in 1864 and Charles W. Eliot became president of Harvard in 1869. Both of these men became distinguished leaders in education. Their work, slowly to be added to by other higher educational leaders, clearly marks the beginning of a new period in the history of the higher learning in the United States.

No effort has been made to present quotations on all the subjects college and university presidents have spoken and written on during the period covered by this study. Obviously, such a task would be impossible. For it should be said, even if it seems a hard saying, that, taken by and large, as the record shows, heads of higher education in this country tend to be a trifle loquacious and discursive on many subjects. And, as one of the guild has himself anonymously asserted, there is no relation whatever between the length and the quality of their speeches.

Those subjects on which presidential statements may be classified and which may show some trends during the past seventy-five years include (1) the college presidency, as this office is described by college presidents themselves; (2) the purposes of higher education, as seen by college presidents; (3) the weaknesses of higher education, as seen by these leaders; (4) the views of presidents on the organization and administration of higher education—the college of arts, the curriculum, student relations, finance, religious life, athletics; (5) faculty relations —academic freedom, research, and teaching; (6) obligations to the social order—to the schools below, for the education of women, for the education of Negroes in the Southern States, during the World War, for adult education, and on state and federal relations in education.

Interpretation of these statements has not been attempted; but some interpretation may appear in the classification and organization of the material. The quotations, more than six hundred from more than two hundred presidents of more than one hundred higher educational institutions—eighty-two presidents of forty-four publicly supported and one hundred twenty-six presidents of sixty-two privately endowed colleges and universities—are expected to speak for themselves and to tell their own stories.

Some of the material from which the statements in this study have been drawn was "pedestrian" and fugitive and has been collected from a variety of sources. Most of it is now on file in the Library of the University of North Carolina.

In this material are included a very few statements not made by presidents. But all such statements—whether made by a professor, a journalist, member of a board of trustees, governor of a state, or by an organization—seemed to be pertinent to the subject under discussion and to give emphasis to what the presidents themselves said.

The study has been made under the auspices of the Carnegie Foundation for the Advancement of Teaching, with funds allocated for the purpose by Carnegie Corporation of New York.

In addition to the officers and staff members of the Foundation and Corporation, I am indebted to Dr. H. P. Smith for assistance in locating, abstracting, and classifying the quotations, to Dr. Fred K. Elder for assistance in checking and verifying the references, and to Mrs. Mabel Thompson Hill for assistance in preparing the material for the printer.

EDGAR W. KNIGHT

Chapel Hill
August, 1939

ACKNOWLEDGMENTS

GRATEFUL acknowledgment is made for permission from the following persons, periodicals, and publishing houses to use material controlled by them:

Amherst Graduates' Quarterly; American Academy of Political and Social Science (*The Annals*, XXII); American Council on Education (*The Educational Record*); American Association of University Professors (*Bulletin*); American Association for Adult Education (*Adult Education in Action*, ed., Mary L. Ely; *Journal of Adult Education*); American Association of Collegiate Registrars (*Bulletin*); Association of American Universities (*Journal of Proceedings and Addresses*); Antioch Press (*Educating for Democracy*); Association of American Colleges (*Bulletin; The Effective College*, ed., R. L. Kelly); Association of American Universities (*Proceedings*); Bureau of Publications, Teachers College, Columbia University (Snow, *The College Curriculum in the United States;* Tewksbury, *The Founding of American Colleges and Universities Before 1860*); Coker College (*The Coker College Bulletin*); Frank Aydelotte and James B. Conant (*The Mission of Endowed Universities*); Columbia University Press (*The Rise of a University*, Vol. I, ed., W. F. Russell; Vol. II, ed., E. C. Elliott; Schmidt, *The Old Time College President*); Cornell University (*Proceedings of the Inauguration of Edmund Ezra Day*); Council of Church Boards of Education (*Christian Education*); Duke University Press (Garber, *John Carlisle Kilgo*); *The Educational Forum; Harper's Monthly Magazine; Hearst's International Cosmopolitan; Harvard Alumni Bulletin;* Houghton Mifflin Company (Cubberley, *Readings in Public Education in the United States*); *Journal of Education; Journal of Higher Education;* Lafayette College (*Proceedings of the Second Annual Conference of Trustees of Colleges and Universities*); Louisiana State University Press (Fleming, *Louisiana State University;* Wilkerson, *Thomas Duckett Boyd*); John Henry MacCracken (*College and Commonwealth*); McGraw-Hill Book Company, Inc. (Brubacher, *Henry Barnard on Education*); McGill University (*Installation Proceedings*); Samuel E. Morison (*The Development of Harvard University*); Joy Elmer Morgan (*Horace Mann*); National Association of State Universities (*Transactions and Proceedings*); New York University Press (*The Obligation of Universities to the Social Order*); *North American Review; The Nation;* The National Catholic Educational Association; *The Nation's Schools;* The National Education Association of the United States (*Proceedings*); The National Collegiate Athletic Association (*Proceedings*); *The New York Times; The New York Times Magazine; The American Mercury;* The University of North Carolina Press (Virginius Dabney, *Liberalism in the South;* Charles W. Dabney, *Universal Education in the South*); George Norlin; Robert M. Hutchins; Allison Danzig; University of Oklahoma Press (*Higher Education and Society*); Oxford University Press (Aydelotte, *The Oxford Stamp and Other Essays*); *Popular Science Monthly;* Princeton University Press; W. Carson Ryan (*The Literature of American School and College Athletics*); Howard J. Savage (*American College Athletics*); *The Saturday Evening Post; School and Society; School Review;* Charles Scribner's Sons (J. H. Denison, *Mark Hopkins;* Nicholas Murray Butler, *Scholarship and Service*); Southern Association of Colleges and Secondary Schools (*Proceedings*); Stanford University Press (Wilbur, *Stanford Horizons*); Syracuse University (*Bulletin*); University of Arkansas (*Bulletin*); University of Arizona (*Inaugural Bulletin*); The Johns Hopkins University Press (Isaiah Bowman, *A Design for Scholarship*); Henry M. Wriston (*The Nature of a Liberal College*); Charles E. Beury; Vanderbilt University Press (*The Inauguration of Oliver C. Carmichael*); Ernest H. Wilkins; The Wake Forest College Press (William Louis Poteat, *Youth and Culture*); *The Wake Forest Student; Wesleyan University Bulletin;* C. A. Dykstra; Yale University Press (James R. Angell, *American Educa-*

tion; Robert M. Hutchins, *The Higher Learning in America*); *South Atlantic Quarterly; University of California Chronicle;* Walter A. Jessup (*Thirty-second Annual Report,* The Carnegie Foundation for the Advancement of Teaching); University of Chicago Press (E. D. Burton, *Education in a Democratic World;* William Rainey Harper, *The Trend in Higher Education;* Robert M. Hutchins, *No Friendly Voice;* Robert M. Montgomery, ed., *The William Rainey Harper Memorial Conference*).

CONTENTS

WHAT COLLEGE PRESIDENTS SAY

1

THE COLLEGE PRESIDENCY

The following statements show what some college presidents themselves have said about the college presidency and college presidents. The earliest of these statements is from President Francis Wayland, of Brown University, in 1842. Two of the most interesting statements are anonymous. One appeared in *The Atlantic Monthly* in April, 1900, on the trials and tribulations of a college president. Dr. Bliss Perry, who was then editor of that magazine, wrote November 9, 1938: "My recollection is that it was written by the president of Trinity College, Hartford, Connecticut, . . . whose name I cannot now recall." Frank P. Graves, Commissioner of Education of the State of New York, said in March, 1939, that the article was written by President James H. Canfield, of Ohio State University. The other anonymous statement appeared in *Harper's Monthly Magazine*, January, 1938, but the identity of the author has been revealed. The statement by President William Rainey Harper, of the University of Chicago, was written in 1904, was read by his son, Samuel N. Harper, at the Centennial of Muskingum College in 1938, and was published for the first time that year.

The second part of this section deals with inaugural addresses of college presidents. Although such addresses vary considerably in length and in subject matter, at least two characteristics appear in most of these presidential pronouncements. It is but natural perhaps for new presidents to refer with great respect and affection to their predecessors and to the founders of the institutions. Many of them also tend to point out the need for larger financial support.

College Presidents and the Presidency

"But it may be asked, have not our colleges on the whole, done well for the country, and are they not deserving of the public patronage. I answer most sincerely in the affirmative. They are in the main well officered; and the incumbents are generally able and industrious men."—President Francis Wayland, Brown University, 1842. *Thoughts on the Present Collegiate System in the United States* (Boston: Gould, Kendall and Lincoln, 1842), p. 73.

"The President of the University is primarily an executive officer; but, being a member of both governing boards and of all the faculties, he has also the influence in their debates to which his more or less perfect intimacy with the University and greater or less personal weight may happen to entitle him. An administrative officer who undertakes to do everything himself will do but little, and that little ill."—President Charles W. Eliot, Harvard University, 1869. Inaugural Address, in S. E. Morison, *The Development of Harvard University* (Cambridge: Harvard University Press, 1930), p. lxxvi.

"The Presidents of our American Colleges have from the beginning been men of noble mark, the very elect in their callings, leaders in the Church, not seldom leaders in both Church and State. No other class of men have done more than they to build up our American civilization. . . . Yes, American College Presidents have moulded the life of the State, quite as much as that of the Church. If they have not always been profound scholars, they have been men, whose *characters* educated those under them, . . ."—Dean James O. Murray, Princeton University, 1888. *The Inauguration of President Patton*, Princeton, N. J., June 20, 1888.

"Alumni, don't talk to the man at the wheel! Let him steer. But say 'God speed the ship'; and bear a hand; and give a cheer for Patton the new pilot of Princeton."—Reverend Henry Van Dyke, address at the inauguration of President F. L. Patton, Princeton University, 1888. *The Inauguration of President Patton*, Princeton, N. J., June 20, 1888.

"The old Concord stage stood before the door of the country tavern, surrounded by more than the usual crowd of village idlers. A new driver was to take the box that morning, and there was no little interest in the man and in the occasion. Several stockholders in the line and one or two of the directors were present. . . . The six horses were hooked up—a motley team. One had served its full time for one of the directors, and had been turned in on the company's assets because the director did not quite like to turn it out upon the public, but had no thought himself of making provision for the poor animal's latter days. . . . Another was a freakish thoroughbred, which had come into the possession of the company quite by chance, and had remained there because no man had made an offer for it. By its side was a heavy, slow, honest gelding, which by rights ought to have been before the plough and in the furrow. . . . This was the team that the new driver was supposed so to direct and control and encourage and stimulate as to secure intelligent industry, conscientious coöperation, faithful service, and constantly accelerating speed.

"The load was almost as motley as the team. There was a large amount of dead weight about the coach itself, the pattern of which was sufficiently antique. . . . It was now a queer combination of a past generation and of the present day—the former predominating. . . .

"Meanwhile, all was confusion at the ticket office, or booking office. Instead of a single agent or ticket seller, several representatives of the line were present. Each seemed to be familiar with a portion of the route only, and to be especially favorable to his particular portion. . . . To add to the perplexity of the passengers, every now and then some 'prominent citizen' would throw in just a word of advice: . . .

"The morning run was to be something of an experiment. The news of rapid transit in other portions of the state had penetrated the dense conservatism of this community, and there had come a demand for a betterment of the old stage service. . . . But there was an unintelligent and inefficient restlessness, which was demanding something new, while providing for little or nothing new, and while objecting to the changes which alone could make anything new possible. . . . Some concessions had been secured already: the coach had a new canvas top fastened with some brass-headed nails which glittered in the sunlight, the body and running gear had been repainted a bright red, and several other minor changes had been made—always with a view to catching the public eye with the least possible expenditure of money. . . . One of the directors favored offering extra inducements to children; asserting that two children could be wedged into the seat of one adult, and that the annual report to the stockholders could thus be made to show a large increase of the total number of passengers carried—ages not being mentioned in the reports; but this plan had not yet been adopted.

"The new driver came out of the tavern into the midst of all the outside confusion, and mounted the box. . . . The passengers eyed the driver suspiciously, and one of the older directors began discoursing in a loud tone about how he used to drive, so many years ago—taking care not to intimate the fact that his experience had been entirely limited to a milk wagon on a short route.

"The new driver looked anxious and troubled, as well he might; but he gathered up the reins, felt of his team through the bits, and as the town clock struck nine he gave the word." —"One of the Guild." An anonymous article, by a college president, in *The Atlantic Monthly*, April, 1900.

"How shall this heterogeneous company become an organic unity where the eye cannot say to the hand, I have not need of thee, nor the head to the feet, I have no need of thee? Can it be accomplished most effectually by giving the president autocratic power? This has been affirmed recently in an entertaining article in *The Atlantic Monthly*, by 'One of the Guild,' who maintains that the president of a college should have the same authority that the president of a commercial corporation has over his subordinates. The general policy of the institution, the requirements for admission and degrees, the discipline of students—all should be determined by him, subject only to the trustees. The remedy, in short, for the chief defects in the administration of our colleges is presidential autocracy.

"Nor are illustrations wanting of the practical application of this remedy. 'We have no faculty meetings now,' said a professor in one of our large colleges of recent origin. 'We had them at first, but there was so much quarreling, and so little progress made, that the president decided to have none, and he manages the college now as he thinks best, or through the committees which he appoints. On the whole, it is a relief, and there is less friction between departments.' Said a professor in another college: 'Our president is a good deal of a tyrant, but he succeeds in getting funds and in keeping the college well to the front, so that we are disposed to let him have his own way.'

"Autocracy, however, is a hazardous expedient, and is likely to prove ultimately as pernicious in a college as it is in a state. It induces too great reliance upon the distinctive characteristics of a despot, and too little upon those of a gentleman. Infallibility and omniscience are not the prerogatives of college presidents, and the conceit of them should not appear as their foible. Like men generally, they need to learn the strength or the weakness of their measures in the light of other minds, and to get the broader outlook which comes when a subject is seen from various standpoints.

"Granted that a man of superior intellectual and moral power might effect some desirable changes more speedily than if he were compelled to wait for the tardy approval of those more sluggish and less intelligent, still it may be doubted whether, for the permanent life of the institution, the autocratic spirit will be the most quickening and fruitful. A college is not a mechanism directed by a master workman. Its aim is not the accumulation of wealth, but the development of character and intelligence. This must be accomplished by the exposition rather than by the imposition of opinion, by persuasion rather than by coercion. The most progressive president can afford to tolerate the sometimes tedious discussions of faculty meetings in order to secure that unanimity of thought and sentiment which will make his associate teachers more efficient co-adjutators in the prosecution of his plans. One man power is apt to enfeeble or to alienate those who are subject to it. In educational procedure it is better to lead than to drive. A heavier load can be moved and greater speed made, when all pull together. Successful autocrats are few, and however long their term of service, it is short compared with the life of an institution."—President L. Clark Seelye, Smith College, 1900. Address at the inauguration of President Rush Rhees, Rochester University, 1900, *Educational Review*, December, 1900.

"The college president has enjoyed a rapid evolution in the course of a single generation. Thirty or forty years ago he was a clergyman, as a matter of course; later he was likely to be selected for business qualifications; now he is a member of the faculty who unites executive ability with high scholarship. We seem to have made a further advance at Columbia by the election of a president who is at the outset an educational expert. He alone does not begin as an amateur and can devote himself to his work while cultivating his scholarship. But the demands now made on the university president are so diverse and exorbitant that even when he gives up both teaching and research they can scarcely be met. He can not be *in loco parentis* for 5,000 students; select and control 400 officers; coördinate the conflicting demands of incommensurable schools and departments; arrange diverse curricula in accordance with changing needs; superintend buildings and grounds; manage an estate of $10,000,000 and secure the additional funds always needed; be a public orator and monthly contributor to magazines; attend bicentennials, sesquicentennials and semi-sesquicentennials; occupy positions of honor and trust whenever called upon by the community or nation, and all the rest. It has become necessary to delegate part of these duties to deans and other officers, and it seems probable that the office of president should be divided and filled by two men of different type: one an educational expert, in charge of the internal administration; the other a man of prominence and weight in the community, in charge of external affairs."—J. McKeen Cattell, Columbia University, 1902. "Concerning the American University," Phi Beta Kappa Address at the Johns Hopkins University, May 2, 1902, *Popular Science Monthly*, June, 1902, p. 180.

"A superficial observer will find much to substantiate the very common accusation that the college president is professionally a prevaricator. Do not members of a college faculty distinctly recall many occasions when the president has promised promotion, or increase of salary, or a special appropriation for books and equipment; promises that he has forgotten as soon as the door was closed upon the interview? Is it not true that on many occasions, students, summoned to the president's office to meet charges made against them, have left the office wholly satisfied that these charges had been shown false and firmly convinced that the president was on their side, only to find next day that the verdict declared them guilty rather than innocent?

"How often, too, it has happened that the president in talking with one person, or group of persons, has seemed to entertain a given opinion, whereas in conversation with another person, or group, strangely enough a different opinion on the same subject was expressed. It is reported that the president of a New England college not long since gave up his position because his statements on the same subject to different people varied so radically; in other words, because the truth as he represented it was so multiform. To be entirely just to New England, it must be added, reports of this tenor are not restricted to that section of the country.

"The president of a college or university who succeeds at times in concealing his real thought concerning this man or that subject is politely called a diplomat. Is it diplomacy, or is it lying? Or may a more euphemistic phrase be found to describe the policy which must characterize his dealing with all classes of men, if he is to remain a college president?

"A closer study of the case and the examination of specific instances will furnish evidence that the professor who thought he had been promised promotion or an increase of salary made petition to this effect, was received courteously, and mistook courteous treatment for a business pledge. The student, it will be found, forgot that the president was his judge. A judge is silent until sentence is to be pronounced. The student mistook that silence for acquiescence in his own statement. It is easy enough to imagine that the person to whom one talks has in his mind the thought of the speaker. The next step is easier still, actually to believe that the listener has approved the words of the speaker, or perhaps that he has spoken them.

"Possible, it is, to be sure, that the president in expressing his desire that such and such a thing should be, sometimes makes a statement that is open to stronger interpretation than he intended. It would be strange if he did not occasionally consent to a proposition which, upon later consideration, might appear to be impracticable; or which, however urgently he might present it to the powers that be, would fail to secure their approval. Does he likewise sometimes forget? Unquestionably, for he is human. Does he sometimes really undertake to do the impossible? Surely, and he discovers this fact to his cost. In all these cases, from the point of view of the other man, he is, in the language of the street, a liar. And yet, I dare say, he still supposes himself worthy of the confidence of his fellow-creatures.

"The college presidency is a profession in which a large percentage of one's time and energy is occupied in saying 'no.' Real risk is taken when, for the sake of variation, even in a small proportion of these cases a kindly interest is shown. To be brutal may not be so good a policy at the time, but in the long run it probably pays. One of the most distinguished university presidents now living was noted during a large portion of his career for his extreme brutality. It is altogether probable that the high success which he has achieved is due in no small measure to this fact. He is said to have become greatly softened in his later years. One can afford to practice a policy in later years which would spell ruin in the early career. . . .

"The office of the college president is an office of service. Everything good or bad which connects itself with service is associated with this office. True service everywhere involves suffering for others. In no other profession, not even in that of the minister of the Gospel, is vicarious suffering more common. But one cannot be suffering for another unless one suffer also with that other. A fundamental characteristic of the president must be a sympathetic nature. He is doomed to failure unless he is able to place himself in the position of others with whom and for whom he has been called to work. In the truest sense the position is a representative one. He does many things, not of his own choice, but because he represents his colleagues. He may not do this or that thing according to his own pleasure or his own sense of what is proper. The decision to do or not to do must rest largely upon the possible effect, helpful or harmful, to the institution of which he is head. In short, he is the slave of his environment and must submit to the drudgery as well as the misery of that slavery. . . .

"While it happens that the words as well as the actions of the president are misunderstood by those about him, even by those of his colleagues who stand nearest to him, he is indeed fortunate if a worse thing does not come—the wilful effort to misrepresent him. He cannot exercise the functions of his office honestly without disturbing at times some even of those whom he believes to be his friends. And when this happens, these friends, perhaps unconsciously, will cease to find back of his actions the motives which he himself entertains. It is sometimes pitiful to see how easily men will misunderstand each other and how complacently the misrepresentations of another's thought are spread from mouth to mouth. The reader will say that such things do not happen. Let me assure him that experience demonstrates not only the possibility but the frequency of their occurrence. Three cases of persecution through misrepresentation, which was actually malicious, have occurred within a year. The names of these institutions are well known. . . .

"How does the president of a university spend his time? Largely in seeking ways and means to enable this or that professor to carry out some plan which he has deeply at heart—a plan, if may be, for research and investigation, or for improving the work of instruction. If it is not service for an officer of instruction, it is service for this or that student whose needs, to him at all events, seem very great. If one is selfish, he grows weary of it all; but, if in his heart there is an earnest desire to do for humanity the several services which in his position it is possible for him to render, he learns sooner or later that to no man in any position is there given greater opportunity for service. In a few cases those with whom one comes into contact appreciate keenly and cordially the unselfish service which has been rendered. . . .

"The college president deserves the support of the intelligent man of modern times. His position is a trying one; his burden is heavy, and the reward is, at the best, meager. His effort is always intended to serve the interests that make for truth and the higher life. He is not usually a 'liar' or a 'boss.' He may sometimes seem to be too self-satisfied; one could name a few such. But for the most part he does his work, conscious that he has the shortcomings which mark his kind, realizing keenly that his tenure of office, unlike that of his colleagues, is quite uncertain, yet fully resolved to perform his duty without fear or favor and to allow time to determine the question of his success or failure."—President William Rainey Harper, The University of Chicago, 1904. "The College President," *The William Rainey Harper Memorial Conference* (Chicago: The University of Chicago Press, 1938), pp. 25, 26, 27, 29, 33, 34. This paper, written in 1904, was read by President Harper's son, Samuel N. Harper, at the Centennial of Muskingum College in 1938; published for the first time in the volume above.

"To labor constantly for the world with no thought of self, to find indifference and opposition where you ought to have active assistance, to meet criticism with patience and the open attacks of ignorance without resentment, to plead with others for their own good, to follow sleepless nights with days of incessant toil, to strive continuously without ever attaining—this it is to be a college president. But this is only half the truth. To be associated with ambitious youth and highminded men, to live in an atmosphere charged with thoughts of the world's greatest thinkers, to dream of a golden age not in the past but in the future, to have the exalted privilege of striving to make that dream a reality, to build up great kingdoms of material conquest and make daily life richer and fuller, to spiritualize wealth and convert it into weal, to enrich personal character and elevate all human relationships, to leave the impress of one's life on a great and immortal institution—this, too, it is to be a college president."—Chancellor James H. Kirkland, Vanderbilt University, 1906. "What It Is to Be A College President," address at the inauguration of President D. F. Houston, The University of Texas, 1906, *Educational Review*, April, 1911.

"One test of efficiency the trustees apply to the president; for one purpose is he really selected and coached: he must develop proper skill and tact in securing large legacies, gifts, or legislative appropriations. . . . The fatal defect in the professiorial position is rather thc degrading tenure on which he holds his place. More helpless than the humblest clerk in a department store, infinitely more so than a veteran female assistant in a Brooklyn primary school, he remains by the sufferance, or departs on the practically irreversible decision, of a single despot. . . . In no other calling is a man's life thus in the hands of one other man or woman. Least of all is it fit or needful in the world of pure scholarship, of liberal education."—President William C. Lawton, Adelphi College, 1906. "The Decay of Academic Freedom," *Educational Review*, November, 1906, pp. 399, 400.

"Much has been written and spoken about the 'autocracy' of the present regime, of the 'dangers inherent in the further development of the presidential office in its present temper,' of present conditions as 'tending to undermine the stability of the academic career,' as taking from such career its 'proper dignity, honor, and station'; and some have deprecated 'glorifying the presidency' rather than duly considering 'the menace and evils of this office' . . . and so forth, ad libitum and ad nauseam. . . . As a rule the presidents of those American colleges and universities which with any accuracy can be called representative are well-equipped, well-chosen gentlemen; serving faithfully, intelligently, modestly, and successfully the institutions over which they preside."—J. H. Canfield (Chancellor University of Nebraska 1891-1895, President Ohio State University 1895-1899), Columbia University, 1907. "On 'The Decay of Academic Courage' and Such Like," *Educational Review*, January, 1907, pp. 3, 10.

"President Futrall will probably come to subscribe to the famous dictum of Dr. Jowett, many years Master of Balliol College, Oxford: 'Never retract, Never explain, Get the thing done, Let them howl.' But he will learn also with Jowett not to make the same mistake twice. He will make some small mistakes; the most that the best of administrators can do is to avoid making large ones. He will be all things to all men. He will take counsel of all men and then work out his own counsel in the quiet of his study. He will lead a life of isolation and yet live his life of action wholly in the open. He will find himself a combination of information and trouble clerk. These are some of the demands, these are some of the difficulties. But the compensations far outweigh them. 'Tis a joyous life of service he enters upon, as middle man between the people and their university, between the university and trustees, between trustees and staff, between staff and students, between students and their parents and guardians. He becomes today the senior member of 'a partnership in all science, a partnership in all art, a partnership in every virtue and in all perfection,' and 'as the ends of such a partnership can not be attained in many generations,' to appropriate still further Burke's conception of the state, this partnership is a 'partnership between those who are living, those who are dead, and those who are yet to be born.' "—President O. E. Lovett, Rice Institute, 1914. *University of Arkansas Bulletin*, Inaugural Number, February, 1915, p. 49.

"And we who have been called on to turn a screw here, or adjust a bearing there, have little to do that really matters. Charge the president! He is already charged and surcharged with routine of ten long successful years. It is left for us to oil the machine, to advance or retard the spark, or perhaps to pump a little more air into the shock absorbers. . . .

"Some of you, no doubt, think that I have my metaphors mixed, that it is the president's job to keep the tank filled and crank the car, and when he has the engine running to jump into the rumble and fold his arms and watch which way the trustees and faculty in the front seat go. Or, perhaps, if it is a larger touring car and there are seats for four, the alumni and football coach may have a share in its operation. . . .

"First then, Mr. President, I charge you, lead Alma, or to stick to our motor metaphor, steer Alma. The responsibility for steering implies of course responsibility for steerage way. Whether the wind will fill your sails, if there is any wind, will depend upon the way you hold your helm. How many miles you will get from a gallon will depend on your manipulation of your throttle, and on your judicious admixture of the proper proportion of air and gas.

"Of course, if there is no wind stirring at all, it is idle for you to stay at the tiller, you may as well go out and raise the wind; if there is no gasoline in your tank, you cannot steer by sitting at the wheel, you must either get out and fill the tank or get some one to fill it for you. That is incidental to leadership of any kind."—President J. H. MacCracken, Lafayette College, 1916. Address at the inauguration of President H. M. Crooks, Alma College, *College and Commonwealth* (New York: The Century Company, 1920), pp. 266, 267, 268.

"The speaker [President Livingston Farrand, Cornell University] then diverted in his most humorous vein to a discussion of a suggestion that was made to him that the heads of the colleges in the state form a society in which, behind closed doors, they could talk over all difficulties and all problems confronting the universities. He said there they could give vent to their feelings in stronger words than would be wise or diplomatic in public. He did not appear to be particularly impressed with the idea.

" 'Different colleges have different problems,' he said, 'and it is wise for the university and the community in which it exists to work out its own problem.' "—President Livingston Farrand, Cornell University, 1922. *Inauguration of Charles Wesley Flint as Chancellor of Syracuse University* (pamphlet made from newspaper clippings, 1922), p. 24.

"The relations which the American college president holds are more numerous, diverse, and complex than those of any other educational officer. . . . A college presidency is not a profession."—President Charles F. Thwing, Western Reserve University (1890-1921), 1925. *The College President* (New York: The Macmillan Company, 1926), pp. 10, 234.

"When a captain takes charge of a ship he assumes vast responsibilities. Unto him much is given, and of him shall much be required. He must know maritime law so that he will respect the rights of other ships upon the seas, and as far as in him lies render aid to those in need. He must understand marine insurance and the laws of clearance for every port which he shall touch. He must be able to handle the ship, manage the ship's family, and apply the rules governing the operation of the crew. He must know where he is going, and what course to follow to reach his port of destination. He should make sure that his gyroscopic compass has not become magnetized by the iron of the vessel, lest its tutored needle cause a deflection of the ship and bring it to ruin upon the rocks. . . . I have been asked to captain the good ship Boston University over educational seas. . . . Our port of destination is Unselfish Service-for-the-Sake-of-Others."—President Daniel L. Marsh, Boston University, 1926. *Bostonia*, July, 1926.

"We are entering into a period of the most searching criticism of education, and particularly of higher education, which we have had in this country from its beginning. For one to assume the presidency of a tax-supported institution at this period is a somewhat different responsibility than it was formerly. The university today must face a slump in public confidence, a slump due to criticisms not from enemies of education but from the friends of education, who in many cases are saying, 'I want to have my faith in education renewed, but as I look about me I find it difficult to defend it on the basis of its present product.' "—President F. J. Kelly, The University of Idaho, 1928. *School and Society*, November 24, 1928.

"Not far from one hundred college presidents go out of office each year, and an equal number come in. The average length of the term is about five years. Of course there are long terms, . . . But these lengths are the exceptions. The days and the years of a college president may or may not be full of trouble, but at any rate they are few. . . .

"College presidents have come, and still continue to come, from no less than four large groups. Historically, the office is recruited largely from the ministry. Such an origin is natural. For the first American colleges were founded as theological training schools. . . .

"A second source of supply, and one more popular than the ministry, is the professorship. In fact, about one third of all the presidencies are drafted from the teaching staff. . . .

"A third source of supply is found in the deanship. This source of supply is less affluent than the two already named, the ministry and the professoriate. For the deanship in the American college is a new office, borrowed from the church. . . .

"But in addition to these chief sources of supply, presidencies, deanships, professorships, the ministry, there are several other sources which, though making small offerings, are to be noted. Among them are editorships, secretaryships, diplomacy, public school superintendencies, general executive work and research laboratories.

"It is . . . uncertain whether college presidents are born or made or are both born and made, or, as the pessimist might add, neither born nor made. . . .

"And yet to say that a college presidency is one of the happiest of all callings would by many be regarded as a deceptive euphemism. For it is to be confessed that too many presidents do find the calling not at all happy. . . . The strains of office are heavy. Its demands are many, rigorous, exhaustive. . . . Conflicts, too, with the board of trustees or regents are not uncommon, especially in the state universities. . . ."—President Emeritus C. F. Thwing, Western Reserve University, 1932. *School and Society*, January 2, 1932, pp. 1 ff.

"There is the classic story of the new college president who expressed to a seasoned veteran the thought that his first year would be the hardest. 'Such was not my experience,' replied the other. 'My third year was the hardest. It was in that year that the faculty found out that I was a liar.' This story I am inclined to discount. A good executive would not have let the faculty find it out."—President H. W. Dodds, Princeton University, 1936. Address at the inauguration of President W. A. Eddy, Hobart and William Smith Colleges. Typescript copy in the library of the University of North Carolina.

"Judging from these reports [of sixty-five college presidents for 1936], contrary to popular belief, the most striking thing about the American college president is his awareness of this changing modern world, with its enormously complex and difficult problems; its magnificent opportunities; its ever expanding horizons; its staggering challenge to men of intellectual and moral power, men of invincible good will. The presidents are men of conscience, courage, and determination. When orderly processes of law and government are endangered, they speak out, as witness their unanimous opposition to 'teachers' oath bills,' and in specific instance, the courageous championship of the New Jersey courts by the men of Princeton."—Martha T. Boardman, Editorial Assistant, Association of American Colleges, 1936. *Journal of Higher Education*, June, 1936.

"Consider the job of a president of a college or university. As the duties of the position have developed in the United States the post is almost too unrealistic and romantic to be filled by one single specimen of human clay. I once saw a complete job specification drawn by the trustees of a university in search of a president. Talk about dual personalities! The gifts of a financier, business man, scholar, preacher, salesman, diplomat, politician, administrator, Y. M. C. A. secretary, were some of the qualifications enumerated in addition to high moral character and a happy marriage to a charming wife. But various efforts to modify the mutually exclusive demands of the presidential office having failed, the only course is to accept it for what it is, a queer vocation, infested with worries but rich in satisfactions and opportunities."—President H. W. Dodds, Princeton University, 1936. Address at the inauguration of President W. A. Eddy, Hobart and William Smith Colleges, 1936. Typescript copy in the library of the University of North Carolina.

"There are presidents for everything. . . . But 'Prexy' is peculiarly the title of a college administrator. It suggests emotion, often affection. . . . In this day of vigorous vocational advice, the college presidency is one job which has not been analyzed at all. If you want to become a president, there are no courses to take in preparation. . . . You might read a few books. . . . Being a professor or a dean is a help; training as a public speaker is very much worth while. As for the rest—it seems to depend on chance.

"Yesterday almost all college presidents were ministers. . . . Today only those colleges with strong church ties look to the ministry when choosing a president. . . . Presidents do not change from one presidency to another as much as formerly.

. . . If there is no general rule for the previous training of a president, there certainly is none for the method by which he is selected. . . . In times of difficulty for a president his wife often suffers more than he does. . . . Presidential salaries are usually not large. . . . When Texas appointed a football coach at $15,000 a year, . . . there were some citizens who felt it regrettable that this was nearly twice the President's salary. . . . Long presidencies are fairly frequent in the East, but nationally they are decidedly the exception, not the rule. The average length of presidential service on one campus is just under four years. About fifty new presidents are elected annually; last fall there were sixty-three. Usually ten per cent 'fail,' at least in the judgment of the Trustees. A few die in harness; . . . There are those who maintain that no president is a good judge of the time to retire. . . . The American college has many able leaders today. . . . Wilson and Eliot were national figures; Butler is today. . . . Hutchins (Chicago) is probably the most colorful of us all. . . .

"Are there as many able college executives today as in past decades? Probably not. Teaching now attracts many men who previously would have chosen administrative work. The presidency is more complicated and less revered, than it was. In the State University field we have many able leaders today, but they are not, I fear, the equal of those of yesterday. . . ."—President James L. McConaughy, Wesleyan University, 1938. *The Educational Forum*, May, 1938.

"Only very rare individuals will be mature and experienced enough before the age of forty-five to assume such responsibilities. Fewer still will be elastic enough after reaching fifty-five. Ten years would seem to be the ultimate term of constructive usefulness in any one position. With exceptions so rare as to be startling, no university presidents have made any really important contributions after passing a decade in one position. It is not merely a matter of chronological or biological age, though the average age at which men become university presidents is just about fifty, so that most have reached sixty at the end of their first decade. It is much more a matter of weariness of spirit so that struggle becomes distasteful. Without struggle, obviously there is stagnation. . . .

"College and university presidents and boards of trustees could and should unite in formulating an orderly personnel program for exchanging current information as to promising young men coming up in the profession. Until that is done, favoritism in one form or another will dictate the selection of many presidents, and accident will play a disproportionate role. But this does not relieve the aspiring young man of his fundamental obligation even under existing conditions, and that is to refrain from becoming a candidate in the sense that school superintendents and athletic coaches are candidates."—President H. G. James, Ohio University, 1938. "How to be a University President," *American Mercury*, January, 1938.

"It is a mystery to most of us college presidents why the public is so interested in us. To those few of us who are a bit pompous this public concern seems quite logical. But most presidents are relatively simple folk, anxious to do a good job on a college campus; to us the public spotlight is often as irritating as it is surprising.

"Whatever a college president does seems to have some degree of public interest. If he loses his job special news writers are sent to cover it 'adequately.' If he loses his driver's license that gets headlines, too. . . . We are asked to speak on every subject imaginable, before all kinds of audiences; and usually there is no honorarium. . . . A college president's job is a varied one. . . . It is never a monotonous job—and I would not swap it with another. Some of us look like presidents; many do not —and the latter enjoy it more. . . . Most of us are married. . . . A president's success is measured by his ability to deal with his trustees, his faculty, his students, his alumni. Truly he has a host of bosses. . . . Presidents gather and hobnob on various occasions. . . . The informal gatherings in the corridors are, however, more popular than the lecture hall. . . . Most of us speak our minds frankly on public affairs, often even on matters in which we have no competency. . . . The president's freedom of speech often gets him into trouble. . . . There are many pitfalls which may destroy a president's usefulness. . . . Athletic problems, chiefly football, often hamper a president's success. . . . Two tests of presidential effectiveness are: Can he say 'no' graciously without offending? . . . Second, can he wait patiently, quietly, to accomplish his plans, or is he the type who drives ahead ruthlessly over opposition, unwilling to wait and win.

"We presidents are proud of our profession. We are humble about our abilities. We think the public often thinks too much of us and our colleges. We would like you to understand clearly what sort of folk we are. Please do not expect the impossible of us; we cannot educate your sons and daughters unless they have the capacity for self-education within them. . . . We do not want the public to consider us supermen. . . ."—"Prexy," by a college president, 1938. An anonymous article in *Harper's Monthly Magazine*, January, 1938.

"A university president is supposed to go down town and get the money. He is not supposed to have ideas on public affairs; that is what the trustees are for. He is not supposed to have ideas on education; that is what the faculty is for. He is supposed to go down town and get the money."—Milton S. Mayer, 1939. "Hutchins of Chicago," *Harper's Monthly Magazine*, March, 1939.

Inaugural Addresses

General Characteristics

"Not only is this occasion in itself momentous; it is made so for me by the fact that it is the first time I have been inaugurated as a university president, and being less assured of my wisdom than those who have had theirs passed upon by time and academic experts, I approach this test as a freshman does his first examination, having prepared for it by a comprehensive review of the authorities; in this case by a careful reading of the words of the great and near great in some twenty institutions throughout the country as expressed in their inaugural addresses. I found that these might be divided into three general classes:

"1. The encyclopedic type, setting forth in verbose detail the community's resources, the facilities of the institution, its past accomplishments, and achievements, no less certain, of the future.

"2. The technical type, explaining in scholarly and sometimes masterly fashion how to teach, the content of a liberal education, the quality of the academic life, or some equally important and stimulating subject.

"3. The omniscient type, settling all the problems of all the people of all time. . . ."—President Robert G. Sproul, The University of California, 1930. "The Educational System of California," *School and Society*, November 8, 1930.

"What does an inauguration mean? Like all the rich old words which have come down to us overlaid with the patina of man's varying experiences and adaptations, inauguration has taken to itself various meanings. . . . The College of Augurs, the highest class of official diviners in ancient Rome, ranked next after the Pontifical College. Its sole duty was the interpretation of signs and portents. For good or ill, life has ceased to be as simple as that, although at times it must have been restful to trust one's destiny to the chance flight of birds.

"I have found no record, for the College of Augurs apparently managed without minutes or executive secretaries, when and where the inaugural address first became a part of the inaugural ceremonies. A spokesman must be found, since it was impractical for several to speak at once. And although he was, and is, no wiser than his fellows, it is for him to interpret the significance of the occasion."—President Stanley King, Amherst College, 1932. *School and Society*, December 3, 1932.

"There is probably no form of self-expression more treacherous than the inaugural address. The inherent promise, the one article which requires no proof, is that nothing which the speaker says has yet been measured in practice. . . . Valedictories are far more seemly and certainly more instructive. . . ." —President Dixon Ryan Fox, Union College, 1934. *School and Society*, October 20, 1934.

"You may remember that Lord Acton once, in talking to a young Cambridge don, said, 'If ever you make the mistake of entering upon a discussion of an educational problem, remember also to begin with a platitude, because then the clever people in your audience will go to sleep and you will have no criticism from them, and all the stupid people will say, "This is a sound man," and you will have their support.' "—President Charles Seymour, Yale University, 1937. *Journal of Proceedings and Addresses of the Association of American Universities* (Chicago: The University of Chicago Press, 1937), p. 98.

"In the whole library of academic documents, none is more dangerous than the inaugural address. Conceivably it can revive old conflicts, once settled happily. By omission or by overemphasis it can offer affront to sensibilities that, in academic circles, are always acute. It can confound well-established policy, and oftentimes will commit the institution to something which, because of misguided enthusiasm, temporarily seems attractive. Innocently, it can sow the seeds of future embarrassment. . . ."—President Levering Tyson, Muhlenberg College, 1937. *School and Society*, October 23, 1937.

"There has never been an inauguration and there has never been any ceremony of any kind. A man was elected President by the Board of Trustees and moved in the house assigned him and went to work. The ideals seemed to be, judging by the action of the Presidents, to choose good professors and to have the subjects taught as well as possible. . . . There was no course in Education and so we were not learned in the language of the modern educationists. . . . However, our graduates made a name for themselves and reflected credit upon the institution. . . ."—President R. E. Blackwell, Randolph-Macon College,

1938. Letter from President Blackwell to Dr. H. P. Smith, March 8, 1938.

"We meet at one another's inaugurations too. These are often occasions of academic glamour as we march in our many-colored gowns and hoods. The speeches vary little; presidents are usually more interested in the length of the inaugural address than in its contents. . . . Sometimes we pay academic debts by conferring honorary degrees on one another; the president most recently chosen may get his first honorary hood at the first inauguration he attends as his college's president delegate. Friendly rivalry exists among us thus to honor one another. . . ."—"Prexy," by a college president, 1938. An anonymous article in *Harper's Monthly Magazine*, January ,1938.

"Faith of Our Fathers"

"They have labored, and we have entered into their labors. And though we may not rest in their labors; though for us as for them our work must be in the actual present, our hope in the future, and our confidence and our reward in God, yet we may justly look to the achievements of the past as a witness of what the College has done for the community; as an inspiration to present effort; and as a promise of continued prosperity. . . ."—President W. D. Hyde, Bowdoin College, 1886. Inaugural Address, *Addresses at the Inauguration of President Hyde*, Bowdoin College, June 23, 1886.

"*President Dickinson* was the first; in office less than a year, dying untimely in the ripeness of his learning, of great practical wisdom, with every gift to guide successfully the fortunes of the young institution. Succeeded by *President Burr*, who brought to his official work, high powers of organizing and administration. . . . Then came the greatest of names among American theologians, *Jonathan Edwards*, who by his untimely death, just after induction to office, has left here only the legacy of his illustrious name. After him *Samuel Davies*, that foremost of American preachers . . . in office only two short years, but wielding a noble and powerful influence in behalf of the College abroad and at home, building his own character into it even in that short time. Next *Samuel Finley*, the man of various learning, an eminent divine, . . . *John Witherspoon*, whose services as an American patriot and signer of the Declaration of Independence only bring into more conspicuity, his distinguished administration of the college presidency. . . . *Samuel Stanhope Smith*, the man of elegant culture, infusing into the college life its refining power. . . . *Ashbel Green*, that born leader in the American Presbyterian Church, the intimate friend of the saintly Bishop White. . . . *James Carnahan*, sagacious, laborious, in executive work, less of the scholar than most of his predecessors, but wise enough to bring into the Faculty such men as Joseph Henry, Stephen Alexander, Albert Dodd, John Torrey, Joseph Addison, and James W. Alexander *par nobile fratrum. John Maclean*, whose name as I speak it calls up that venerated form so lately vanished from his native town, whose life is one long record of devotion to the college, whose courage and faith stood true in the dark hours of its history, the courtly, benign, beloved, thrice-beloved of teachers and Presidents. Lastly, and how nobly crowning the succession, *James McCosh*, who would have been famous in philosophy, had he not been president, but whose twenty years in Princeton constitute the most distinguished era in its history.

"And to-day we add another, the twelfth of these apostles of learning and religion, President Patton."—Dean James O. Murray, Princeton University, 1888. *The Inauguration of President Patton*. Princeton, N. J., June 20, 1888.

"And in days quiet and troubled alike Princeton has stood for the nation's service, to produce men and patriots. Her national tradition began with John Witherspoon, the master, and James Madison, the pupil, and has not been broken until this day."—President Woodrow Wilson, Princeton University, 1896. Inaugural Address, *The Forum*, December, 1896.

"The success that has been met with is the surest testimony to the wisdom of its founders and projectors. Grateful we are to the kind friends of the North who put the University here; grateful, too, that this trust was committed to one so wise, so prudent, so far-seeing as the first President of the Board. The impress of his grand character will long rest on all the University organization, and his memory will remain fresh in the hearts of all the officers whose privilege it was to be associated with him. After a work so gloriously done, under the shade of magnolias that his own hand planted, he sleepeth well. To my predecessor, too, in the office of Chancellor, is due no small part of the credit for the wise organization and equipment of this institution. His presence on this occasion forbids that I should speak as I would like to do of his services."—Chancellor James H. Kirkland, Vanderbilt University, 1893. Inaugural Address. Typescript copy in the library of the University of North Carolina.

"The illustrious man who inspired this foundation has eternal honor here. Here he lived, here they laid his mortal body, and here dwells in ceaseless energy his immortal spirit."—President Edwin A. Alderman, The University of Virginia, 1905. Inaugural Address. Typescript copy in the library of the University of North Carolina.

"There is an old Spanish maxim which warns us to beware of entering where there is a great gap to be filled. But he whose withdrawal has made this wide gap has done the work of his hands so wisely that the task of his successor is greatly lightened. Under his guidance the traditions and ideals of the College have been established in right directions. He has led it out of the wilderness and put the song of progress in its mouth. Moreover, I take comfort in the fact that the wisdom and generosity to which I am deeply indebted are still within reach of my perplexity. I hail him today with honor and affection, and felicitate him that his name is written large on the brightest page of Wake Forest history."—President William Louis Poteat,

Wake Forest College, 1905. Inaugural Address, in *Youth and Culture* (Wake Forest: Wake Forest College Press, 1938), p. 12.

"This is not a celebration of an accession to office. It is of an investiture with one of the most sacred of responsibilities this State can put upon a man—the care, under its laws, of its most precious possession. Accepting this investiture, I but widen the horizon of the pledge that I gave ten years ago to the city of New York and its college—a pledge that I can keep without disloyalty to that city and that college which have been all my world and now continue a part of it—and I speak my deepened, strengthened faith in the succeeding, despite all the obvious failures, of the sublime endeavor of a democratic people to rise to nobler, happier life through the education of its children. I carried into my office a few days ago the image of a youth who typifies to me that great host through whom this State has this hope. What I would have for him I would have for his generation. He is the witness of my pledge, the hostage of my faith."—President John H. Finley, The University of the State of New York, 1914. *Proceedings of the Inauguration of John Huston Finley, as President of The University of the State of New York and Commissioner of Education* (Albany: New York State Education Department, Tenth Annual Report), IV, 49.

"The soundness of the principles laid down by President Seelye, the extraordinary degree to which he succeeded in giving form and application to these principles, the brilliant achievement of President Burton in carrying on their development, and the appreciation by the country of the value of the educational opportunities created by these two men—all these might be taken as justifying their successor in conceiving his duty as one of tending a well-running machine and in general of keeping his hands off."—President William Allan Neilson, Smith College, 1918. *The Inauguration of William Allan Neilson as President of Smith College*. Northampton, Massachusetts, 1918.

"We are very proud of this College. It has had a noble record. President Seelye was the directing genius for a generation. He

managed its affairs like a great educator, and he also showed the vision of a great statesman. He would have made a great chancellor of the exchequer of any country in the world. I doubt if there is another educational institution anywhere that continued for thirty-five years without any deficit. And then he was succeeded by a man of fine administrative talent; he was succeeded by Doctor Burton. And these two men have transmitted the College to their successor, who is being inaugurated to-day and who receives a college that makes a more nation-wide appeal, if we may judge from the places from which its students come, than any other college in America."
—Governor Samuel Walker McCall, Massachusetts, 1918. *The Inauguration of William Allan Neilson as President of Smith College.* Northampton, Massachusetts, 1918.

"Such responsibilities can never be lightly assumed: but to succeed in the presidency a man like William DeWitt Hyde, in such critical and uncertain days like these, is made possible only by the generous assurance of support and coöperation from the Governing Boards, from the Faculty, and from the students, alumni, and friends of Bowdoin. I should like here also to thank representatives of other colleges in New England and our guests whose presence with us today shows that we are working out our academic problems together:

> " 'We share our mutual woes,
> Our mutual burdens bear;
> And often for each other flows
> The sympathizing tear.' "

—President K. C. M. Sills, Bowdoin College, 1918. *Addresses at the Inauguration of Kenneth Charles Morton Sills as President of Bowdoin College, June 20, 1918* (Brunswick, Maine, 1918), p. 13.

"But this morning I must speak of those whose burden has but now been laid down. . . . President Frost has brought to thousands of people a Christian education, which, but for him, would have been an impossibility."—President W. J. Hutchins, Berea College, 1920. Inaugural Address. Typescript copy in the library of the University of North Carolina.

"The University of North Carolina, product of the vision and the aspiration of generation after generation of the citizenship of this State, . . . declares anew at this hour her firm purpose to be worthy of it all.

"With reverent gratitude her heart goes out to those who since her second founding have presided over her destiny. Never has an institution been granted wiser guidance, never richer devotion. There is no one of them, her leaders, to whom she does not owe a richer and fuller life; no one who did not leave her greater and stronger than he found her; no one who did not lay deep and broad foundations on which those who came after him might build."—President H. W. Chase, The University of North Carolina, 1920. Inaugural Address, *The State University and the New South.* Chapel Hill, 1920.

"For twenty-two years President Hadley has served the University with untiring devotion. Under his leadership Yale has grown marvelously in material wealth, in intellectual power, and in educational prestige. I make no attempt, Sir, at this time to rehearse the many contributions which you have made to the history of Yale; but on behalf of all her sons I offer you the tribute of warmest gratitude, unqualified admiration, and sincere affection."—President James R. Angell, Yale University, 1921. Inaugural Address, *American Education* (New Haven: Yale University Press, 1937), p. 1.

"It is appropriate at the very beginning of this address for me to acknowledge the solemn and yet inspiring sense I have of standing today in a great succession. Giants have labored here, and their works do follow them. Words of devotion they wrote with long and ill-paid service. . . . Time would fail to mention the men of this college who, through faith, subdued kingdoms of difficulty, wrought righteousness in a land where evil contested every foot of the way, obtained promises (on some of which they collected), waxed mighty in the holy war of Christian education, and put to flight the armies of the opposition. Perhaps the best tribute we can give them is to adopt as our own the noble words:

" 'Faith of our fathers, holy faith,
We will be true to thee till death.' "

—President John L. Seaton, Albion College, 1925. *Albion College Bulletin*, October 15, 1925.

"For the fourth time this university inaugurates a president. Those who have served hitherto in that high office have been master builders. Their work stands like a great cathedral—imposing, forceful, symmetrical, gigantic, but unfinished, waiting for another master builder to take up the plans and make real the entire vision."—President John L. Bates, Board of Trustees, Boston University, 1926. *Bostonia*, July, 1926.

"I believe in education. . . . I believe in William Fairfield Warren. . . . I believe in Boston. This 'darling town' has been peculiarly favored by divine blessing. . . . I believe in Boston University. . . . I believe in that vast company of men who have out of the rich treasures of their hearts, their faith, their love, and by their large gifts from limited resources, and their self-sacrificing labors, carried this institution through the early years of doubt, difficulty, and discouragement. . . . I believe in Bishop Anderson (Applause). . . . I believe in Boston University . . . for the next twenty-five years I would rather be the President of Boston University and live in Brookline than be an archangel and live in Heaven!"—President L. H. Murlin, DePauw University, 1926. Address at the inauguration of President Daniel L. Marsh, Boston University, 1926, *Bostonia*, July, 1926.

"Out of the past, historic with struggles of freedom and democracy, come figures, living and dead, to stand by us in this inaugural hour in the woods where Davie, the founder, in the eighteenth century stood under the poplar and raised the standard of a people's hope. The lives of the presidents reassure us all with their spiritual presence and power: Caldwell, the first president, in whose administration for the first time in America a modern language was given curricular equality with an ancient language and the first observatory was established in an American college, and whose communicated social passion sent Murphey to lay the foundation of the state's public schools, and Morehead to build railways to bind the East and West in bonds of iron; Swain, in whose time the University advanced to a high leadership in the South, and who, in the closing war days and reconstruction, was a conciliatory spirit in an age of hate; Battle, dauntless father of the reopening of the University, deviser of a separate group of graduate courses in the curriculum fifty years ago, and founder of the first university summer school in America, whose gay kindliness will ever pervade this place and whose noble spirit still walks in these woods; Winston, lying stricken in this village today, a casualty of the life militant, champion of religious freedom and educational democracy who synthesized the classical and scientific, the cultural and vocational, in his own varied and brilliant life; Alderman, lately and deeply lamented, who in his last days with something of a premonition of the end returned in filial memories to alma mater, her sons, and her scenes where his eloquence long stirred the creative imagination of the people of a commonwealth and caught the ear of the people of a nation; Venable with his passion for soundness of scholarship and integrity of life, the symbol of the group of scientific scholars whose research and teaching won recognition among the scholars of the world, with us still in modest retirement these later years gathering flowers from his garden for his friends in the village where he once gathered truth from test tubes for all mankind; Graham, major prophet of university extension and interpreter of culture and democracy to the people, his name memorialized in a students' building on the campus whose ideals he helped to mold and whose life he passionately extended all over the state as he identified a democratic state university with the life of the people whose sustaining power has returned a hundred fold since his going; and Chase, under whose leadership came the greatest material expansion and intellectual advance, whose administration gathered up the momentum and values of the past, added high values of his own, and worked a synthesis of many, champion of the freedom of scientific inquiry in testing times, genial, leader and friend, now president of the University of Illinois but always at home in Chapel Hill."—President Frank P. Graham, the University of North Carolina, 1931. Inaugural Address, *The Alumni Review*, December, 1931.

"Inspired by the noble conceptions and the heroic sacrifices of the founders and sustained by the fidelity of their faithful followers, who have served and been served here, we march on with steady step and renewed confidence and hope that the Heavenly Father will continue to guide the destinies of this institution and that He who takes note of the sparrow's fall will watch over us as we make our flight through the illimitable air, lone wanderings, perhaps, but not lost."—President G. G. Singleton, Hardin-Baylor College, 1937. Inaugural Address. Typescript copy in the library of the University of North Carolina.

"On the occasion of the formal opening of this University on the 7th of October 1868—sixty-nine years and one day ago—the first president, Andrew Dickson White, in whom the University was so rarely blessed, delivered a notable address. For a generation the ideas set forth by President White in this opening statement were Cornell's educational magna charta. Even today the ideas bear so significantly upon the structure and policy of the University that I venture to present them once more."—President Edmund E. Day, Cornell University, 1937. *Proceedings and Addresses at the Inauguration of Edmund Ezra Day, Fifth President of Cornell University*, Ithaca, 1937.

"One fact impressed itself upon me most strongly. Each of these four stalwarts—Muhlenberg, Sadtler, Seip, and Haas—

in his own way made distinguished contributions to the record. Their combined efforts established the present educational policy of the college. Tenacity of purpose, disregard of discouraging influences and faith in ultimate success mark every page of that record. . . . The early foundations were well laid. . . . How well my distinguished predecessor accomplished his task, a host of proud alumni, an able and loyal faculty, a progressive community, and a beautiful campus pay silent eloquent tribute today."—President Levering Tyson, Muhlenberg College, 1937. *School and Society*, October 23, 1937.

"DePauw University stands at the end of a century of distinguished achievement. . . . DePauw was conceived in faith and born into a situation where adversity was a frequent and familiar experience. The virtues demanded by the first century were faith, vision, sacrifice, patience, courage, and intelligence. . . . DePauw was founded in this faith; she was nurtured in this confidence. We have not been this way before . . . but if to the faith of the fathers can be added the increased knowledge of the sons, we can face the exacting demands of our second century with the confidence and joy of those who with a shout greet the golden colors of the dawn—for after all our college color is—Old Gold."—President Clyde Everett Wildman, DePauw University, 1937. Inaugural Address. Typescript copy in the library of the University of North Carolina.

"To assume the administrative leadership of a college or university is, in every instance, a grave responsibility, but to follow in the footsteps of so great a leader as my predecessor, whose administration is unparalleled not only in length but in quality of service, is an undertaking in the presence of which one must feel, to an unusual degree, a sense of humility."—Chancellor O. C. Carmichael, Vanderbilt University, 1938. *The Inauguration of Oliver C. Carmichael*, Nashville, Vanderbilt University, 1938.

Money! Money!! Money!!!

"And what is the cry that comes up from every college large and small in the land, but 'money! money!! money!!!' The religious press rings with appeals for gifts and endowments, alumni of colleges pour in large offerings of love and gratitude, noble men and women dying, bequeath rich legacies to favorite institutions, but still the cry is 'money, money, money! . . .'

"We are all so busy with farms and our merchandise, we so dote upon our great mills, factories, and warehouses, we are so engrossed with cent per cent, and the fluctuations of the exchange; we fall down and worship so many 'gods of gold, of silver, of brass, of iron, of wood, and of stone,' that we forget the higher life of the spiritual existence in a swelling sea of earthly troubles and triumphs. . . .

"You have your choice as yet between the one, great, rich, free, populous, cosmopolitan university which shall be your chief pride and joy, and the dozen or more petty, starveling, ill-appointed affairs, in which as a *people* you will have no common interest. And you can take your choice between educating your artisans and professional men here, on your own soil, and sending them to Yale, to Harvard, to Ann Arbor or Madison; for depend upon it, whatever you may think about it, the young men and women are going where the brains are, and the means of instruction, fullest and freest."—President W. W. Folwell, The University of Minnesota, 1869. Inaugural Address. Typescript copy in the library of the University of North Carolina.

"What can the community do for the University? It can love, honor, and cherish it. Love it and honor it. The University is upheld by this public affection and respect. In the loyalty of her children she finds strength and courage. The Corporation, the Overseers, and the several faculties need to feel that the leaders of public opinion, and especially the sons of the College, are at their back, always ready to give them a generous and intelligent support. Therefore we welcome the Chief Magistrate of the Commonwealth, the Senators, Judges, and other dignitaries of the State, who by their presence at this ancient ceremonial bear witness to the pride which Massachusetts feels in her eldest university. Therefore we rejoice in the presence of this throng of the Alumni, testifying their devotion to the College which, through all changes, is still their home. Cherish it. This University, though rich among American colleges, is very poor in comparison with the great universities of Europe. The wants of the American community have far outgrown the capacity of the University to supply them."—President Charles W. Eliot, Harvard University, 1869. Inaugural Address, in S. E. Morison, *The Development of Harvard University* (Cambridge: Harvard University Press, 1930), p. lxxvii.

"And though it is true the funds to-day are insufficient; though in view of decreasing income from investments, and imperative necessity of immediate extension of our teaching force, the need is sore and pressing, yet I enter on this work in full faith that the needed funds will not be wanting. . . . Bowdoin's history is worth more than thousands of dollars; her sons are better sureties of her future prosperity than bonds; the community which she has done so much to form is a safer recourse than a bank account."—President W. D. Hyde, Bowdoin College, 1886. Inaugural Address, *Addresses at the Inauguration of President Hyde*, Bowdoin College, June 23, 1886.

"Aside from the help given by our founder, and continued by his descendants for two generations, but little has been done for Vanderbilt University. . . .

"The food that universities thrive on is gold. Without that, nothing can be achieved; with this, all things are possible. The sustenance that this University has had in the past has produced wonders, but it is not sufficient for the future. . . ."—Chancellor James H. Kirkland, Vanderbilt University, 1893. Inaugural Address, 1893. Typescript copy in the library of the University of North Carolina.

"If there is danger of America being absorbed in money getting for its own sake, there is also danger that college presidents may catch the same disease."—President J. H. MacCracken, Lafayette College, 1916. Address at the inauguration of President H. M. Brooks, Alma College, *College and Commonwealth* (New York: The Century Company, 1920), p. 268.

"Our program for the future is determined in no small measure by the new economic situation. The high cost of learning is a twin brother to the high cost of living. We may congratulate ourselves upon being a corporation with something like $2,000,000 worth of property, but when we stop to think that more than one-third of this is not income-producing and that the normal charges for its upkeep have more than doubled in the last five years, and when we stop to think again that the portion of it which does bring us an income—some $1,200,000—is only the equivalent of less than half that sum before the war, we are at once brought face to face with our most pressing problem, the urgency of which I cannot overestimate. Twenty-five years ago my distinguished predecessor in this office in his inaugural address declared that the first need of the college was an endowment yielding income enough to meet current expenses. The need today is as urgent as it was then. The great task to which we should immediately set our hand is the adding of a second million dollars to our endowment. . . .

"There are other needs, but I do not propose to tax your patience farther on this occasion. There always will be needs—a college is a perpetual mendicant—and that will indeed be a sorry day for Bates College when she has enough and to spare. Enlarging needs ought always to be the corollary of enlarging usefulness. The material resources of Bates College are still seriously limited and she is poor, compared with the almost unlimited wealth enjoyed by some institutions of learning, but she is rich in her noble ideals and traditions, rich in the affection of those who have learned to love her in proportion as they have sacrificed for her welfare, rich in the useful lives of her sons and daughters who throughout the length and breadth of this land and across the seas are exemplifying the high ideals of consecrated service to state and nation which they learned in these halls. Today we stand on the threshold of this new epoch in our history and we face the future years with noble purpose, with high hope and with unshaken confidence because of our faith in One whose wisdom is better than our own and because we know that the God who led our fathers will continue to guide and inspire their successors."—President Clifton Daggett Gray, Bates College, 1920. Inaugural Address, *Bates College Bulletin* (Lewiston, Maine), December 1, 1920.

"Dr. Livingston Farrand, president of Cornell, himself in office but a year, offered the friendship and coöperation of Cornell to the new Syracuse chancellor. He also pointed out that the present problem of the modern university is to obtain the support it deserves from society.

" 'Dollars and cents are always factors in a university's problem,' he said. 'The university contributes endlessly to the prosperity and welfare of society; it is right that society should contribute something in return. The cost of higher education should not be borne by the comparatively few who actually study in the colleges, but by the society which generously benefits from it.' "—President Livingston Farrand, Cornell University, 1922. *Inauguration of Charles Wesley Flint as Chancellor of Syracuse University* (Pamphlet made from newspaper clippings, 1922), p. 19.

"I shall expect from the community—Boston and all New England—financial assistance; for Boston University is in very great need of improved and enlarged facilities and increased endowment, and I cannot believe that men and women to whom God has entrusted money will allow an agency of so great service as Boston University to be cramped and hindered in its operations by lack of funds."—President Daniel L. Marsh, Boston University, 1926. *Bostonia*, July, 1926.

"My second counsel is, That you *pay heed to the balance of the Ledger*. You will sometimes receive counsel to the contrary.

Once a man said to me that debts and deficits were signs of expansion and of healthy growth. Later I discovered that according to that principle he himself was positively robust! For twenty-three years this University has balanced its budget and at the end of each twelve months period has had only the debt of learning and love. That policy has commended itself to business men and philanthropists. . . . Debts that stand for income-bringing assets are one thing : debts that represent frozen assets are often no more available than their great cousin, the North Pole! The General Education Board is rightly conservative about assisting an institution that lives beyond its means, even as bankers are conservative about loaning to a man of like character. The Carnegie institutions are naturally cautious in their aid for 'pot-boiler' institutions,—meaning by that peculiar phrase those schools that depend much upon the boarding-house and rooming-house method, or upon the profits from sales to their own students. . . . A college is no place for frenzied finance. . . . When an institution casts herself down from the pinnacle of the financial temple in the presumptuous hope that God will bear her up, it often takes a lengthy period for the arrival of the fiscal angels. . . ."—Bishop E. H. Hughes, at DePauw University, 1928. *Inauguration of G. Broomley Oxnam as President of DePauw University*, DePauw University, 1928.

"Happily, the wells of philanthropy have not yet been drained, and, somehow, those of us who know the American spirit cannot believe that they will be. The long procession of noble men and women who have fed the living streams of learning in this country with their benefactions is not ended, nor will it end. Patrons of humanity in its finest purposes, they have merged themselves into the immortality of American colleges. Moved by affectionate confidence they have seen in each a personality, whose worth had little relation to size or outward grandeur. As it scans the long roll of its benefactors the small college, in its sentiment of gratitude and its conviction of responsibility, finds impulse there, if there were no other, to maintain and to increase its high service to mankind."—President

Dixon Ryan Fox, Union College, 1934. Inaugural Address, *School and Society*, October 20, 1934.

"Now that Muhlenberg has been established firmly, shall we let her languish for lack of proper sustenance? This is the issue we face. I don't believe any element in our constituency will answer that question except with an emphatic negative. That constituency may ignore her needs, but they will pay a heavy price in the end if they do."—President Levering Tyson, Muhlenberg College, 1937. *School and Society*, October 23, 1937.

2

THE PURPOSES OF HIGHER EDUCATION

In the quotations given in this section appear the purposes of higher education as these are seen by college presidents. It appears that, for nearly two centuries after the founding of Harvard, "discipline and the furniture of the mind," as President Jeremiah Day, of Yale College, said in 1828, were considered the primary purposes of higher education in this country. To lay broad foundations of general culture, "to prepare for life and not for making a living," were the aims and ends of collegiate materials and methods of education. Since the introduction of the elective system after 1869, the purposes of education, as seen by college presidents, have changed, although as pointed out in Section IV of this study, the College of Arts is still regarded as the "heart" of higher education. "Mental discipline which ranked first sixty years ago, . . . now ranks twenty-second among the twenty-five avowed purposes of our institutions of higher learning," in the opinion of three hundred presidents who were asked to list, in the order of their importance, what they believed to be the purposes of the institutions over which they presided, according to a statement by President Robert M. Hutchins, of the University of Chicago, in 1938. But there are presidents today who say that mental discipline is the best thing the college can do for students.

In the Nineteenth Century

"The two great points to be gained in intellectual culture are discipline and the furniture of the mind. The former of these is, perhaps, the most important of the two."—President Jeremiah Day, Yale College, 1828. Report on the Course of Instruction in Yale College by a Committee of the Corporation and the Academical Faculty. New Haven, 1828. Quoted in L. F. Snow, *The College Curriculum in the United States* (New York: Teachers College, Columbia University, 1907), p. 143.

"The object then for which I suppose these encouragements to a liberal education are given is, to furnish means for the most perfect development of the intellectual treasures of the country. In order to the most perfect condition of any society, it is necessary that, whenever unusual talent of any kind exists, it be so cultivated as to be able to accomplish the highest results of which it has been made capable. This talent is very equally distributed among the various orders of society, least of all is it limited to the rich. But the means for the thorough and radical training of a human mind are very expensive. They involve the cost of libraries, philosophical apparatus, laboratories, and a formidable array of teachers of distinguished ability. Were these to be provided by individual enterprise, the expense would be so great that none but the rich would be educated and by far the larger part of the talent of a country must perish in useless obscurity. Hence arises the reason why a large portion of these means, all that which involves the outlay of considerable capital, should be the property of the public, and why it should be open to the use of all who might by the use of it be rendered in any way benefactors to the whole. The design therefore of university establishments so far as the public is concerned, is not to furnish education to the poor or to the rich, not to give away a modicum of Greek and Latin and Geometry to every one who chooses to ask for it, but to foster and cultivate the highest talent of the nation, and raise the intellectual character of the whole, by throwing the brightest light of science in the path of those whom nature has qualified to lead."—President Francis Wayland, Brown University, 1842. *Thoughts on the Present Collegiate System in the United States* (Boston: Gould, Kendall and Lincoln, 1842), pp. 47, 48.

"Here in college is to be fashioned, in the highest attainable perfection, the scholar, the citizen, the good man, the Christian gentleman."—President Charles King, Columbia College, 1849. Inaugural Address, in *Addresses at the Inauguration of Mr. Charles King as President of Columbia College, New York.* New York, 1849.

"Without the refining influences of education, wealth grows coarse in its manners, beast-like in its pleasures, vulgar and wicked in its ambitions. Without the liberalizing and uplifting power of education, wealth grows overweening in its vanity, cruel in its pride, and contemptible in its ignorance. Without the Christian element in education, wealth grows selfish in the domestic circle, tyrannical in the State, benighted and bigoted in the church, and everywhere impious toward God."—President Horace Mann, Antioch College, 1854. *Inaugural Address* (Yellow Springs, Ohio, 1854), p. 16. Quoted in E. I. F. Williams, *Horace Mann: Educational Statesman* (New York: The Macmillan Company, 1937), p. 316.

"Columbia College believes that even for this technical and professional work, it is well for a man to lay the broad foundation of a general culture, but she does not refuse to recognize the specializing tendencies of the times, and to permit those who will to obtain the one without the other. Nevertheless she does say that, if a man can spare the time, he is throwing away part of his life and part of his power in the years to come if he does not submit at the beginning to the disciplinary training which cultivates the mind before he begins to plant the particular seed which he wishes especially to grow. Columbia College believes that the specialist, because he is a specialist, ought first of all to be a broadly developed man."—President Seth Low, Columbia University, 1890. *Installation of President Low, February 3, 1890.*

In the Twentieth Century

"The American college, as it existed thirty years ago or more, and as it still exists in some quarters, is distinctly a school for personal culture. Its strongest agency has been the personal influence of devoted men. It has made no effort to give professional training. It has made no pretense of leading in scientific research."—President David Starr Jordan, Leland Stanford Junior University, 1902. "University Building," in *Popular Science Monthly*, August, 1902, p. 330.

"The object of the undergraduate department is not to produce hermits, each imprisoned in the cell of his own intellectual pursuits, but men fitted to take their places in the community and live in contact with their fellow men. . . ."—President A Lawrence Lowell, Harvard University, 1909. Inaugural Address, in S. E. Morison, *The Development of Harvard University* (Cambridge: Harvard University Press, 1930), p. lxxix.

"The business of the college, as has been said a thousand times, is to prepare for life and not for making a living."—President Nicholas Murray Butler, Columbia University, 1927. *Report for 1926-27*. Quoted in *The Rise of A University*, Vol. II, ed. Edward C. Elliott (New York: Columbia University Press, 1937), p. 234.

"To expound my faith more concretely, I would say that Education should do three things for us: it should give us Insight, it should bring us Inspiration, and it should enable us to relate ourselves to our fellows in Service to a common end.

"Education should result in Insight. To be educated we must learn to see the forest *and* the trees, and to discover that trees may come and go while the forest continues. We must learn that man is worth more than things, that his life is more important than food and clothing, houses and machines, that things are of value only as they contribute to life, and that in the pursuit of things life may be lost. Somewhere we must learn to see and appreciate excellence. We must learn that the fine and the clean and the true are as real as the coarse, the filthy and the false."—President A. A. Shaw, Denison University, 1927. Inaugural Address, *Inauguration of President Shaw, Denison University, Granville, Ohio.*

"Our ideal is the scholar who can be of practical service and the workman who brings the scholarly attitude to his work. And this ideal can be attained at all levels of intelligence from that of the humblest craftsman to the most erudite philosopher.

"This ideal can be well worked out in the program of The College of the City of New York. Beside the liberal arts college, we have our schools of technology, of education and of business. All these schools must impart professional instruction, but their work rests on a broad cultural base. They aim to produce effective workers to be sure, but also cultivated, broad-minded citizens of the democracy."—President F. B. Robinson, College of the City of New York, 1928. *The Inauguration of Frederick Bertrand Robinson as Fifth President of the College of the City of New York.*

"The first problem, of course, is as to what education should be, and what the university should have as its objective. There is no subject under the sun which admits of so much discussion and dispute. Perhaps it might be well to remind ourselves first of what the word education means, for there seems to be a very common, persistent, and official misunderstanding of that elementary matter. Education is conceived as entirely a process of imparting or pushing in knowledge to the human mind. Actually the word means the opposite. To educate is not to push in but to lead or draw out. It is true that these processes are inseparable, but the major process is not to induce but to educe. The true object of education is not to load the young mind but to excite it. An educated man is not primarily one who can produce facts, but a man who can think and sort them out. He is not one who can solve cross-word puzzles without reference to a dictionary, but one who by long training in learning, thinking, and doing realizes approximately the extent of his ignorance and incapacity. Education is shown far more by the ability to ask intelligent questions than to supply pat answers. True education first discovers, then leads natural ability. And as God fulfills Himself in many ways, so does the inspired teacher. The trouble in the modern world is that so many experts sit on the throttle of his inspiration.

"It is one thing, however, to say what education should be and should aim at; it is another thing to say what instruments it should employ, or stake out the path by which it should approach its objective. It is here that educators dispute endlessly, rage, and utter vain phrases. If you asked the professors at the University of California what each one regarded as the proper means by which to achieve the purposes of that institution, you would have almost as many answers as there were professors, both as to purposes and means. With the varying philosophies of life that mankind has developed, it is not surprising that there should be no unanimity of opinion regarding a philosophy of education. But some things should be clearly defined and generally accepted, as to what we are seeking and the means by which we may attain it. Time and money, strength and genius, are being wasted because of the absence of these. An educational survey of the United States would disclose vast sums wasted on duplicated courses and huge plants and equipment that need never have been. So would such a survey of California. There is no reason why every junior college, college, and university should cultivate all fields of knowledge, or the same fields of knowledge. More to be commended is a careful restriction of instruction and research, so that, within its estimated income and its community requirements, each institution may support comfortably the departments of known value and established need. . . .

"Furthermore, largely because objectives are not clear and methods are uncertain, all institutions of higher education that I know have student bodies so lacking in homogeneity, so varying in mental power, as to be almost unteachable, as a whole. And size of student body affects this problem but slightly in degree and not at all in kind. In the universities of today we are attempting to be all things to all men, and are about as comfortable as a chameleon on a Scotch plaid. Some of our students are as brilliant and ambitious for learning as any scholar of medieval times. Some have the mind but little desire to use it. Some are beautiful but dumb, and some are not even beautiful. But we try to educate them all by similar means—an unattainable purpose. And yet, if we sorted them, and grouped them into homogeneous units, most of them might be educated profitably."—President Robert G. Sproul, The University of California, 1931. "Three Problems of the American University," *University of California Chronicle*, January, 1931.

"The university has two great functions: the discovery of truth, and the injection of that truth into the social life stream. And as in industry so in the university it may be that the processes of production have been more highly perfected than those of intelligent distribution. Certainly the present influence of destructive propaganda and of partial truths makes it evident that there are too few scholars who, like the Galilean, have the power to transmit wisdom so that the common people receive it gladly. Piled up at the mine mouth is a mass of knowledge which has never been utilized for the uplift of society.

"Today the university is called upon as never before to fulfill its obligation to the social order not merely by promoting the effectiveness and wisdom of those within its gates, but by lifting the entire community which surrounds it to a constantly greater appreciation and love of truth."—President William Mather Lewis, Lafayette College, 1932. In *The Obligation of Universities to the Social Order*, ed. H. P. Fairchild (New York: New York University Press, 1933), p. 398.

"Coming out of an obscure past, universities have always eluded precise definition, and never more so than today. They represent the embodiment in each nation of its highest ideals of scholarship. They afford a recruiting ground for its men of learning, and in the Occident they have for centuries been looked up to as the capstones of the educational system. Conservative, but still plastic, they have exhibited phenomenal vitality. They have seen dynasties rise and fall, governments come and go, civilization itself undergo profound modification, and

still they endure. The last century has witnessed the birth of many new universities, sometimes in response to public demand, sometimes as the expression of private beneficence seeking a worthy outlet. Particularly in the Western World, where the faith in education as a social panacea is sublime (albeit at times pathetic, if not tragic), has the multiplication of these institutions been conspicuous—some of them doubtless unworthy of the great name they have assumed, but others surely deserving to be received into the ancient sisterhood of the elect."
—President James Rowland Angell, Yale University, 1932. In *The Obligation of Universities to the Social Order*, ed. H. P. Fairchild (New York: New York University Press, 1933), p. 7.

"A university is an institution in which the advancement of knowledge is deliberately and officially fostered, an institution which is committed not only to the higher forms of instruction but also to research, and which rests its reputation on the quality of its scholarly output. The institution may be large and of complex organization. It may be very small and confine its teaching and investigation to a few fields, or even to a single field. Whether it be as large as Columbia or as small as Clark University is of no significance in determining its university status. It does not have to be called a university in order to be one; witness the Massachusetts and the California Institutes of Technology. A university, then, is distinguished chiefly by its polarization; by its devotion to inquiry and to intellectual creation. Ideally, all of its educational activities, on whatever level they may be conducted and towards whatever practical ends they may be directed, are informed by the spirit of research, are made to square with the standards of intellectual integrity set by the research scholar."—President Samuel P. Capen, The University of Buffalo, 1932. In *The Obligation of Universities to the Social Order*, ed. H. P. Fairchild (New York: New York University Press, 1933), pp. 58, 59.

"All social engineering must rest eventually upon some education. It is infinitely better that social change should be guided by trained and informed intelligence rather than by untutored emotion or uninformed politics. And therein lies the challenge of the new day for the universities."—President Lotus D. Coffman, The University of Minnesota, 1932. In *The Obligation of Universities to the Social Order*, ed. H. P. Fairchild (New York: New York University Press, 1933), p. 38.

"In my opinion the college should round out the student's general education in such a way as to give him some understanding of the social order and of the contributions of arts and science to the progress of society. He should have a knowledge of fundamentals of government and of the economics of government. The college should assist the student in intelligent choice of a vocation in which he will be interested, and for which he is fitted. It should cultivate an attitude of open-mindedness, a sense of proportion, and the habit of relating problems to fundamental principles, and it should give encouragement to the cultivation of tastes which will enrich life. In a word, the college, I believe, should produce high-quality citizens prepared to meet responsibilities, and thus prepared for their jobs in life, whether the job be a business, whether it be housewifery, or whether it be a professional career."—Harold W. Swift, President of the Board of Trustees, The University of Chicago, 1932. In *The Obligation of Universities to the Social Order*, ed. H. P. Fairchild (New York: New York University Press, 1933), p. 74.

"The conceptions of a university have not changed materially at St. Andrews in a hundred years. Figuratively speaking, it sits on Mt. Olympus free from the pressures of the world, studying the things that the flocks in the valley below need, and shedding luster and learning upon them according to their need. It is one of the most magnificent conceptions of what a university should be, one that we should keep constantly in mind lest we dissipate our intellectual strength by chasing the lures and social vagaries of the times. . . .

"It is so easy for the universities of America to be diverted from their real purposes that we must restate them time and again. A university, for example, studies politics, but it will not advocate fascism and communism. A university studies business, but it will not engage in commerce. A university studies social relief, but it will not undertake to administer it. A university studies engineering, but it will not build bridges. A university studies stocks and bonds, but it will not operate an investment house. A university studies military tactics, but it will not promote war. A university studies peace, but it will not organize crusades of pacifism. It will study every question that affects human welfare, but it will not carry a banner in a crusade for anything except freedom of learning."—President Lotus D. Coffman, The University of Minnesota, 1935. "Building a University," *Higher Education and Society* (Norman: University of Oklahoma Press, 1936), pp. 311, 312.

"Education implies teaching. Teaching implies knowledge. Knowledge is truth. The truth is everywhere the same. Hence education should be everywhere the same. . . . If education is rightly understood, it will be understood as the cultivation of the intellect. The cultivation of the intellect is the same good for all men in all societies. It is, moreover, the good for which all other goods are only means. Material prosperity, peace and civil order, justice, and the moral virtues are means to the cultivation of the intellect."—President Robert M. Hutchins, The University of Chicago, 1936. *The Higher Learning in America* (New Haven: Yale University Press, 1936), p. 66.

"The Antioch idea is a marked departure in educational method and philosophy. This departure is primarily a change in emphasis. I believe that most of the novel and important steps in the growth of human culture are due to changes in emphasis and attention, rather than to the introduction of explicitly new principles or concepts. Conversely, in such cases, all distinctive value may be destroyed by loss of emphasis, without open repudiation of the principles involved. The maintenance of distinctive emphasis depends fully as much upon emotional realization of value as it does upon intellectual understanding and acceptance. . . ."—President Arthur E. Morgan, Antioch College, 1936. "Not by Eastern Windows Only: The Dawn of a New Education," *Antioch College Bulletin* (Yellow Springs, Ohio), March, 1936, p. 5.

"A great university should be a place in which there are relatively undisturbed opportunities to live with ideas. Much of life is otherwise engaged. But on campuses such as this thoughtful men and women, of faculty and student body alike, should be led to seek out all sorts of ideas: ideas that are deeply rooted in human experience; ideas that, like constellations in the intellectual firmament, have guided the earlier mariners of human thought; ideas that have more recently opened the doors of new knowledge of nature and of man; ideas that afford the foundation of our systems of law and order, of justice and liberty. Men and women on a campus like this should learn how knowledge is gained and wisdom won. They should through practice improve their command of the difficult art of critical thinking. They should come to know something of the nature of imaginative and creative thinking. They should acquaint themselves with the race's heritage of accumulated wisdom. They should strive for intelligence. They should learn what it means to abide with reason. They should through sustained effort, achieve accessions of intellectual power. They should, in brief, through their common interests and activities here in this university, come to know what is really meant by the intellectual life.

"This is no academic plea. Nor is it an ideal that need not be too seriously taken. The place of intelligence in culture is being currently challenged in ways that may well give us all pause. When men in power conclude that ideas should come from authority and not from thought, men of reason must give battle. The liberal tradition to which the democratic peoples the world over owe allegiance cannot survive in a climate unfavorable to free inquiry. If the liberal tradition is to be sustained there must be an unswerving belief in the capacity of the people for intelligent action; there must be a readiness on the part of the people to follow intelligent leadership; and there must be, wisely protected and adequately supported, centers of higher learning in which intelligence is assiduously cultivated and has free play."—President Edmund E. Day, Cornell University, 1937. Inaugural Address, *Proceedings and Addresses at the Inauguration of Edmund Ezra Day, Fifth President of Cornell University* (Ithaca, New York, 1937), pp. 29, 30.

"The universitity is not a pep meeting. It is a place devoted to the discovering and dissemination of the truth. The dissemination of truth! To me this means *more* than the mere publication of truth. It concerns dealing with the minds of those who come to us. It concerns putting truth at the disposal of youth. Youth, if it is cynical, if it has lost faith in much of our institutional civilization, if it questions much of what to us seems fundamental, still appears to have some faith in the instrument we call the university. The continued coming of youth in such numbers is some evidence of this fact. To youth we are still a vital agency of civilization—perhaps the only one. . . .

"Doubtless this thought was in the mind of President Van Hise when he said 'If the university does not become the center of the cultivation of the highest capacities of the human mind where is the work to be done in this country?' I believe we all recognize that money, physical equipment, instructors and students are vital in a university solely because they are the means by which we hope to cultivate these 'highest capacities.' If we have doubts in the premises, they concern the *nature* of that cultivation.

"At this point there is divergence of opinion among those who discourse on what is called 'the higher learning.' What have we to say to the 11,000 who will be with us as students during this academic year? . . .

"Well, here are the youth—11,000 of them. You will recall a hymn of your childhood called 'The Ninety and Nine.' One out of the hundred of the sheep was far away on the hills and the shepherd went after it. He was especially interested in this researcher into new fields and new experiences. But he did look after and tend the ninety and nine. He saw that they were cared for and nourished and *then* he set out to guide the one lone creature. Ninety-nine out of one hundred of our students will become part and parcel of the working world that is to be—the great controlling force in our society. Will they help to leaven it from the bottom up in these many communities into which they go? In some degree we who teach on the campus will help to answer that question. That is, I believe, a responsibility of our 'community of scholars.' . . .

"And so I ask you to think with me about the problem of where we are in education and where and how we are going. I do not have the answers. Perhaps together we can find them. The problem of today and tomorrow must be approached as we approach our own segregated problem in the laboratory or the library—prepared to find what the evidence dictates. We are a *community* of scholars. In this brief moment I have emphasized the community aspect of the phrase. It is the *whole* university that demands our allegiance and our cumulated efforts. That which is best for the whole university in its relation to the whole of life must be our absorbing task today. I referred earlier to an aspect of scholarship which I pictured as the lonely pine on the distant hill. Here in Wisconsin we have also the myriad fields of grain ripening from green to gold, from gold to harvest ministering to the needs of man in a thousand places. Who is to say which picture tells the lovelier story? We have both and both are beautiful. I ask today for no neglect of the distant pine as I draw your attention to the fact that the vineyard and the harvest field *calls also* for those who can trim and prune and reap. I believe that this is the essence of the Wisconsin tradition. I go forward with you in that tradition."—President Clarence A. Dykstra, The University of Wisconsin, 1937. Address to the faculty, October, 1937. Mimeographed copy in the library of the University of North Carolina.

"Five of the major elements in the Antioch program . . . are as follows.

"1. Course of study. Antioch tries first of all to give its students a solid intellectual foundation by requiring a broad cultural program in the liberal arts and sciences, plus proficiency in a field of concentration. That is, academically the student should acquire a cultural base broad enough to make him aware of the major intellectual interests of the race, and he should also have the experience of more concentrated and thorough work in one field of his own choice. Recent modifications in the curriculum have been aimed at giving this purpose greater meaning in the student's life.

"2. The coöperative program. Antioch believes in the program of alternate work and study as a means of encouraging the student to develop initiative, maturity, and judgment, and of helping him to find that vocation for which he is best fitted and in which he will be happiest. Current developments in the plan are pointed toward better integration between the student's work experiences and his academic experiences, and toward more effective counseling and placement.

"3. Character. Antioch attempts to strengthen and refine the character of its students less by rules and exhortation than by the contagion of example and by making clear the issues involved and giving the students responsibility, under guidance, for their own personal and social welfare. This policy of education through active responsibility is gaining increased emphasis in the Antioch program.

"4. Health. Antioch believes in educating for life in the matter of health. By unifying the health and physical education programs, and by securing more accurate information about the health knowledge of incoming students, the College aims to give better health training and service.

"5. Research. The College regards the presence of active research on the campus as stimulating both to faculty and to students. The program of scientific research, independently financed, has been extended in scope and personnel, and has materially added to College facilities."—President A. D. Henderson, Antioch College, 1937. "A Continuing Heritage," *Antioch College Bulletin* (Yellow Springs, Ohio), September, 1937.

"The amount of knowledge which a student can accumulate in his college years is limited in any case, and to us at Swarthmore it seems clear that the most useful thing the college can do for him is to train his mind and develop his power of thought, to the end that he will go on through life acquiring as thorough a mastery of subjects in which he is interested as his abilities and opportunities make possible."—President Frank Aydelotte, Swarthmore College, 1937. Quoted in the *Bulletin of The American Association of University Professors*, March, 1937, p. 251.

"The task of education today is more than ever before in the field of morals. The attitude of a man toward his job in the world is much more important than his intellectual equipment for the job. If he does not approach the world with an intelligent social altruism and with the willingness to impose upon himself a high degree of social discipline under which he will forego some of the individual prerogatives which he once could claim, then he is not yet educated."—President James Rowland Angell, Yale University, 1937. "The Vital Task of Education," *The New York Times*, June 20, 1937.

"There is no debate on the relative importance of facts in education. To consider their acquisition as the end of education is fatal. The significant goal of the educative process is the development of the ability to think. In addition to acquiring facts and learning to think a real love of and desire for knowledge are necessary if scholarship is to be effective. However promising intellectually one may appear on graduation day he may not qualify as really educated if he has failed to acquire deep and permanent intellectual interests. But even these are not enough. With scholarly interests must be fused active social interests which provide the urge to action. This fact has been overlooked too often in educational planning. Socialization, in the sense of adjustment of the individual to society, is not the real objective. A sense of social responsibility, devotion to public welfare, and a recognition of the principle that giving and not getting is the true way of life should be the result of higher learning.

"It is the dynamic quality of scholarship that the colleges and universities should seek to develop. It is doubtful if general education, consisting of rhetoric, logic, mathematics, and the classics, plus three years in the study of principles would accomplish it, for it would seem to require that study be associated with vital human interests, that it be concerned with needs that stir the imagination, and with real problems, the solution of which would challenge the best efforts of the student."—Chancellor O. C. Carmichael, Vanderbilt University, 1938. "Some Issues in the Higher Learning," *The Educational Record*, July, 1938.

"The problem of 'culling the natural aristocracy from every condition of our people' is much more complex and difficult than Jefferson imagined. We have only begun to envisage the ways and means of approximating his ideal. We must not only perfect our methods of selecting those most suitable for certain types of higher education but arrange for a different type of training for those not so 'culled.' Selection is not a 'weeding out process'; it is one aspect of educational guidance which has as its aim the direction of every youth into a fruitful field of labor. Only a relatively few should proceed through the long and somewhat tedious process of 'book learning' that leads to the professions. The others should receive a training which not only equips them for work in certain vocations but prepares them for life as well-rounded, intelligent, and useful citizens in a democratic society.

"Clearly the basic conditions for the differentiation of higher education are universal elementary education and universal opportunities for secondary education. Toward the first goal we have made great strides in the past fifty years. Though much more remains to be done, the groundwork has been laid. Relatively little talent is lost to the country because of a lack of educational opportunities at the lowest level. When we consider high school, college, and university, however, the case is quite otherwise. It has been stated that 63 per cent of the persons between the ages of fourteen and seventeen now attend public or private high schools; only 11 per cent of those between eighteen and twenty-one attend colleges or universities.

"The proportion of the population which is now receiving a higher education may be too large or too small. This is not an easy question to answer without defining carefully what we mean by 'higher education.' But only the most unrealistic optimist would believe that the accidental interplay of social and economic forces has resulted in the selection of the right 11 per cent of our youth for college work. And no one who thinks in terms of adapting the education to the student would imagine that the same type of training would be desirable for the entire 100 per cent of boys and girls of college age even if it were felt advisable for everyone to go to college."—President James B. Conant, Harvard University, 1938. "The Future of Our Higher Education," *Harper's Monthly Magazine*, May, 1938.

"Some three hundred college and university presidents recently answered a questionnaire in which they were asked to list, in the order of importance, what they regarded as the purposes of their institutions. Mental discipline, which ranked first sixty years ago, according to a recent analysis of the college catalogues of that day, now ranks twenty-second among the twenty-five avowed purposes of our institutions of higher learning. It is preceded by such objects of higher education as good manners. 'Good manners' have no place in the program of higher education. 'Personality' has no place in the program of higher education. 'Character' has no place in the program of higher education. College develops character by giving young people the habits of hard work and honest analysis. If it tries to teach character directly, it succeeds only in being boring."—President Robert M. Hutchins, The University of Chicago, 1938. *The Saturday Evening Post*, January 22, 1938.

3

THE WEAKNESSES OF HIGHER EDUCATION

The first part of this section deals with general criticisms of higher education. In these criticisms appear also, at least by implication, purposes of higher education, noted in the preceding section. These criticisms began to be made much earlier than the beginning of the period covered by this study. One of the earliest to be found came from Amherst College in 1827 and one of the latest from the president of the University of Chicago in 1938. In 1842 President Francis Wayland, of Brown University, pointed out many points of weakness in the collegiate system of the United States. In 1853 President James Walker, of Harvard, said that there was more cant in this country on the subject of education than on any other subject except religion.

The second part deals with criticisms of competition among the colleges and the need for coöperation. These criticisms run all the way from statements of President Philip Lindsley, of the University of Nashville, in 1829, President Francis Wayland, of Brown University, in 1842, President Josiah Quincy, of Harvard, in 1845, President Henry P. Tappan, of the University of Michigan, about 1850, President F. A. P. Barnard, of the University of Mississippi, in 1856, to the report of President Walter A. Jessup, of the Carnegie Foundation for the Advancement of Teaching (formerly president of the State University of Iowa), for the year ending June 30, 1937.

In that report President Jessup criticized the growing competition among the colleges of this country and the effect of competitive exploitation upon the students. Competitive pressures which seemed to have marked higher education for many decades "may become very much greater than they are at present."

General Criticisms

"The complaint is, and if our ears do not deceive us, it daily waxes louder and louder, that while everything else is on the advance, our colleges are stationary; or, if not quite stationary, that they are in danger of being left far behind, in the rapid march of improvement."—Faculty of Amherst College, 1827. Two Reports of the Faculty to the Board of Trustees of Amherst College, 1827. Quoted in L. F. Snow, *The College Curriculum in the United States* (New York: Teachers College, Columbia University, 1907), p. 155.

"Whoever has studied the history, genius, character, government, modes of instruction, endowments, revenues, and all the concentrated ways and means and facilities of communicating knowledge, which distinguish the most celebrated European universities, will be able to comprehend our meaning when we speak of them as an order or species of institution altogether unknown in the United States. We have nothing like them or approaching them. . . . Whether we ought to essay the creation of precisely such institutions among us, or whether, if established, they would be duly patronized and sustained by our busy, restless, speculating, money-making people, are questions open for discussion. . . ."—President Philip Lindsley, The University of Nashville, 1827. *The Works of Philip Lindsley*, ed. L. J. Halsey (Philadelphia, 1864), I, 404. Quoted in D. G. Tewksbury, *The Founding of American Colleges and Universities Before the Civil War* (New York: Bureau of Publications, Teachers College, Columbia University, 1932), p. 3.

"It seems to me then that our literary institutions in this country, are greatly deficient in this important element of a well arranged Collegiate system. . . . I firmly believe that if our system of Collegiate education can be improved it will be received with greater favor than at present; and with increasing favor in proportion to the value of the improvement.

"And, again, in suggesting changes I am very far from believing that any wholesale revolutions could be effected immediately without great injury. Such revolutions in matters of civil government are never effected without great peril and seldom without social disorganization. It is the same with respect to anything which has been long established, which has taken deep root in the feelings of men and become interwoven with the usages of society. . . .

"First, the number of studies pursued during the College course, might be limited in such manner that whatever is taught may be taught thoroughly. The College would in this case be open only for persons who are candidates for degrees. The standard of attainment may be as high as is considered desirable. The difference aimed at would be this, that, instead of learning many things *imperfectly*, we should learn a smaller number of things *well*. I am sure that every man in active life would, on retrospection, wish that his education had been thus conducted. By learning one science well, we learn *how to study*, and how to master a subject. Having made this attainment in one study, we readily apply it to all other studies. We acquire the habit of thoroughness, and carry it to all other matters of inquiry."—President Francis Wayland, Brown University, 1842. *Thoughts on the Present Collegiate System in the United States* (Boston : Gould, Kendall and Lincoln, 1842), pp. 97, 104, 108.

"Next to religion, there is no subject on which there is so much cant as education."—President James Walker, Harvard University, 1853. Inaugural Address. Quoted in S. E. Morison, *Three Centuries of Harvard* (Cambridge: Harvard University Press, 1936), p. 294.

"What an enormity it is that our Colleges which annually send forth hundreds of young men to the rostrum, the forum, and the pulpit, should ever be guilty of overt acts of treason against the highest welfare of the community by fitting depraved men for positions of emolument and power."—President Horace Mann, Antioch College, 1857. Baccalaureate Address.

Quoted in Joy Elmer Morgan, *Horace Mann: His Ideas and Ideals* (Washington: National Home Library Foundation, 1936), p. 139.

"The subject of education is one which has occupied the most thoughtful minds of every age; and it is probable that the fundamental principles which should direct a truly liberal education may be as clearly deduced from the writings of Aristotle, of Seneca, or of Quintilian, as from those of the most judicious thinkers of modern times. And yet there is probably no subject in regard to which, were we to judge from the controversial literature to which it has given rise, we might be led to infer that there is so little that is settled, and so much that is uncertain or doubtful. Within the past twenty or thirty years, our long-tested and successful system of collegiate instruction has, in particular, been so persistently decried and so seriously menaced, as to fill the friends of sound education throughout the country with alarm, and to compel them to discuss the whole theory and practice of our higher education with anxious earnestness and by the light of first principles."—President F. A. P. Barnard, Columbia College, 1864. *Proceedings at the Inauguration of Frederick A. P. Barnard, S.T.D., LL.D., as President of Columbia College.* New York: Hurd and Houghton, 1865.

"We have heard much of our educated men keeping aloof from politics; the examples of the older nations would lead us to believe that were scholarly young men trained steadily in political questions from the outset, they would enter public life at such an advantage that this charge would be brought to naught."—President Andrew D. White, Cornell University, 1878. "Political Education," *Report of Commissioners to the Paris Universal Exposition, 1878*, p. 380.

"A liberal education without this fundamental idea of character-development amounts to nothing. It is not enough to say that it is imperfect; it does not in the true sense exist at all." —President Arthur T. Hadley, Yale University, 1899. *The Cosmopolitan*, November, 1899, p. 105.

"The future will witness the lifting up of professional education and a closer identification of the professional schools with the universities. The great law-schools and medical schools of our country . . . are not law-schools and medical schools which stand alone, independent of university connection. They are rather those schools which share the *high ideals* of the university, and are under university management. The majority of law and medicine schools in this country are stock companies, organized for pecuniary profit; . . . The great theological seminaries of the future will be those which are identified, directly or indirectly, with the universities. . . . It is enough to say that the ordinary theological seminary cannot today provide the curriculum of study demanded by those who are to do the work of the ministry during the next quarter of a century. . . .

"This union of professional education with the university, which is rapidly taking place in all great centres of the country, means two things: (1) the uplifting of this work, its broadening, and its acceptance of higher ideals; (2) the separation, to a greater or less degree, of the control of this work from the particular professions."—President William Rainey Harper, The University of Chicago, 1902. "The Trend of University and College Education in the United States," *North American Review*, April, 1902.

"Some universities are deaf to the cry of suffering humanity; some are exclusive and shut up in themselves; but the true university, the university of the future, is one the motto of which will be: Service for mankind wherever mankind is, whether within scholastic walls or without those walls and in the world at large."—President William Rainey Harper, The University of Chicago, 1902. *The Trend in Higher Education* (Chicago: The University of Chicago Press, 1905), p. 28.

"There are two prominent difficulties that obstruct the growth of education in the South. The first is the lack of an educational conscience; and the second is the lack of sound educational doctrines and correct educational ideals.

"It may sound a bit rude, even unkind, to say that the South has as much education as it wants, but unfortunately this is the truth. Not all are satisfied, for there are many chafing spirits, but they are in the minority. Ignorance in any part of America at this time is voluntary. It is, therefore, no malicious criticism to say that the South has all the education it wants. The traditional apology of poverty caused by the war cannot be sincerely urged any longer as an adequate excuse. The growth of wealth in the South has been marvelous, while the growth of education has been slow and tedious. What has been accomplished is the result of persistent struggle on the part of a few leaders. There has been no general and enthusiastic spirit behind these efforts."—President John C. Kilgo, Trinity College (North Carolina), 1903. "Some Phases of Southern Education," *South Atlantic Quarterly*, April, 1903, p. 137.

"There is hardly any conceivable limit to the ingenuity and genius of the advertising spirit in many of our colleges of today. Some institutions are engaged in the work of 'university extension' for the publicity it gives them, professing to do 'at long range' what they have never learned to do thoroughly within their own walls. Others are emphasizing, from this same motive of self-advertisement, 'correspondence study,' which frequently amounts to nothing more than a travesty upon the name and purpose of college discipline."—President George H. Denny, Washington and Lee University, 1904. *Papers and Addresses of the Association of Colleges and Preparatory Schools of the Southern States, 1904*, pp. 10, 11.

"The university must be as free from narrowness and partisanship in its moral attitude as in its presentation of scientific truth. No one wishes it turned into a Sunday School or into a Salvation Army corps. But there are certain moral resources not objectionable to any, on which universities might draw far more copiously than most have yet drawn.

"Instruction in ethics could be made more inspiring and concrete. Professorships could be created for giving instruction, of course in a purely scientific and non-sectarian way, in Old and New Testament literature—that body of ancient tractates rammed with life far beyond most else which men have written. . . ."—Chancellor E. B. Andrews, The University of Nebraska, 1905. *Transactions and Proceedings of the National Association of State Universities, 1905.*

"When colleges were small and universities non-existent, it was possible—but very unusual—to have a faculty composed throughout of men of exceptional ability and distinction. The rapid growth and multiplication of colleges and universities, however, has necessarily drawn into their service men of every type and kind, and of these mediocrity has claimed its full share. One main difficulty with which the higher institutions of learning throughout the world have to struggle today is militant mediocrity. . . . The searching question is being asked, where are to be found fit successors to the scholars of the generation that is now passing off the stage? Many are sought, but few are found."—President Nicholas Murray Butler, Columbia University, 1907. *Report for 1909-10*, p. 22.

"A glaring defect of the American civilization is the national mania for bigness and blind faith in numbers. . . . At least ten years ago every college in the state should have taken the chance of reduced numbers, and refused admission to all students who had not completed a high school course. I should not speak of this now if I felt sure that there had been made an end to this evil."—President William P. Few, Duke University, 1909. "Constructive Educational Leadership," *Proceedings of the North Carolina Teachers' Association*, 1909.

"Moreover the change from the life of school to that of college is too abrupt at the present day. Taken gradually, liberty is a powerful stimulant; but taken suddenly in large doses, it is liable to act as an intoxicant or an opiate. No doubt every boy ought to learn to paddle his own canoe; but we do not begin the process by tossing him into a canoe, and setting him adrift in deep water, with a caution that he would do well to look for the paddle. Many a well-intentioned youth comes to college, enjoys innocently enough the pleasures of freedom for a season, but released from the discipline to which he has been accustomed, and looking on the examinations as remote, falls into indolent habits. Presently he finds himself on probation for neglect of his studies. He has become submerged, and has a hard, perhaps unsuccessful, struggle to get his head above water. . . ."—President A. Lawrence Lowell, Harvard University, 1909. Inaugural Address, in S. E. Morison, *The Development of Harvard University* (Cambridge: Harvard University Press, 1930), pp. lxxxvi, lxxxvii.

"Any careful student of higher education in the United States must be struck by the lack of coördination and system of definite standards and of properly sustained ideals. The absence of efficient supervision and regulation both on the part of the national and state governments has been in great measure responsible for this state of affairs. The consequent abuses, waste of money and of power, and the really criminal injury to the youth of the country have been our crying shame.

"These abuses have formed an old and disgraceful story, and we are still far from through with them. The open traffic in degrees, professional and honorary, together with the glowing advertisements of institutions . . . has been partly suppressed. But we still have multitudes of unendowed, unequipped, wretchedly named institutions, facetiously classed as 'monohippic,' which profess to give a high education at a low cost and which grant degrees with a freehandedness truly democratic but somewhat demoralizing."—President F. P. Venable, The University of North Carolina, 1910. "What Factors Shall Mould Higher Education in the United States?" *The University of North Carolina Record*, April, 1910.

"Everyone agrees that there is waste of time. Everyone agrees that we begin our professional education too late. . . .

"I want to point out one more thing. There is an assumption that all boys are to proceed with their education at the same

6

rate of speed. . . . One of the chief defects, I think, in our education is that of carrying all children at the same rate of speed. . . .

"That brings me to my second point—the only other point. Why should we not have diversity in our universities? There is a tendency in education to standardize, and this is taken to mean that all universities should be alike. . . ."—President A. Lawrence Lowell, Harvard University, 1914. *Journal of Proceedings of the Association of American Universities*, 1914.

"The university man has not had his traditions subjected to any such keen appraisal as that which fell upon the elementary school during the last part of the nineteenth century or that which now registers itself upon the secondary school. A rigid and thorough going appraisal of college and university is now due. In fact, it is overdue. There has been much current criticism of higher schools during the last ten years, both from lay and professional minds; but it has been partial in character and lacking in a fundamental point of view. A critique which is basic and thorough is welcome at this time when our academic minds are so completely stirred that the profession is eager for rational assistance. Some reconstruction of the American college is coming. The wisdom of the immediate reconstruction depends upon the analysis of society's requirements of the institution and upon an unbiased judgment of the worth of existing collegiate attitudes and processes."—President Henry Suzzallo, The University of Washington, 1920. "Foreword" to Jay W. Hudson, *The College and New America*. New York: D. Appleton and Company, 1920.

"Our system of credits makes the course an end, instead of the means to an end; leads the student to aim at passing a course instead of acquiring knowledge, and the instructing staff to fix their attention upon carrying through a process instead of attaining a result. Passing a course is a very different thing from learning a subject, and measuring knowledge in terms of the courses traversed a very different thing from measuring difference between estimating the amount of gasoline in a tank by computing the number of gallons poured into it when there are holes in the tank, and measuring the actual amount of gasoline there. Students who know that their progress depends upon the courses passed are apt to look on getting through with it as the object of a course. They are like Cook's tourists in the picture galleries of Europe, checking off in their guide-books the pictures they have hastily seen and straightway forgotten. Everyone knows how rapidly the knowledge acquired in a single course upon a subject fades away if there is no motive for keeping it fresh. A well educated Englishman is said to be one who has forgotten Greek; and perhaps Americans ought to be regarded as particularly well educated, because of the number of things they have barely touched upon in their school days and then forgotten."—President A. Lawrence Lowell, Harvard University, 1920. Address at the inauguration of President Harry W. Chase, of the University of North Carolina, 1920. *The State University and the New South* (Chapel Hill, N. C., 1920), pp. 29, 30.

"So far as education is concerned, there has been overorganization for a long time past. Too many persons are engaged in supervising, in inspecting and in recording the work of other persons. There is too much machinery, and in consequence a steady temptation to lay more stress upon the form of education than upon its content. Statistics displace scholarship. There are, in addition, too many laws and too precise laws, and not enough opportunity for these mistakes and failures, due to individual initiative and experiment, which are the foundation for great and lasting success."—President Nicholas Murray Butler, Columbia University, 1921. *Report for 1920-21.* Quoted in *The Rise of A University*, vol. II, ed. Edward C. Elliott (New York: Columbia University Press, 1937), p. 66.

"All of our colleges are now greatly overcrowded, partly as a result of the emphasis given collegiate training by the war, but partly also, we may as well confess, as a result of congestion due to lowered standards. Not every institution has succumbed to this craze for numbers with little regard for quality, but certainly in all institutions the rush of hordes has been felt and the student body is no longer primarily composed of those who are there for the development of their intellects or character, and every one will concede that many are trying to enter college who really lack the necessary brains or industry.

"Several college presidents have, of late, called attention to those conditions and suggested that collegiate education should be limited to an 'aristocracy of the best minds.' And, of course, they are right."—President F. P. Graves, The University of the State of New York, 1922. *Inauguration of Charles Wesley Flint as Chancellor of Syracuse University* (Pamphlet made from newspaper clippings, 1922), pp. 42, 43.

"University education is distinctly a hybrid phenomenon. The college of arts and sciences deals only to a limited extent with strictly university materials. At least fifty per cent of the work done in it ought properly to be classified as secondary education and rightly belongs to the secondary school. Because of this fact both the teaching methods of the college and its disciplinary regime are adapted rather to immature boys and girls than to men and women who have entered upon the serious preparation for their life work. Time is therefore wasted not only below the college, but still more prodigally in the college." —Chancellor Samuel P. Capen, The University of Buffalo, 1922. *The Inaugural Address of Samuel Paul Capen* (Pamphlet, 1922).

"It is a sad commentary on many of our colleges that their graduates return from college, not only out of touch with the young people's group which has grown up during their absence, but out of touch with the church itself, with the ideals and its mission. Much blame, no doubt, rests on the church, in not having kept in friendly contact with its absent young people, but more blame, I am convinced, rests on the colleges, where the Church, its aims, its work, are relegated to an obscure and little frequented chamber of the mind. A Christian College of Liberal Arts will surely glorify the Church, magnify its importance, and by intelligent participation in the life of the local churches, and in its curriculum, will prepare young people to go back more keenly alive to the majestic opportunities of the Church, and better fitted to take an active part in its service. . . .

"There are few colleges and universities where Religion does not have a place outside the curriculum. Even in State institutions many extra-curricular religious activities are found. The Christian College has an opportunity to give Religion a commanding place in its teaching."—President A. A. Shaw, Denison University, 1927. Inaugural Address, *Inauguration of President Shaw, Denison University, Granville, Ohio.*

"Education, like religion, politics and the weather, seems to be a subject upon which any one, regardless of age, sex or previous condition of ignorance, is permitted to speak without let or hindrance . . . we all generously share with others our observations upon the purposes, the materials, the methods and especially the failures of education. Some of us theorize at large, with a vague, yet none the less insistent dogmatism, while others, especially the professors of education, entrench themselves within a barbed-wire entanglement of pedagogical terminology into which few normal beings have the hardihood or even curiosity to penetrate, and from which they at intervals emit a portentous fusillade of doctrines and statistics."—President Arthur S. Pease. Amherst College, 1927. Inaugural Address, *School and Society*, December 3, 1927.

"One other phase of the question of fundamentals in college seems to me of utmost importance, although I think it is not so often in the minds of our friendly critics. Undergraduate students are devoting their time to highly differentiated aspects of subjects at the expense of a broad understanding of those studies fundamental to the proper appreciation of our common life and to our continuous intellectual growth. This tendency to spread college courses over the whole field covered by a given department is the result of a conception of education which I think is unsound."—President F. J. Kelly, The University of Idaho, 1928. *School and Society*, November 24, 1928.

"This is not a thoughtful age. There is a tendency to substitute sentiment and emotion for clear, fearless thinking. It is an age inclined to confuse every change with real progress, scientific theory with established fact; an age inclined to scientific bigotry, to deny any reality unless discernable through the medium of natural science. It is inclined to canonize cynicism and doubt by sending its young men and women to search for beauty and truth, without telling them where they may be found or how they may be recognized.

"It is inclined to overcome old vices by the simple expedient of changing their names into new virtues and then admitting them as guests-elect into the family circle. The ancient names were sensuality and lust. Frankness and self-expression of youth are the new names. What was called by the definitive name of concubinage now hides the lie and the shame under the title of companionate marriage. It is an age inclined to make of morality and religion two chameleon-like things, ever obligingly changing and adjusting themselves to fashion and convention, to the whims and weaknesses of human nature. . . ."—President William M. Magee, S.J., Marquette University, 1928. *Inaugural Address* (Milwaukee: Marquette University Press, 1928), pp. 15, 16.

"Why does not a more vital education come out of our conventional schools? Why does not schooling produce, in a more nearly automatic and inevitable fashion, uniformly great and dependable citizens, with free minds, curious spirits, and a fixed determination to make some creative contribution to the future of American democracy? And what can we do about it?

"I think this situation all grows out of the fact—overlooked by the early enthusiast for democracy and education—that our schools are controlled by adults. These adults are, in the main, dominated by points of view that came out of the education of another generation when other problems confronted American democracy. The intellectual life of many of these adults stopped the day they received their diplomas. . . ."—President Glenn Frank, The University of Wisconsin, 1929. *Adult Education in Action*, ed. Mary L. Ely (New York: American Association for Adult Education, 1936), p. 38.

"That university man is rare indeed who would claim that the present system of higher education is adequate, yet we stick to it because it is easier than to make a radical change. The lockstep is hard to break. The faculty develops younger men to follow in its footsteps, selecting teachers on the basis of their conformance to the tradition of the men who trained them. Generation after generation we go through the same rigamarole, and all too seldom do the augurs glance at one another and solemnly wink. The curious thing is that the men who, in education, accept what has been done traditionally, in their own fields recognize that knowledge is changing constantly and they are always experimenting in the hope that they may contribute to the changes. Why should we not look on education as a problem for experimentation just as we so look on a problem in physics or astronomy? Why, when we recognize the importance of theories and experimentation in every other field, should we accept, with such complaisance, our present system of education? The reason is that most of us give no thought to the theory underlying the system of education we support, or we seem to think that education is an exception to the rule that every subject must rest on some cardinal theory. . . ."—President Robert G. Sproul, The University of California, 1930. "The Educational System of California," *School and Society*, November 8, 1930.

"For the purpose of technical scholarship the extreme 'subjectizing' of material is helpful; for purpose of liberal education it is, in my judgment, harmful. The educational success of even the extreme integration of the curriculum of the Experimental College, as far as the students in this particular venture are concerned, is, in my judgment, clear beyond question."—President Glenn Frank, The University of Wisconsin, 1930. "The Experimental College," *The Journal of Higher Education*, June, 1930.

"Whoever heard of a meeting of college alumni to improve library facilities? Whoever heard of a conference of alumni on the research problem of a university? Whoever heard of a meeting of alumni that confined its discussions largely to the promotion of the moral and spiritual and ethical welfare of the student body? Whoever heard of a meeting of alumni whose primary purpose was that of improving scholarship within the institution? And yet these are the things that constitute the sole excuse for a college or university."—President Lotus D. Coffman, The University of Minnesota, 1931. *Bulletin of the Association of American Colleges, 1931*, p. 50.

"The last ten years have seen an influx of students that has almost overwhelmed the undergraduate departments of American universities. The ambition of parents, increased wealth, the attractiveness of college life, assumed vocational advantages, and, above all, social prestige, have transformed and reinforced the motives which formerly led students to college, and have resulted in the present vogue for the 'collegiate' among great groups of young men and young women who really have little idea as to what it is all about. The cultural influence of alma mater seems to many to have been swamped by the ever-increasing waves of young people demanding the delights and advantages of a university education without the labor and the application necessary to attain in reality that desirable distinction."—President Robert G. Sproul, The University of California, 1931. "Three Problems of the American University," *University of California Chronicle*, January, 1931.

"One of the commonest assertions of current discussion is that the colleges do not engender in students a love of books and that when the undergraduate receives his diploma he bids farewell to mental recreation and becomes a golf enthusiast. He may keep himself abreast of his technical field if he is in a profession, or of the literature of his particular business, but he will not be an active general reader. . . ."—President H. M. Wriston, Lawrence College, 1931. *Bulletin of the Association of American Colleges, 1931*, p. 345.

"Whatever influence has helped to standardize Southern colleges at the level of the best American practices and traditions has been a distinct contribution to educational progress and to Southern civilization. I say this recognizing, as we all do now recognize, that objective educational standards and standardizing agencies are not the unmixed good that they were once thought to be."—President William P. Few, Duke University, 1933. *Proceedings of the Southern Association of Colleges and Secondary Schools, 1933*.

"Then, too, so it seems to me, we are practically a nation of economic illiterates. Certainly the great body of the American public knows little or nothing about the principles of economics. Indeed, it is even doubtful whether professors of economics have known much about the principles of economics until recently. Our failure to teach the principles of economics is due either to our ignorance of these principles or to the fact that we were afraid to teach them. Practically every student goes from us today uninstructed and ignorant of exchange, currencies, commerce, and the part which gold and commodities must play in maintaining credit and world trade. Not only are we ignorant of these matters but as a people we have become the victims of the grossest and most inexcusable exploitations."—President Lotus D. Coffman, The University of Minnesota, 1933. In *The Obligation of Universities to the Social Order*, ed. H. P. Fairchild (New York: New York University Press, 1933), p. 34.

"Instead of admitting students on the basis of years in school, grades acquired, courses taken, and credits accumulated, I should prefer to admit to the University of Chicago any student who can read and write and who is recommended by somebody who knows something about him as a person who deserves a chance at a collegiate experience."—President Robert M. Hutchins, The University of Chicago, 1933. *Bulletin of the American Association of Collegiate Registrars*, July, 1933, p. 335.

"The chief handicap of the American college at the present time is the difficulty of finding students properly qualified by native ability, previous training, and social attitude to profit by what it has to offer. The result has been that colleges generally have accepted large numbers of students who are not really interested in their work and who make no worth while use of the opportunities provided."—President D. J. Cowling, Carleton College, 1934. *Bulletin of The Association of American Colleges*, December, 1934, p. 466.

"The collapse in the business world has brought colleges face to face with new problems. These are financial and also educational. Almost every institution is now facing an obligation

(1) to halt expansion
(2) to reduce expenditures
(3) to appraise justly its own work
(4) to contribute something to the solution of public problems
(5) to develop courses of study that prepare students for a part in government, in economic development, in world adjustment
(6) to develop a social conscience that makes possible a new social order wherein dwelleth righteousness."

—Chancellor James H. Kirkland, Vanderbilt University, 1934. *Bulletin of The Association of American Colleges*, December, 1934, p. 471.

"Does it not seem strange to you, that with all our elaborate modern equipment, we are not providing a much greater proportion of intelligent leaders in our country than we did far back in post-revolutionary days, and, indeed, that we are not providing markedly more intelligent followers? Far too many citizens of this and other states are still superstitious, they still believe the words of the noisest demagogue, they are still swayed by emotion, they are easy victims of crude propagandists; they are, in short, not educated."—President Lee Paul Sieg, The University of Washington, 1934. Inaugural Address, *Addresses at the Inauguration of Lee Paul Sieg, President of the University of Washington, October 5, 1934.*

"I think . . . college graduates very commonly, if not almost characteristically, are deficient in a sense of social responsibility. There is altogether too much short-sighted, not very intelligent selfishness on the part of the graduates of our institutions."—President F. D. Farrell, Kansas State College, 1934. *Transactions and Proceedings of the National Association of State Universities, 1934.*

"There are books on all the things that are wrong with the schools and very seldom are there any books telling about the things that are right with them. I think most of the things in the schools are all right."—President John J. Tigert, The University of Florida, 1934. *Transactions and Proceedings of the National Association of State Universities, 1934.*

"Too few of the university graduates become or remain effective leaders. Nearly every representative of the learned professions experiences an intellectual let-down a few years after he leaves college. No matter how conscientious professional leaders are, the gap between what they know and what they ought to know widens."—President Lotus D. Coffman, The University of Minnesota, 1935. "Building a University," *Higher Education and Society* (Norman: University of Oklahoma Press, 1936), p. 317.

"This is the position of higher learning in America. The universities are dependent on the people. The people love money and think that education is a way of getting it. They think too that democracy means that every child should be permitted to acquire the educational insignia that will be helpful in making money. They do not believe in the cultivation of the intellect for its own sake. And the distressing part of this is that the state of the nation determines the state of education.

"But how can we hope to improve the state of the nation? Only through education. A strange circularity thus afflicts us. The state of the nation determines the state of education. How can we break this vicious circle and make at last the contribution to the national life that since the earliest times has been expected of us? We can do so only if some institutions can be strong enough and clear enough to stand firm and show our people what the higher learning is. As education it is the single-minded pursuit of the intellectual virtues. As scholarship it is the single-minded devotion to the advancement of knowledge. Only if the colleges and universities can devote themselves to these objects can we look hopefully to the future of the higher learning in America."—President Robert M. Hutchins, The University of Chicago, 1936. *The Higher Learning in America* (New Haven: Yale University Press, 1936), pp. 31, 32.

"If what I have said about American education is true, if it is confused and chaotic, then the taxpayers of the United States ought to be rather irritated. For they are spending two and a half billion dollars a year on education and they are not getting their money's worth. But they ought to be intelligent about their irritation. For irritation may lead to such irrelevant action as the demand for 'loyalty oaths' and legislative witch hunts.

"Loyalty oaths and witch hunts are based on the mad notion that the schools are un-American. Far from being un-American, they are guilty of all the distinctively American shortcomings. An intelligent investigation of the schools, if our publishers and legislators were capable of making one, would reveal that the taxpayers are wasting their money by demanding precisely the kind of education the schools are providing. . . .

"The clamor for vocational training is as loud as it ever was. Certain industries are demanding that children be prepared for their shops at public expense. School boards, including the one in my city, are boasting of their plans to accommodate these industries on an even larger scale than at present. In response to pressure by vocational teachers and industrialists, the governments, national, state and local, are appropriating larger and larger funds for such courses."—President Robert M. Hutchins, The University of Chicago, 1937. *The Saturday Evening Post*, December 25, 1937, pp. 10, 11.

"Democracy would be wise if it would curb the education of thousands of our present school population. For hundreds of thousands today a high school education is largely a waste of time, a waste of public funds, but for those with ability, no barrier of poverty or race should exist."—President James L. McConaughy, Wesleyan University, 1937. "Education in a Democracy," *The New York Times*, August 31, 1937.

"Two sets of forces operate to make it difficult for our universities to maintain the primacy of the intellectual function. The forces of the first set are external: they inhere in the nature of the surrounding culture.

"Reference has already been made to the current eclipse of the liberal tradition. Force is in the field, armed, aggressive and arrogant. War in some quarters has become so natural a phase of governmental action that it no longer has to be declared. The outlook for peace-loving peoples is in certain respects most ominous. The life of the university is inevitably affected by this world situation.

"Another external force of great potency is the love of money. To a dangerous degree we have come to regard the accumulation of wealth as the hallmark of individual success. Perhaps this was an unavoidable consequence of the stress laid in conquering our continent on ideals of free individual enterprise. But the love of money has dominated our social psychology to such an extent as to make the intellectual life appear to many pale and academic. The basic work of the universities becomes increasingly difficult as the intellectual life loses social esteem.

"Closely affiliated with the love of money, though by no means identical with it, is the widely prevalent insistence upon vocational results in American education. Not that vocational aims are not to be granted a place in the organization of formal education. As a matter of fact, vocational interests constitute an invaluable aid over a wide range of educational undertaking. At times, and with certain types of students, education apparently cannot be made effective except as it is made primarily vocational. The essential difficulties arise from the fact that vocational interests are in many instances narrow in outlook and distressingly short-sighted as to the ways and means by which a durable vocational competence is to be developed. The best training for a position may be an enhancement of intelligence and intellectual power without explicit reference to the more technical skills the position requires. It is quite likely that most of these technical skills should be taught on the job, not in the school or college. In so far as the cultivation of the intellectual life in our universities is put under narrow vocational pressures, the primary purposes of the university are in some measure defeated.

"This same type of consideration arises in connection with all sorts of practical demands upon our institutions of higher learning. Let me not be misunderstood. It is the duty of a great university to serve the society in which it carries on. But it is equally the duty of the university to apply its resources so as to maintain that service permanently. It is for the long pull that our universities exist. . . . Practical men commonly want quick results. As a people we are afflicted at times with attacks of unwarranted impatience. Even our leaders sometimes succumb. All through our political and economic life are evidences of the virus of immediacy. We forget that the course of civilization has been one long struggle to recognize the greater wisdom and efficiency of doing things in roundabout ways that are ultimately timesaving, but initially time-consuming. Our universities, like our social institutions, suffer at times from too great outside insistence upon quick practical results. Thus another external force is added to those which make it difficult for the university, even when its vision is clear, to adhere strictly to its fundamental purpose."—President Edmund E. Day, Cornell University, 1937. *Proceedings and Addresses at the Inauguration of Edmund Ezra Day, Fifth President of Cornell University* (Ithaca, New York, 1937), pp. 31, 32.

"My experience with college, as student, teacher and commencement orator, convinces me that the following persons should not go to college:

"Children whose parents have no other reason for sending them than that they can afford to.

"Children whose parents have no other reason for sending them than to get them off their hands for four years.

"Children whose characters are bad and whose parents believe that college will change them for the better.

"Children who have had no other reason for going to college than to avoid work or have a good time for four years.

"Children who have no other reason for going to college than to have a stadium in which to demonstrate their athletic ability.

"Children who have no other reason for going to college than the notion that it will help them achieve social or financial success in later life."—President Robert M. Hutchins, The University of Chicago, 1938. *The Saturday Evening Post*, January 22, 1938.

"Agitation for the reduction of college enrollment used to be confined to those who believed, along with the late Governor Berkeley of Virginia, that 'learning has brought disobedience and heresy and sect into this world.' Interests which have reason to fear general enlightenment have always advocated restriction of educational opportunity. Those interests are still at work; but they now have some new allies: the educators themselves."—President Robert M. Hutchins, The University of Chicago, 1938. *The New York Times Magazine*, June 12, 1938.

Competition and Coöperation

"Colleges rise up like mushrooms in our luxurious soil. They are duly lauded and puffed for a day, and then they sink to be heard no more."—President Philip Lindsley, The University of Nashville, 1829. Quoted in D. G. Tewksbury, *The Founding of American Colleges and Universities Before the Civil War* (New York: Bureau of Publications, Teachers College, Columbia University, 1932), p. 24.

"A principal cause of the excessive multiplication and dwarfish dimensions of Western colleges is, no doubt, the diversity of religious denominations among us. Almost every sect will have its college, generally at least one in each State."—President Philip Lindsley, The University of Nashville, 1829. Statement concerning the increase in higher educational institutions, 1829, *The Works of Philip Lindsley*, ed. L. J. Halsey (Philadelphia, 1864). Quoted in D. G. Tewksbury, *The Founding of American Colleges and Universities Before the Civil War* (New York: Bureau of Publications, Teachers College, Columbia University, 1932), p. 4.

"The colleges have but little connexion with each other." —President Francis Wayland, Brown University, 1842. *Thoughts on the Present Collegiate System in the United States* (Boston: Gould, Kendall and Lincoln, 1842), p. 41.

"Harvard College is represented as a society combined and laboring for the propagation of Unitarianism; as an association of infidels, without belief in the awful mystery of Christ's incarnation, placing no reliance on his propitiatory death, and deriving no assurance of a future state for his glorious resurrection and ascension; denying his divine mission, not acknowledging him either as Mediator or Redeemer, but resting all their hopes of a future life and happiness on their own merits; 'not mentioning Christ in their prayers,' and 'openly denying the Lord who bought them!' . . . Parents, who are found contemplating sending their sons to Harvard, are beset by the Calvinistic preachers or missionary in their neighbourhood, and entreated not to jeopardize their children's hopes, both as respects the present and the future life, by subjecting them to the temptations and dangers to which an education at Harvard College would inevitably expose both their bodies and souls. . . .

"There is no question that systematic calumnies like these, circulated very openly and boldly, as I am informed, in the Middle, Southern, and Western States, have a powerful influence in turning young men from Harvard to other Colleges; and that they are the main cause of the diminished influx of students from these States, and from foreign countries, into Harvard, and of the comparative increase of their numbers in other Colleges. In Yale, Brown, Dartmouth, Williams, Amherst, and Harvard, there are *four hundred and fifty* students derived from these sources; of whom Yale has 201, the other four Colleges 146, and Harvard only 103. That such are the effects of representations like those above stated, assiduously made, circulated, and believed in those States, is notorious; and that these representations are utterly false is, in this vicinity, equally notorious.

"It is now more than sixteen years since I accepted the office of President of Harvard College, and I here openly and unequivocally declare, that, so far from the influence of Harvard College being devoted to the propagation of Unitarianism, or the labors of its teachers being directed to this object, this has never, so far as I have seen, known, or believed, been made the chief or any special object of their thoughts or labors at all. For the purpose of avoiding, as much as possible, the communication of any peculiarities of religious opinion to the students, writings free from such an objection by the universal consent of all classes of Christians, such as 'Baley's Evidences,' and 'Butler's Analogy,' are selected as text-books. Episcopalian, Baptist, Calvinist, Unitarian, and every other denomination of Christians, have ever stood before the Corporation and Faculty in the same equal light, been treated with the same deference and respect, and have received an equal share of the College honors and beneficiary funds. . . .

"Let the people of Massachusetts understand that the attempt now making by leading Calvinists in Boston and its vicinity is not merely to get Unitarianism out of Harvard College, but to put Calvinism into possession of it; that this has been their purpose and struggle for these forty years past; and unless their projects be counteracted and defeated by the vigilance and spirit of the community, they will ultimately be successful, though it cost a struggle of forty years more. The alliance recently, to all human appearance, entered into on the floor of the Senate-chamber of Massachusetts is a pregnant evidence of their aim and tact. The predominating influence of Calvinism is stamped, in characters not to be concealed or mistaken, on at least seven institutions for education in New England,—Yale, Williams, Amherst, Bowdoin, Dartmouth, Middlebury, and Burlington. There is also another highly endowed institution in Massachusetts, in which every article of the creed of this sect is riveted down for ever on the seminary by a subscription of faith required of the professors, to be renewed every five years. Yet with all this power they are not content. All this influence 'availeth them nothing, so long as' Harvard is not also in their possession. . . ."—President Josiah Quincy, Harvard University, 1845. Quoted in S. E. Morison, *Three Centuries of Harvard* (Cambridge: Harvard University Press, 1936), pp. 258, 259.

"The tendency to the undue multiplication of Colleges at the West is notorious, and by none more deplored than by the members of this Board. The whole influence of the Society has been to terminate the day of college building, having its origin in the pecuniary interest of individuals or localities, and to place every movement, having such an object in view, upon a broader scale."—Society for the Promotion of Collegiate and Theological Education at the West, 1847. *Seventh Report of the Society for the Promotion of Collegiate and Theological Education at the West*, pp. 38-39. Quoted in D. G. Tewksbury, *The Founding of Amer-*

ican Colleges and Universities Before the Civil War (New York: Bureau of Publications, Teachers College, Columbia University, 1932) p. 7.

"The idea of fitting our colleges to the temper of the multitude does not promise great results. . . . We have cheapened education so as to place it within the reach of everyone; we have retained the short term of four years, so that no great portion of life need be spent in study; and we have made the terms of admission quite easy enough. . . . The multiplication of colleges after the same model only serves to increase our difficulties. We set about putting up the same kind of buildings; we create the same number of professors, to teach the same things on the same principle; we get together a few books and some philosophical apparatus; and then we have the same annual commencements, with orations and poems, and the conferring of degrees; and we get under the same pressure of debt, and make the same appeals to the public to get us out of it; and then with our cheap education, to induce many to get educated, we experience the same anxiety to gather in as many students as possible; and since, where we cannot get money it is something to get appearance, we show the same readiness to educate for nothing those who will submit to be educated, but who cannot pay. In all this we are improving nothing; but we are taking away all dignity from our system of education, and proving its inadequacy. . . ."—President Henry P. Tappan, The University of Michigan, *ca.* 1850, in *University Education*, New York, 1850. Quoted in D. G. Tewksbury, *The Founding of American Colleges and Universities Before the Civil War* (New York: Bureau of Publications, Teachers College, Columbia University, 1932), p. 8.

"The University as a whole treats us ungenteelly, and with but little of that courtesy due an honorable inferior. . . . We are a state institution equal in every respect to Chapel Hill as to privilege. . . . If Chapel Hill has wealth in its interest, we have the mass of people in our favor. We can certainly succeed much better with your favor, but we can certainly live in some way without it. Speak of us respectfully, treat our recommendations honorably, and try them as others do, and if we visit you, treat us as gentlemen, and you will have no more important ally than Normal."—President Braxton Craven, Normal College, North Carolina, 1854. Letter to President D. L. Swain, The University of North Carolina, May, 1854. Quoted in L. L. Gobbel, *Church-State Relationships in Education in North Carolina Since 1776* (Durham : Duke University Press, 1938), p. 37, note.

"Nearly all our colleges are, furthermore, the creations of the different religious denominations which divide our people. They are regarded as important instrumentalities, through which the peculiarities of doctrine which distinguish their founders are to be maintained, propagated, or defended. It is this which has led to the great multiplication of collegiate institutions in our country, and which is daily adding to their number."—President F. A. P. Barnard, The University of Mississippi, 1856. "On Improvements Practicable in American Colleges," *American Journal of Education and College Review*, January, 1856, p. 176. Quoted in D. G. Tewksbury, *The Founding of American Colleges and Universities Before the Civil War* (New York : Bureau of Publications, Teachers College, Columbia University, 1931), pp. 4, 5.

"It is one of the glories of our American colleges, that their doors are alike open to all classes in society, and that the only nobility known within their walls has its basis in intellectual power, high attainment and moral worth, . . . Within the walls of an American college all factitious distinctions vanish. . . ."—Theron Baldwin ("Father of Western Colleges"), 1856. *Thirteenth Report of the Society for the Promotion of Collegiate and Theological Education at the West.* Quoted in D. G. Tewksbury, *The Founding of American Colleges and Universities Before the Civil War* (New York: Bureau of Publications, Teachers College, Columbia University, 1932), pp. 4, 5.

"There has arisen, within a few years, an earnest, not to say violent, competition among several religious denominations in respect to their educational arrangements. Each denomination seems anxious to out do the others in the number of its Colleges and Schools. This spirit of rivalry has proved itself contagious, as well as debilitating."—Director Absalom Peters (1836-1842) Union Theological Seminary, 1858. Quoted in D. G. Tewksbury, *The Founding of American Colleges and Universities Before the Civil War* (New York: Bureau of Publications, Teachers College, Columbia University, 1932), p. 76.

"Our own little commonwealth never before contained so many institutions of learning.

"We believe the field is not yet so crowded that the laborers must turn their weapons against each other.

"There is room for all."—President James H. Carlisle, Wofford College, 1860. Quoted in *Coker College Quarterly Bulletin*, December, 1936.

"The annalist who should be faithful in respect to those obituary records could hardly fail to swell the list to somewhat formidable proportions—and if a headstone were put up for each bearing the inscription 'In Memoriam,' the traveller, after lengthened journies by lake and forest, and prairie, might find himself still within the enclosures of this apparently limitless burial ground."—Theron Baldwin ("Father of Western Colleges"), 1864. Quoted in D. G. Tewksbury, *The Founding of American Colleges and Universities Before the Civil War* (New York: Bureau of Publications, Teachers College, Columbia University, 1932), p. 24.

"But we are told that there are too many colleges; and that this result is due to the voluntary system. In a free country, how can this be helped? There are just now too many banks, too many railroads, too many ships, too much iron; but the law of supply and demand is the only possible corrective for the evil. If a college attracts to itself patronage and endowment, it has a right to live; if it does not, it will die. The law of natural selection applies to colleges as well as to the animal and vegetable world. . . . Time alone can determine whether a college has the right to live."—M. B. Anderson, The University of Rochester, 1877. *Voluntaryism in Higher Education.* New York, 1877. Quoted in D. G. Tewksbury, *The Founding of American Colleges and Universities Before the Civil War* (New York: Bureau of Publications, Teachers College, Columbia University, 1932), pp. 8, 9.

"Are there too many colleges? There are not too many for the whole country with its constantly widening area and its rapidly extending population. But they are inconveniently crowded together and many are therefore practically useless because they are unavailable for those who need them. They are worse than useless, so far as many who need them are concerned. They hinder rather than aid one another by their jealous rivalries; . . . The most thoughtless if not criminal stupidity is often manifested in founding new institutions in a city or vicinity that is already over supplied. It is not difficult to obtain a large gift from some plethoric donor who is ambitious to connect his name with a new college or university, or by means of it to dignify the place of his residence or nativity. In his simplicity he thinks it as easy to found a university as it is to build a cotton mill, and he finds no difficulty in securing the coöperation of a zealous board of trustees and the praises of a gratified if not a grateful public."—President Noah Porter, Yale College, 1878. *The American Colleges and the American Public.* (New Edition. New York: Charles Scribner's Sons, 1878), p. 254.

"We are poor. It is as much as this state can do to keep the smallest number of institutions with their heads above water. Shall we then scatter and thus squander and dissipate our resources and means among a number of feeble, struggling and impotent agencies or concentrate them as much as possible and put at least one institution on a respectable footing? From the former policy we can hope nothing."—President W. P. Johnston, Louisiana State University, *ca.* 1881. Quoted in W. L. Fleming, *Louisiana State University, 1860-1896* (Baton Rouge: Louisiana State University Press, 1936), p. 402.

"Within the past half-century a system of state universities and schools of science has come into existence. This intrusion into the field of higher education has been viewed by many most worthy citizens with doubt and disfavor. By some these institutions have been denounced as Godless and infidel. This sentiment has been entertained by so many persons that it seems worthwhile, even at this late day, to face the question, 'What right have such schools to exist, and can their work and influence be beneficent?' "—President W. W. Folwell, The University of Minnesota, 1883. *Education*, III (1883), 513.

"We are bringing Trinity nearer our State University, geographically speaking, and I urge that we bring it nearer to that honored institution in sympathy and in earnest coöperation in the advancement of the general educational work of the State. . . .

"I appeal to the friends of these two institutions and to those of all other institutions of learning in the State to see to it that no jealousies shall rise up among any of them."—Governor T. J. Jarvis, North Carolina, 1890. Address at the laying of a cornerstone at Trinity College, 1890. *State Chronicle*, November 13, 1890. Quoted in L. L. Gobbel, *Church-State Relationships in Education in North Carolina Since 1776* (Durham: Duke University Press, 1938), p. 127, note.

"We charge you to remember that this is the peoples' institution. Renounce forever all servitude to ecclesiasticism and partyism and set out to be the ruling and the shaping force among the energies that stir the people and are making of the old fields a new earth, of our long slumbering land a resounding workshop. . . . In consecrating yourself to this, swear that the 'day of compromise is done.' To every mendicant tradition that asks favors of you; to every narrow ecclesiastical prejudice that shall demand tribute; most of all to the colossal inertia that you inherit, in whatever form they come, in whatever guise they present themselves—to them all say with kindness:

" 'Go honored, hence, go home
Night's childless children: here your day is done,
Pass with the stars and leave us
With the sun.' "

—Walter Hines Page, 1891. Address at the inauguration of President G. T. Winston, The University of North Carolina, 1891. Quoted in K. P. Battle, *History of the University of North Carolina* (Raleigh: Edwards and Broughton Printing Company, 1912), II, 466.

"The work of higher education is really just beginning to be properly taken hold of by the American people. . . . Our work is not done; only a fair beginning has been made. . . .

"I do not care to discuss the question whether education should be carried on by the Church or State; in fact, I have little sympathy with that discussion in the abstract. Theoretically both sides can make out a satisfactory case. The fundamental principles of both sides are right, and from their respective standpoints both Church and State have a right to devote themselves to this work. The truth is that education is an interest so vast and so vital that it justifies every honest and unselfish effort for its advancement. . . .

"The State should not be led by any outburst of national enthusiasm to provide in duplicate what is already sufficiently provided for. . . .

"Nor should denominational zeal lead to the establishment of an over-supply of poorly equipped colleges, which drag out a meager existence, gather patronage together only by the application of the Church whip, and serve at the same time to starve the bodies of their professors and the minds of their pupils. In educational institutions what we need now above all things is not quantity, but quality. . . ."—Chancellor J. H. Kirkland, Vanderbilt University, 1893. Inaugural Address. Typescript copy in the library of the University of North Carolina.

"It is believed and will be urged that in the present condition of our State every cent of money raised by taxation that is available for educational purposes ought to be expended in increasing the efficiency of the Common School System; and that all higher education ought to be cared for by private enterprise, and supported, so far as necessary, by private munificence."—President C. E. Taylor, Wake Forest College, 1894. *How Far Should a State Undertake to Educate?* (Raleigh: Edwards & Broughton Printing Company, 1894), p. 15.

"What should be the relations of the Ideal Christian College to sister institutions of learning? They should, most assuredly, be relations of amenity, of cordial coöperation, mutual helpfulness, honorable competition. If anywhere in the world petty jealousies, heartburnings, bitterness, clamor, evil speaking and appeals to passion would seem to be out of place, it is in the wide republic of the liberal arts."—President C. E. Taylor, Wake Forest College, 1895. Baccalaureate Address, "The Ideal Christian College," *The Wake Forest Student*, March, 1916.

"I yield to no man in doing honor to those who have given of their means to endow educational institutions, but, if the people desire to have the scholarship of these United States in grateful sympathy with their own interests, I think that their safest policy will be to provide sufficient means to give every man and woman an opportunity for the highest culture in institutions supported by public taxation."—President Charles D. McIver, Normal and Industrial Institute for Women, 1898. "Democracy In Education," *Addresses and Proceedings of the National Education Association, 1898*, p. 266.

"By consent, there has been to some extent a division of labor, an appointment of the work among several agencies. Elementary training is left almost exclusively to private and public schools. Theological education is assigned to the several denominations, while professional education is largely given over to the state. As time rolls on, I opine that this accord will strengthen, and that any disposition toward a clashing of interest will be averted."—President James K. Powers, The University of Alabama, 1901. *Proceedings of the Association of Colleges and Preparatory Schools of the Southern States, 1901*, p. 8.

"The future will bring a sharper distinction than has ever yet existed between the higher education maintained by the state and the higher education conducted on private foundation. . . . It cannot be said that the best interests of education at large would be secured if the state, as such, were to abandon its present policy of maintaining and directing the higher educational work. It would be just as great a mistake if, on the other hand, the non-state institutions were to disappear. Each of these great divisions possesses sources of strength to which the other may not lay claim. Both have been thoroughly established; both will develop side by side through and beyond the twentieth century; each will correct the weaker tendencies of the other; each will supply something which the other cannot furnish."—President William Rainey Harper, The University of Chicago, 1902. "The Trend of University and College Education in the United States," *North American Review*, April, 1902.

"Institutions can not be graded by the number in attendance. This is the most frequent and most vulgar gauge of relative standing. The rank of an institution is determined no more by the number of its students than by the number of rocks on its campus."—President David Starr Jordan, Leland Stanford Junior University, 1902. "University Building," *Popular Science Monthly*, August, 1902, p. 334.

"In the rush to increase patronage educators have used superlatives with reckless extravagance. School catalogues are not intended to quadrate with strict moral standards. Much must be understood as advertisement, and there is an advertising, as well as a poetic, license. Commercial morals are not as strict as personal morals. 'Our great university' is a Southern descriptive often used with more positive assurances than a German would employ in his comments on Berlin or Leipsic. It is reported on good authority that a college official at a recent commencement in the South said, 'Ladies and gentlemen, I am about to confer the greatest literary degree in the world—the Master of Arts of this institution.' That university may well afford to take a rest while Berlin, Cambridge, and Harvard catch up. Such expressions as, 'Our great colleges and universities,' and many others of the same sort, have been much overworked by educators in the South. Why should a people who are already at the head of the procession make further efforts at enlarged expenses? False statements cannot produce high aims, and to wound with the truth is far better than to lull with error."—President John C. Kilgo, Trinity College (North Carolina), 1903. "Some Phases of Southern Education," *South Atlantic Quarterly*, April, 1903, pp. 145, 146.

"I may be permitted to remark incidentally that, as regards this personal factor in education, the small college has the advantage of the large. Not necessarily, as I think, for the average number of students to each teacher need not be larger in the large college than it is in the small. Besides, special devices may be available to check the tendency in the larger institutions towards estrangement between teacher and student, as for example, the preceptorial system lately introduced at Princeton. In any case, I shall hope that the increase in our numbers here, which I confidently anticipate, with the consequent widening of our service, will not involve the loss of the cordiality of friendly intercourse between teacher and student which for the years has characterized this institution. It must not."—President William Louis Poteat, Wake Forest College, 1905. Inaugural Address, in *Youth and Culture* (Wake Forest: The Wake Forest College Press, 1938), p. 15.

"Professor Park, of Andover, used to divide one's theological holdings into two classes . . . those for which a man would go to the stake, and those for which a man would not go to the stake. I announce in advance that I am not prepared to go to the stake on the size of a college."—President William J. Tucker, Dartmouth College, 1906. "Small vs. Large Colleges," *School Review*, December, 1906, p. 717.

"I should like to see Tulane the best endowed University in the United States, but the General Assembly cannot appropriate one dollar to the Tulane University without recognizing it as a State University."—President Thomas D. Boyd, Louisiana State University, 1906. Quoted in Marcus W. Wilkerson, *Thomas Duckett Boyd: The Story of a Southern Educator* (Baton Rouge: Louisiana State University Press, 1935), p. 352.

"We are informed that your Senator ——, is still hesitating to vote for an appropriation to the women's department of this University, the Sophie Newcomb College. I beg, therefore, that you may use your utmost endeavor to secure from your leading citizens and his political supporters a petition urging him not to rob the women of this State of advantages such as are offered to the women of no other State, simply because the Faculty and friends of L. S. U. are opposed to the measure. The success of Newcomb College can in no way interfere with the success of L. S. U., because they have no Woman's College.

"In behalf of the women of this State I beg you to protest against this outrage. . . .

"Many of the friends of L. S. U. are becoming ashamed of this narrow, selfish and shortsighted policy. But for the fatal policy of the L. S. U., that institution would have received $216,000, instead of what it is likely to receive, $100,000, and at the same time Tulane would have received $50,000 a year. If the Presidents of our education institutions could be induced to work in harmony, all our institutions would receive ample appropriations. . . . I may also add that I have all along urged liberal support for the L. S. U., and that I am in no way responsible for this fratricidal strife."—President E. B. Craighead, Tulane University, 1906. Letter to influential women in Louisiana. Quoted in Marcus W. Wilkerson, *Thomas Duckett Boyd: The Story of a Southern Educator* (Baton Rouge: Louisiana State University Press, 1935), pp. 245, 246.

"I am not an enemy of the Tulane University. I have no desire to see its growth retarded or its revenues reduced in any manner whatever. On the contrary, I wish the Tulane University far greater success than it has ever achieved or than it can ever achieve by continuing its present policy; but it is my earnest conviction, born of many years of experience in educational work in this state, that it is not well for Tulane, nor well for New Orleans, and not well for Louisiana that Tulane should be a state university."—President Thomas D. Boyd, Louisiana State University, 1906. Quoted in Marcus M. Wilkerson, *Thomas Duckett Boyd: The Story of a Southern Educator* (Baton Rouge: Louisiana State University Press, 1935), p. 257.

"The highest promise and the fullest potency of educational efficiency are in the recognition of the personal and the ethical in education. Church, state, and private institutions, with antagonisms disappearing, are swinging into their orbits in a national galaxy about the full-orbed character-education.

"The University of Chicago has given a great impetus to this movement. Fifteen short years ago, in a period of competition, the great state and other universities watched with some degree of anxiety the establishment of this University, with promised extensive affiliation and endless endowment.

"Today, in a period of coöperation, these same universities, stimulated by its deeds and ideals, rejoice in its prosperity and share in its success. The world is constrained to recognize this Middle West as not only an agricultural, industrial, and commercial, but also as a collegiate, center. The largest increase in the attendance of college students is in this region, while the attendance is relatively stationary in the far East and West. Educational movements also originate in these North Central states."—President G. E. Maclean, The State University of Iowa, 1907. *The University of Chicago Record*, April, 1907.

"I venture to express a suspicion, and it is only a suspicion, that, if one were to count up the graduates of the small colleges of America who have rendered efficient service to the commonwealth and to humanity, and if one were to count up the graduates of the large colleges who have rendered efficient service to mankind and to the state, and if one were to compare these numbers with the whole number of graduates of the colleges of the two classes, it would be found that, great and lasting and noble as are the services given by the sons of the large colleges, the services rendered by the sons of the small colleges would be seen to be even greater and more beneficent."—President Charles F. Thwing, Western Reserve University, 1910. *A History of Education in the United States Since the Civil War* (Boston: Houghton Mifflin Company, 1910), p. 159.

"Whatever may be the privilege and the function of the private institution, there will always rest upon the state university a duty to consider first and above all the needs of its own state and of its own people. Much harm has already been done in some of our states by the attempt to model a university after the pattern of some other institution in some other state where conditions are very different. No feeling of pride, no striving after ideals impossible of realization should ever swerve from its real purposes and its plain duty an institution founded and supported by the people."—President John C. Futrall, The University of Arkansas, 1914. *University of Arkansas Bulletin*, Inaugural Number, February, 1915, p. 28.

"The relation between the University and the colleges ought to be close."—President J. H. Reynolds, Hendrix College, 1914. *University of Arkansas Bulletin*, Inaugural Number, February, 1915, pp. 38, 39.

"You chance to be here in Raleigh, and to be responsible to the Baptist church, and to be teaching young women; while we happen to live in Greensboro, or Boone, or Chapel Hill, and to be responsible to the State at large, and to be teaching men, perhaps. These are merely the variant but converging lines along which we work; for the saving grace (if you will pardon the expression)—the saving grace of all of our work depends on the insight, vigor, and patient sympathy with which, each of us, each in his own place and after his own kind, sees that work as directed toward the common end of the whole, abundant life of the State, and to make that as fully and richly fruitful as may be."—President Edward K. Graham, The University of North Carolina, 1916. "Greetings from the State Colleges," at the inauguration of President Charles E. Brewer, Meredith College, Raleigh, North Carolina, 1916, *Education and Citizenship and Other Papers* (New York: G. P. Putnam's Sons, 1919 [also University of North Carolina Press]), pp. 192, 193.

"We shall need to be on our guard lest institutional loyalty betray us into the practical fallacy of regarding our institutions as ends in themselves rather than as apparatus and means for the education of all the people. The common task is too sacred and too large for jealousies and the rancor of competition. Competition? A lady standing on the beach quite ready for the surf explained why she did not go in by saying, 'Another lady is using the ocean.' "—President William Louis Poteat, Wake Forest College, 1920. At the inauguration of President Harry W. Chase, of The University of North Carolina, 1920. *The State University and the New South* (Chapel Hill, N. C., 1920), p. 72.

"Once more the great free West has put New York in its place. No sooner does Columbia University announce an enrollment of 32,240 with the modest commentary that this seems to give our city the largest university in the world, than the University of California proclaims a student body of 43,266, 'without including the university farm.'

"The idea of a University seems to have been greatly expanded in recent decades. Columbia, for example, has some 2,800 undergraduates and 8,200 graduate and professional students; the remaining 21,000 are counted in Summer school and extension courses. Girls to whom a Summer in New York is the only alleviation of the humdrum routine of school teaching in a small town, and to whom Columbia Summer School is the only excuse for a trip to New York, go to swell the total, as well as the immense hordes who go in for the various forms of 'extensions.'

"Meantime, salutations to California, which has assembled the greatest grand glittering galaxy of students known in all history, and without the added attraction that brings so many to a Summer school located in New York City. The University of California covers the state with its extensions: from Shasta's icy mountain to Coronado's coral strand, where Mack Sennett's bathing beauties play in the golden sand. A worthy incarnation of the greatest of States, where no frost can damage the crop of superlatives."—"The Greatest on Earth," Editorial in *The New York Times*, March 12, 1922, concerning conflicting news items earlier in *The New York Times* on the sizes of Columbia and the University of California.

"It is not my province in this address to offer a panacea for the ills of education, or even to suggest many individual remedies. I would invite your attention to the reams of reports and addresses to be found in print, and you may select the remedy which appeals to you. I can see no reason for attempting to recover a ground which has already been worn threadbare. I am, therefore, going to present some of the problems relating to administration and management which confront the University of Maine. It should be understood, however, that the most of these problems are not limited to us, but are common to institutions of our type and many of them are common to all classes of institutions. In studying such problems it should be kept constantly in mind that, whether we desire it or not, there is a certain degree of interdependence between all institutions of higher education that can not be side-stepped. When an institution attempts to build a wall around itself and forgets this relationship it is taking a backward step. To be sure, each state has its own problems, but we should be careful that we do not reverse the saying of the old Quaker 'All people are peculiar except thee, and me, and sometimes thee is a little peculiar.' "—President H. S. Boardman, The University of Maine, 1926. *Inaugural Address by Harold Sherburne Boardman, President University of Maine, June 12, 1926* (Pamphlet), pp. 4, 5.

"Among the faulty generalizations and half-truths which clutter our thinking on social problems, a familiar one deals with a distinction often made between state-supported and privately endowed colleges and universities. The idea is prevalent that the state schools, in comparison with others, are necessarily more vulnerable to the machinations of politicians who would use the schools for their own selfish purposes. This opinion is the result partly of a lack of information, but it is supported also by examples, some of them representing the worst which can happen to higher education, of political interference with state educational programs.

"Private schools are controlled entirely or in large part by a select group of executives and patrons, and state institutions are more directly and generally responsible to the whole body of citizens. This does not mean, however, that it is wise for the private school to limit its services to society according to the whims of a few individuals, no matter how powerful, nor does it signify that responsibility to the citizens of a state necessarily delivers the state university into the hands of the politicians. In fact, those administrators of state schools, and there are many, who have traded control of the curriculum, staff appointments, and admission requirements for appropriations are guilty of having betrayed a public trust. Responsibility to the people means that the interests of all of the citizens are to be served to the extent to which facilities are provided, not additional perquisites to those who are able, astute or fortunate enough to be elected to carry on the business of government. The state university is frequently pressed to grant special privileges to the politically powerful, but it is doubtful if this pressure is any greater or more embarrassing than that exerted by important alumni and patrons of the private school."—President A. G. Ruthven, The University of Michigan, 1937. "The Role of the State University in American Higher Education," in *Proceedings and Addresses at the Inauguration of Edmund Ezra Day, Fifth President of Cornell University* (Ithaca, New York, 1937), pp. 21, 22.

"For the present it is my own firm conviction that privately endowed institutions and state-supported institutions should be engaged in a common task on a common level for a common group of students. If any other theory ultimately prevails it would seem to me that a state would be compelled by the logic of the situation to close its state university and pay the tuition charge for its students at the privately endowed institutions where they might have the benefit of private endowment."—President F. J. Kelly, The University of Idaho, 1928. *School and Society*, November 24, 1928.

"With the University today stand all the state and denominational schools, colleges, and the neighbor university. Not in antagonism but in all friendliness and rivalry in excellence we would work in this region and build here together one of the great intellectual and spiritual centers of the world."—President Frank P. Graham, The University of North Carolina, 1931. Inaugural Address, *The Alumni Review*, December, 1931.

"So I am not as worried as I might be over the fact that California is a large university. Indeed, I am disposed to approve mass education—so long as it does not become herd education. The important point is that the qualifications of entrants to do university work be maintained, and that the standards of the university be not impaired, either from within or without, with a view to making it possible for larger numbers to meet the requirements. Subject to those limitations, I believe that the University should welcome all who desire to come to it. The State cannot but profit by serving the splendid group of young men and women who seek an education on the various campuses of the University. An increase in that number, if quality be maintained, cannot but be desirable."—President Robert G. Sproul, The University of California, 1931. "Three Problems of the American University," *University of California Chronicle*, January, 1931.

"It is plain that, historically, practically, and theoretically, American opinion is strongly in favor of continuance and prosperity of both church and non-church schools, supported wholly by gifts and fees. It is equally plain that American opinion is heartily in favor of supporting out of taxes much more education than can be supported by means of gifts and fees. . . . The practical limit to tax supported education will mainly be set by public finances; the pupils are likely to demand and to need more education than can be paid for out of the public treasury or otherwise."—President N. Y. Benedict, The University of Texas, 1932. "What Education Should be Paid for Out of Taxes?" *Texas Outlook*, August, 1932, p. 15.

"In the confusing situation in which education in common with other social institutions finds itself, there still is a highly important place for the small college."—President F. W. Johnson, Colby College, 1932. *School and Society*, February 6, 1932.

"The chief danger inhering in university circles is that they will become so intellectualized and standardized that their pliability and usefulness as educational institutions will be minimized, if not destroyed. This does not mean that there may not be persons on any campus who work best and accomplish most when they are freest from social contacts, nor does it mean that these institutions should be so neglectful of standards and requirements as to be cheap imitations of a university. Certainly any university that loses step with current movements, that fails to give consideration to the sweeping changes that are occurring in every part of the world, will soon become archaic and incompetent to educate youth for the exercise of leadership.

"The State universities of America today are gravely concerned about their future status and usefulness. They behold a movement for tax reduction affecting all institutions alike without regard to their importance in the present crisis. If the programs and incomes of the State universities are to fluctuate up and down with every political wind that blows, then both public welfare and the economic life of the commonwealth they are maintained to serve will suffer."—President Lotus D. Coffman,

The University of Minnesota, 1932. In *The Obligation of Universities to the Social Order*, ed. H. P. Fairchild (New York: New York University Press, 1933), pp. 28, 29.

"No State university could survive in a sheer intellectual empyrean. State universities do not reside upon a hill. Their professors do not enjoy a cloistered life far from the marts of trade and the maddening crowd. They are constantly renewing their strength by returning to the springs from which the sources of strength flow. They are constantly measuring themselves by the extent to which the life of the people whom they are serving has been changed and improved. They are constantly evaluating their effectiveness by the developing and expanding social points of view of their graduates. They share with all universities the common responsibility of advancing the cultural life of the people they serve."—President Lotus D. Coffman, The University of Minnesota, 1932. In *The Obligation of the Universities to the Social Order*, ed. H. P. Fairchild (New York: New York University Press, 1933), p. 25.

"When the biographies of *Who's Who* are explored, the witness of the past is strongly reassuring to the smaller colleges. Judged in proportion to their total number of graduates, the independent colleges show a high rating of distinction, at least as it is recognized in that familiar work. In the first fifteen, out of seventy considered, are Amherst, Wesleyan, Trinity, Hobart, Williams, Haverford, Hamilton, Bowdoin and Union—and Lafayette, Dartmouth, Rutgers and Colgate are not far behind. These figures may be crude, but gloss them as you will the small college, so far, has no cause for shame in the essay of American alumni. The graduates of the good small college have for generations sent their sons back to its care, knowing its value in their own lives. . . ."—President Dixon Ryan Fox, Union College, 1934. Inaugural Address, *School and Society*, October 20, 1934.

"We shall not forget, then, that the University is a servant to the State. Our highest ambition is to do our work so well in instruction, in research, and in spreading knowledge by means of the extension service and through faculty participation in the economic and cultural life of the State, that we, like those pioneer schools about which the historian wrote, shall merit the continued support of 'government and the best of men.' In 1830 it was said that the citizens of Maine took the 'utmost pains to promote and improve the school system.' So today their descendants must see to it that education is properly supported. In saying this I am not thinking in terms of the University alone. The University shares with the public schools, private academies, normal schools, and the colleges of the State, the hope that by working together they may provide educational opportunities worthy of a State that is noted, above everything else, for the high quality of its human resources. . . .

"Service to the State, coöperation with all its educational agencies, the maintenance of high standards in everything we undertake, emphasis upon those elements in our university life that make for good citizenship and abundant living; these are the goals we set before us. Toward their attainment I pledge my best efforts."—President Arthur A. Hauck, The University of Maine, 1934. "The University and the State," *The Maine Bulletin* (Orono, Maine), December, 1934, p. 18.

"First I may say that for a long time we have said that denominational colleges in our state were not competitors of the state university, that we joined in a common cause, and that we extended our assistance in any way we could to these denominational institutions."—Chancellor E. A. Burnett, The University of Nebraska, 1934. *Transactions and Proceedings of the National Association of State Universities, 1934.*

"Particularly does the standard of student enlistment in the modern colleges differ from that of twenty years ago. Some of the student enlistment today is being very finely done, amounting to an actual appraisal of the intellectual calibre of student material, and some of it is being very badly done, amounting to little more than a commercial cat fight in the hope of persuading Student 'A' to go to one college instead of to another."—President Irving Maurer, Beloit College, 1934. *Bulletin of the Association of American Colleges*, December, 1934, p. 476.

"I think the people in America are very fortunate in having the three types of higher education, the independent colleges like Harvard and Columbia, the church colleges, and the state colleges. The independent colleges can initiate programs with greater facility than we can who have to depend upon public opinion. We are more or less bound down and cannot do the pioneer work that the independent institutions can do."—President L. T. Baker, The University of South Carolina, 1934. *Transactions and Proceedings of the National Association of State Universities, 1934.*

"It seems to me, gentlemen, that if we grant that higher education is desirable in the public interest and that it should be widely available, it is easy to demonstrate that state-supported higher education, notwithstanding its imperfections, has justified itself."—President F. D. Farrell, Kansas State College, 1934. *Transactions and Proceedings of the National Association of State Universities, 1934.*

"The independent four-year college is no longer the dominant institution in the field of American higher education. It is high time for any college which wishes to survive for any considerable period, and with any considerable degree of vitality, to face courageously the conditioning factors of general social and general educational change; and to take thought for the building of its own future rather than for the defense of its own past or its own present—even if the building of its own future involves the disturbance of forms and customs beloved by those to whom they are familiar."—President E. H. Wilkins, Oberlin College, 1934. *Bulletin of The Association of American Colleges*, December, 1934, p. 475.

"The present generation has witnessed a continuous expansion of the role of government. There are those who urge that the day of private charity and private education is past. This viewpoint is illustrated by the sentiment which favored the removal of the usual educational exemptions from the tax measures at the last session of Congress. It is a most dangerous doctrine. Education must not become a state monopoly."—President H. W. Dodds, Princeton University, 1935. *Report for 1934-35*, p. 2.

"In the United States the state universities and the endowed universities are, of course, attacking the same problem. They have the same task. They can help each other best by trying to do all that they can to rival and stimulate each other. In these days, when charity is passing from private to public hands, and when the sphere of government control is being so rapidly enlarged, I think it would be nothing less than a calamity if education were to be entirely supported by the state. But the endowed universities are expensive and they will continue to prosper, of course, only if they justify themselves."—President Frank Aydelotte, Swarthmore College, 1936. Address at the Harvard Club in New York, June 9, 1936, in *The Mission of the Endowed Universities* (Pamphlet).

"The colleges of South Carolina are bound together in a common task with a common purpose, and with common problems and difficulties.

"They are engaged in a common war against the foes of our own household : ignorance, illiteracy, near-illiteracy, prejudice, intolerance and narrowness of vision."—President J. R. McKissick, The University of South Carolina, 1936. Quoted in *Coker College Quarterly Bulletin*, December, 1936.

"I take it that it is agreed that there is no hostility between the privately endowed colleges and universities on the one hand and the state universities on the other. We are all working for the same end, the advancement of higher education in America. But we do believe that in the first place history shows that the privately endowed institutions are likely to act as pace makers for the publicly endowed institutions. In the second

place, . . . the private institutions are, and we hope will continue to be, peculiarly the citadels of freedom. They are free from that political influence which may dominate at times the public institutions. In the third place, the endowed universities are less prone to be moved by utilitarian considerations, and there is less danger that they will substitute vocational training for real education. We are confident that they at least will uphold the cause of higher education, that they will value the diligent search for the truth for its own sake, that they will continue to carry on the great tradition of advancing knowledge."
—President James B. Conant, Harvard University, 1936. Address at the Harvard Club in New York, June 9, 1936, in *The Mission of the Endowed Universities.* (Pamphlet.)

"We all know that higher education as conceived in the United States calls for both tax-supported and privately endowed and supported universities and colleges. One of the great functions of the tax-supported institution is, of course, to preserve the democratic ideal in higher education. The truth is that the privately endowed universities and colleges in origin were not democratic. They were organized to serve the conscious needs of particular groups or interests. They remain today more easily able to hew their own paths, less governed by popular clamor because they are responsible to a more restricted constituency than are agencies supported by governmental appropriations.

"It is the private institution which is free to limit enrollments, to set requirements where it will, to indulge in experimentation, and to preach the doctrine that education rightly conceived is essentially not a leveling process. . . .

"The tax-supported university, of course, cannot escape a political responsibility, nor does it wish to do so. Unfortunately the responsibility as enforced is sometimes to low politics rather than high politics. For this reason we should continue to view with concern the injection of politics into boards of control of tax-supported institutions. In several instances there is still much to be accomplished in the divorce of boards of regents from low politics."—President H. W. Dodds, Princeton University, 1937. *Journal of Proceedings and Addresses of the Association of American Universities* (Chicago: The University of Chicago Press, 1937), pp. 82, 83.

"It is obvious that the universities were not founded and cannot be maintained simply to keep the professors busy and the students out of mischief. When we refer to our original charters, almost without exception in the case of the colleges and generally in the case of the universities, the obligation of producing graduates capable of serving the state, of providing the commonwealth with citizens qualified to serve the public welfare in this or that field, has always been emphasized.

"It is equally certain that in the future, unless that obligation of service be fulfilled by the universities, they will not be allowed to survive in their existing forms. State institutions will be radically reorganized; privately endowed institutions will disappear."—President Charles Seymour, Yale University, 1937. *Journal of Proceedings and Addresses of the Association of American Universities* (Chicago: The University of Chicago Press, 1937), p. 98.

"When I examine the history of higher education in America in the last fifty years and note the growth of the publicly supported institutions,—the increase in student body, in plant and in capacity for scholarly and professional work of the highest order,—I can arrive at only one conclusion. During the next century of academic history, university education in this republic will be largely in the hands of the tax-supported institutions. As they fare, so fares the cultural and intellectual life of the American people.

"From this obvious prediction, arrived at by extrapolating the recent trends in American history, I by no means conclude that the role of privately endowed institutions is in the future to be relatively insignificant. On the contrary, their function I believe to be as important as ever for they must both supplement and assist the tax-supported institutions in rounding out the whole picture of American life. This function, as I shall endeavor to show, although quantitatively small is qualitatively a matter of the greatest consequence.

"In the first place it seems to me that privately endowed educational institutions,—schools, colleges and universities alike,—have a peculiar role to play as truly national centers of learning. The tax-supported university or college must have, by and large, a local clientele. The university *independent* of state aid may, on the other hand, quite properly use its funds for the education of boys and girls from all parts of the country. Such an institution has the opportunity,—perhaps I should say has imposed upon it the duty,—of being one of the centers where sectional prejudice may be rapidly disintegrated by the action of social and educational forces. If the student bodies of the privately endowed colleges and universities are true geographic cross sections of the country, these institutions can fulfill a unique and vital function in American education. The point is obvious and has been long recognized; to stress it further before this audience would be to force the proverbial open door.

"The second and perhaps more important function of a privately endowed institution is to act as an innovator and pacemaker. On the whole, a university which receives its income from endowment is more favorably situated in this regard than a tax-supported institution. The size of the student body can be limited, the pressure to undertake various purely utilitarian and vocational lines of endeavor can be more readily resisted. With less dependence on the immediate support of a mass of voters, new departures along certain lines can be achieved more rapidly or entered into with less caution. There are dozens of examples of educational experimentation which I could use to illustrate the significance of the privately endowed university as a proving ground for new ideas. . . ."—President James B. Conant, Harvard University, 1937. "The Role of the Endowed University in American Higher Education," *Proceedings and Ad-*

dresses at the Inauguration of Edmund Ezra Day, Fifth President of Cornell University (Ithaca, New York, 1937), pp. 15, 16.

"No institution that approaches the problem of selection sincerely can free itself from pressing questions. The president of one of the most famous of our colleges, after an examination of the resources, capacities, and ideals of the institution, said frankly that he didn't see how he could get students in numbers sufficient to operate if the institution maintained so selective an ideal. If the distinguished executive head of a richly provided college expresses doubts such as these, we need not be surprised at the compromising with ideals that goes on in weaker institutions. The president of a small college recently said, 'We know that we are accepting students who cannot do our work. We know that we are carrying these students forward to graduation. In our present situation we are under such pressure that we feel we have no other choice. Our campus morale is affected by numbers and a reduction in attendance is looked upon as a slump—as though the institution were losing ground.' It is of the utmost significance that so many of the oldest and most powerful institutions in this country are directing attention anew to the importance of wisely selecting their students. The competitive pressures among institutions may become very much greater than they are at present. Fortunate will be the college that knows what it can do and that has educated its constituency to a recognition of its institutional capacities and its institutional integrity. Such a college can be confident of an honorable future. Colleges are means, not ends."—President Walter A. Jessup, The Carnegie Foundation for the Advancement of Teaching, 1937. *Thirty-second Annual Report* (New York City, 1937), p. 11.

"The growth of the junior college has been the most startling development in the field of higher education in the last two decades. . . . At the same time, professional schools are more and more commonly taking students after two years of college work. This situation is obviously menacing for the independent college. . . ."—President E. H. Wilkins, Oberlin College, 1937. Quoted in *Bulletin of the American Association of University Professors*, March, 1937, p. 250.

"In a country with forty-eight States generalizations are dangerous. The reader may feel that I am painting much too dismal a picture of the fate of the poor boy, and that I am overlooking the existence of our great State-supported universities. No one can be unmindful of the value of their work. It is true than an education can be obtained at these centers at very low cost. Furthermore, earning one's way through college is still both possible and fashionable; probably easier at our State universities than at the privately endowed institutions, but still possible at both.

"Nevertheless, I submit the following facts to support my plea for a greatly enlarged scholarship policy for the country: (1) the statistics in regard to the income of the families of the country (less than 3 per cent with $5,000 or more, 80 per cent with incomes of less than $2,000) and the number of students of college age in our colleges or universities (11 per cent) as compared with the high-school figure of 63 per cent; (2) the fact that, with the unemployment situation as it is today, working one's way through college is much more difficult than in former times; (3) the empirical evidence collected incidentally during the past few years in connection with the administration of the Harvard National Scholarships in certain States in the Middle West. The Dean's Office has found case after case of a most likely candidate for university work—a young man of outstanding ability and personality—who could not afford to go even to the publicly supported university of his State. A scholarship which would pay the total cost of his education away from home would enable such a boy to go on; otherwise his higher education would consist only of high-school work or the instruction offered in a local academy. These youths are lost to the professional leadership of the country. They are lost to the advancement of knowledge and its application to the needs of society. No one can estimate the potential gifts to civilization which are yearly squandered by cutting off the further education of boys and girls for financial reasons."—President James B. Conant, Harvard University, 1938. "The Future of Our Higher Education," *Harper's Monthly Magazine*, May, 1938.

"The issue between State-supported and privately endowed institutions seems destined to become more sharply drawn in all regions except the East. If the Federal Government makes grants for higher education, as has been proposed, these grants will probably go primarily to institutions under State control. If the amounts are large, private colleges which now offer an educational opportunity to at least half of the American boys and girls going to college may suffer severely. If the Federal Government is going to subsidize higher education in part, it is to be hoped that an effect will not be the weakening or eliminating of hundreds of colleges independent in their control." —President James L. McConaughy, Wesleyan University, 1938. *The New York Times*, January 2, 1938.

"The institutions all alike serve the public, and in that sense are equally public. We must all stand or fall together. The success of one is the success of all and the failure of one is the failure of all. No one of us should be so much engrossed in his own concerns as to overlook the wider good of all."—President W. P. Few, Duke University, March, 1939. Address before The North Carolina Education Association, Raleigh, March 17, 1939. Typescript copy of address; published in part in the *News and Observer* (Raleigh), March 18, 1939.

4

ORGANIZATION AND ADMINISTRATION

Presidential statements concerning the organization and administration of higher education do not lend themselves so easily to classification and organization as their statements on some other subjects. However, the quotations that appear in this section throw some light on their views concerning the College of Arts as the "heart" of higher education; the curriculum and the changes it has undergone; the elective system; student relations, with particular emphasis on discipline and religious life; athletics, especially football; and finance, one of the most persistent problems of all.

The history of the college curriculum in the United States, over which conflicts have often waged, seems to divide itself into three rather definite periods: from the curriculum of Henry Dunster, who brought it to Harvard from Cambridge, England, in 1640, to about the advent of President Charles W. Eliot of Harvard in 1869; between that date and the World War; and since the World War.

The first of these periods was marked by the well known domination of the classics in a fixed curriculum of a very few other subjects that included mathematics, rhetoric, logic, and moral philosophy—the seventeenth, eighteenth and a part of the nineteenth century version of the ancient *trivium* and *quadrivium.* The classical subjects were standard in most of the colleges, slight differences here and there serving only to give emphasis to the similarity of the American college curriculum for two centuries or more. From about 1869 to about 1914 there was a growing tendency away from a fixed curriculum toward a gradual increasing freedom of elective programs, under the assumption, that some thoughtful people believed to be a bit violent, that the college student was sufficiently mature to make wise selections of his courses. The elective system gained wide vogue under the influence of Harvard which was the leading university of the land and therefore identified with the fitness of educational things. Professor S. E. Morison, the official historian of Harvard University, says: "It is a hard saying, but Mr. Eliot, more than any other man, is responsible for the greatest educational crime of the century against American youth—depriving him of his classical heritage."

No consideration of the change in the college curriculum during this period can neglect the significance of the secular upheaval following the advent of the "gilded age," when the colleges and universities appeared to begin to pay "less and less attention to the thunders of the pulpit." Great business leaders were being appealed to for educational endowments and by 1900 the lists of trustees of colleges and universities "read like a corporation directory." The classics which for centuries had been bent mainly toward theological purposes began to wane, religion began to have a smaller place in the program of higher education, and, now released from a prescribed curriculum, college students were soon able to nibble all over the catalogues.

The third period, which roughly covers the past two or three decades, has been marked by strong swing away from freedom of election back to a measure of prescription.

Probably on no collegiate subject have more words been written and spoken by college presidents and others than athletics. Since Rutgers and Princeton played the first game of intercollegiate football in 1869, this popular game has become an increasingly stubborn problem among college presidents. President James Felton, of Harvard, as early as 1860, pointed to some of the evils which were destined to distress the heads of higher educational institutions. President F. A. P. Barnard, of Columbia, as early as 1888, President Charles W. Eliot, of Harvard, as early as 1893, President E. D. Warfield, of Lafayette, as early as 1894, and other presidents said some of the same things that have been said about intercollegiate football in recent years. Deceit and bad faith have often been charged by college presidents, in the area of football, which has become big business and is described as "dementia Americana."

It was noted in Section 1 that college presidents in their inaugural addresses often ask for adequate financial support for their institutions. The subject of finance is also discussed by these educational leaders at other times, especially in their annual reports. Here it should be noted, however, that such reports are not made by all college presidents. In some cases, also, these reports are more or less intimate documents, generally intended only for the trustees and other members of the supporting constituency. But the views of some higher educational leaders on what President W. W. Folwell, of the University of Minnesota, in 1869 called "Money! money!! money!!!" and what Chancellor James H. Kirkland, of Vanderbilt, in 1893 called "the food that universities thrive on," appear in Part 8 of this section.

Changes that took place in higher education in this country between 1914 and 1934 are discussed in the quotations given in Part 9 of this section. In 1934, at the annual meeting of the Association of American Colleges, a number of college presidents compared conditions at that time with conditions in 1914, when that organization was founded.

Some Guiding Principles

"Its Corporation should therefore be men who are incapable of acting from fear, favor, or affection. In all official acts, they should look with equal eye upon the merits of the nearest relative, and upon those of a stranger. They should know no parties either in politics or religion; and knowing nothing but the duties and obligations of their office, should appoint and remove solely and entirely for the good of the institution of which they are the appointed governors. . . .

"If politicians, like Virgil's harpies, will insist on defiling what they cannot eat, I know of no remedy that can be anticipated from that source. Or again, it may be said that there is not interest enough on this subject in the community to carry forward any change in this respect; or that if the theory of the system were changed, it would inevitably fail in practice, inasmuch as it would be impossible to find men competent to such a trial, or that if found competent they would not give to it the time and labor necessary for the successful discharge of its duties. If this be so, I grant the case to be hopeless. The other obstacles might be surmounted. Where there is a will there is a way. But for indifference on such a subject, there is no cure; and we must wait until the community attains a higher sense of social and moral obligation.

"Supposing however, all this to be so, two conclusions will follow. If there exist not in the community, sufficient energy and self denying effort to carry forward institutions of learning, let the blame be laid at the right door. Let not colleges be blamed for not doing what the apathy of the community renders impossible to be done. Instead of changing college courses, and trying experiments on college discipline, let us strive to arouse the nation to a conviction of the importance of the subject. Let us strive to cure the ailing member. If the heart be diseased, let us not persist in blistering the head. If the community will take an intelligent interest in the subject, all the other disorders will easily remedy themselves."—President Francis Wayland, Brown University, 1842. *Thoughts on the Present Collegiate System in the United States* (Boston: Gould, Kendall and Lincoln, 1842), pp. 50, 60, 61.

"To see every day the evil fruit of a bad appointment must be the cruelest of official torments. Fortunately, the good effect of a judicious appointment is also inestimable; and here, as everywhere good is more penetrating and diffusive than evil."—President Charles W. Eliot, Harvard University, 1869. Inaugural Address, in S. E. Morison, *The Development of Harvard University* (Cambridge: Harvard University Press, 1930), p. lxxvii.

"A university is the last place in the world for a dictator.

Learning is always republican. It has idols but not masters."
—President Charles W. Eliot, Harvard University, 1869. Inaugural Address, in S. E. Morison, *The Development of Harvard University* (Cambridge: Harvard University Press, 1930), p. lxxvii.

"The office and value of administration in a modern university are not yet clearly understood. Indeed, administration has been defined by some one whose wit does not wholly hide his aspirations for anarchy as 'doing extremely well what had better not be done at all.' The task of university administration is the clearly defined but difficult one of making an environment in which scholars and teachers can work agreeably, effectively and undisturbed. It is everywhere and always subordinate to the intellectual life and activity of the university, but it is vitally important if the wisest use is to be made of limited resources, if waste and confusion are to be prevented, and if the conditions surrounding teaching and investigation are to be such as to make most easily possible the prosecution of successful intellectual endeavor."—President Nicholas Murray Butler, Columbia University, 1910. *Report for 1909-10*, p. 1.

"There is some measure of truth in the cynical suggestion that administration may best be defined as the doing extremely well of something that had better not be done at all. The tendency not only in universities but in all forms of public business to multiply and to complicate the details of routine administration is as strong as it is mischievous. The whole purpose of university administration is to make it possible for the University's scholars to do their work of teaching and investigation with the least interruption, annoyance or division of interest, and to record and to classify in the simplest way possible the personal performances of those who come to the University as students. . . . Fussy administration manifests itself chiefly through the committee system which is a plural executive with necessarily divided responsibility. Many minds chosen for their representative character and capacity are needed to formulate and to settle questions of policy, but when policies are once formulated and settled, they are far better executed by a single individual than by a number of men acting in consultation."—President Nicholas Murray Butler, Columbia University, 1915. *Report for 1914-15*, p. 1.

"Some years ago the London *Spectator* invited Lord Salisbury, then Prime Minister, to read to his colleagues in the Cabinet the eighteenth chapter of Exodus beginning at the thirteenth verse. The writer pointed out that in that chapter the true principle of civil administration is laid down with a clearness and precision which no subsequent writers on public affairs have ever bettered. The passage in question relates the visit of Jethro to his son-in-law, Moses, in the course of which Jethro observed that the whole of Moses' energy was occupied with the details of administration. He therefore felt compelled to protest and to ask Moses why he was so continually immersed in the details of his work. . . .

"More tractable than most sons-in-law, Moses accepted the good advice of Jethro, and the record tells that in future Moses refrained from interference with matters of detail and occupied himself solely with those of importance. . . . To distinguish between government and administration and then to establish sound principles of administration, are no less important now than in the days of Jethro and Moses."—President Nicholas Murray Butler, Columbia University, 1917. *Report for 1916-17*, p. 41.

"It should be said in passing that the experience of state-controlled universities offers many discouraging illustrations of how far we yet have to go before the machinery of government provides for the wishes of the people in the management of the university. Public interest and political interest have been found too often divergent, and it is little wonder that as yet many thoughtful parents prefer to entrust their children, and philanthropists their money, to these stable, adequately supported, privately controlled universities than to the unstable, less well-supported, state-controlled universities which have been so often subjected to the caprice of small-minded politicians."—President F. J. Kelly, The University of Idaho, 1928. *School and Society*, November 24, 1928.

"The University therefore is a complex organization, bringing together under one central control many agencies of higher education, adult education, and research. It represents a combination of many of the State's non-political functions. As head of the public school system, it must assume the position of a sympathetic and inspiring leader. It should offer to the graduates of our high schools and junior colleges opportunity to acquire a broad cultural foundation and to supplement this with the specialization necessary for a chosen field. It should inspire the few who are capable of leadership to still further endeavor in the graduate field. It should be a leader in the advancement of knowledge, seek to find new facts and to reinterpret old ones. It should gather the wisdom of the ages to the end that it may inspire its students, inform the people, and expand the industries of the region. For industry the University should furnish a resource survey, a fact-finding organization, and a training ground for young men and women. It should be a non-partisan guide and counsellor of the State's economic and industrial systems, looking never to personal or partisan gain but to the present and future welfare of the people."—President Homer L. Shantz, The University of Arizona, 1930. *Inaugural Bulletin* (Tucson, Arizona, 1930), p. 37.

"The success of a large university in providing sound education is primarily a matter of organization. The quality of the faculty, the wide range of opportunities in the way of departments and courses, the splendid facilities in libraries and laboratories, all make the University of California a most attractive place for students. If such a university is able to furnish enough instructors of proper qualifications and sufficient facilities, as we now are, I know of no reason why a very large number of students should not receive an excellent education on its campus. As long as we maintain high standards of admission and graduation there is no need to limit enrollment. As to eliminating the first two years, I should prefer that others make that experiment. We shall observe the results with interest and be guided as to our future policy by them."—President Robert G. Sproul, The University of California, 1931. "Three Problems of the American University," *University of California Chronicle*, January, 1931.

"Academic departments, like nations, should be separated but not isolated, strong but not dictatorial. I regard with a good deal of irritation the increasing emphasis on the kind of nationalism in public affairs and of departmentalism in academic life that is narrow and self-centered. The reintegration of knowledge is as necessary to liberal culture as the reintegration of nationalism is to the general welfare."—President Harry A. Garfield, Williams College, 1932. In *The Obligation of Universities to the Social Order*, ed. H. P. Fairchild (New York: New York University Press, 1933), p. 297.

"The organization of American universities, with sharp division into a multitude of departments, each of which tends to confine itself within definite bounds, and each of which tends to conceive of itself, not as an administrative convenience, but as a reality, with its vested interests and its independent life—all that, I say, tends to emphasize the idea of specialization to a wholly irrational degree.

"Here is one of the great problems before us: How shall we make proper provision in American universities for specialization and the specialist, and, at the same time, prevent culture from leaking through the cracks which develop between specialties as they pull apart? I could wish that our faculties, as a rule, sensed the problem more keenly."—President Samuel P. Capen, The University of Buffalo, 1933. In *The Obligation of Universities to the Social Order*, ed. H. P. Fairchild (New York: New York University Press, 1933), pp. 70, 71.

"If an American university takes seriously its obligations to serve as an example of democratic principles, how, specifically, will it conduct its affairs? First of all it will admit of no tyranny anywhere within its walls. The relations existing between trustees and faculty and between faculty and students will be those of mutual confidence and respect; they will be coöperative relations in the conduct of an undertaking in which all are partners. Government there must be, in a university as elsewhere, and the external framework of the government of most universities is the product of an earlier day; of a pattern more oligarchical than democratic. But in its operation it will be government with the consent of the governed."—Chancellor Samuel P. Capen, The University of Buffalo, 1935. *School and Society*, June 22, 1935.

THE COLLEGE OF ARTS

"For the ordinary purposes of educating boys, generally between the ages of fifteen and twenty-one, we have no hesitation in giving preference to such colleges as we already possess; provided always, that they be made in fact what they assume and profess to be in name. Such institutions, scattered over the land, at convenient distances from each other, are better adapted to the habits, wants, and circumstances of our widely dispersed and comparatively poor population."—President Philip Lindsley, The University of Nashville, 1827. *The Works of Philip Lindsley*, ed. L. J. Halsey (Philadelphia, 1864), I, 405. Quoted in D. G. Tewksbury, *The Founding of American Colleges and Universities Before the Civil War* (New York: Bureau of Publications, Teachers College, Columbia University, 1932), p. 3.

"The question will here be asked what are we to do with the four years course? I answer, it seems to me of but very little consequence whether we do with it or without it. The whole course, originally, like the apprenticeship to trades, extended to *seven* years, at which time the student proceeded to the Master of Arts, with the full liberty of teaching or lecturing wherever he pleased. . . . This has since been abridged to four years, . . . There is nothing magical or imperative in the term of four years, nor has it any natural relation to a course of study. It was adopted as a matter of accident; and can have, of itself, no important bearing on the subject in hand.

"But is it not important to have some standard fixed; and to have this standard as high as possible, to which the candidate for the certificate of a liberal education shall conform. I answer most truly, and I would elevate rather than depress it. I by no means sympathize with the efforts made in various forms to render the requirements for a degree less exact or comprehensive or scholarlike . . . fixing the time to be occupied ostensibly in liberal study, by no means accurately fixes the amount of knowledge required for a degree.

"I am by no means tenacious of the term of four years. I certainly would not have the period curtailed. . . . But I would not have it a matter of time. Instead of fixing upon a period of four or five or six years, I would designate the amount of knowledge and discipline which could be attained by ordinary talent and persevering diligence during that time. But supposing this time to be fixed, the question is how shall it be occupied; in thorough or in superficial study; in full and manly development of the powers of the mind or in merely running over elements. . . . It seems to me that the proper course is marked out by plain common sense. Let the requirements for a degree be high, and let them be high in attainment of knowledge and not in the number of things to be properly learned. . . . What we do let us do well, and then our system will recommend itself." —President Francis Wayland, Brown University, 1842. *Thoughts on the Present Collegiate System in the United States* (Boston: Gould, Kendall and Lincoln, 1842), pp. 101-103.

"In its external aspect, the college is the promoter and conservator of the liberal arts, those subjects which engage the interest of enlightened minds; it is the guardian of the culture of mankind; it is the apparatus by which each generation is brought up into sympathetic appreciation of the total achievement of the race. In its internal aspect, the college is a body of associates in pursuit of the higher things of life, a brotherhood in which character takes form in the atmosphere of culture, in which mind comes to its own in the process of dealing with the finest products of mind—a mutual benefit society yielding dividends in efficiency and character. . . . For the college is at once the minister and the symbol of the supremacy of the ideal world, and the note of idealism shares with the note of fellowship the dominance of college life."—President William Louis Poteat, Wake Forest College, 1905. Inaugural Address, in *Youth and Culture* (Wake Forest: Wake Forest College Press, 1938), pp. 12, 13.

"It is worth our while to consider the nature of an ideal college as an integral part of our University; ideal, in the sense not of something to be exactly reproduced, but of a type to which we should conform as closely as circumstances will permit. It would contemplate the highest development of the individual student—which involves the best equipment of the graduate. It would contemplate also the proper connection of the college with the professional schools; and it would adjust the relation of the students to one another."—President A. Lawrence Lowell, Harvard University, 1909. Inaugural Address, in S. E. Morison, *The Development of Harvard University* (Cambridge: Harvard University Press, 1930), p. lxxxi.

"The college, as we have it, is peculiar to our own national system of education, and is perhaps its strongest, as it certainly is its most characteristic, feature."—President Nicholas Murray Butler, Columbia University, 1902. *Report for 1901-02*, p. 48.

"The college is now as ever a school of culture. It aims to make wise, sane, well-rounded men who know something of the best that men have thought and done in this world, and whose lives will be the better for this knowledge."—President David Starr Jordan, Leland Stanford Junior University, 1902. "University Building," *Popular Science Monthly*, August, 1902, p. 331.

"The college exists to foster sound learning and scholarship, habits of reflection and application, together with mental and spiritual growth and culture."—President Nicholas Murray Butler, Columbia University, 1903. *Report for 1902-03*, p. 31.

"However valuable may be the work of the professional and vocational departments of a university, the heart and soul of any institution for higher learning is its college of liberal arts." —President John C. Futrall, The University of Arkansas, 1914. *University of Arkansas Bulletin*, Inaugural Number, February, 1915, p. 14.

"The reality of the state university's power to liberate the faculties and aspirations of the workers in the productive state depends on the force of that power as generated in it as an association of teachers and students, given wholly to the pursuit of truth and free from the distractions of making a living. The heart of this association, the college of liberal arts and sciences, has as its mission now as always the revelation of the full meaning of life in its broad and general relations, and to fix in the heart of its youth a point of outlook on the field of human endeavor from which to see it clearly and to see it whole. It fears no criticism based on an interpretation of its mission as 'impractical'; but it does regard as fatal any failure to evoke the best powers of its own student body."—President Edward K. Graham, The University of North Carolina, 1915. "Inaugural Address," *Education and Citizenship and Other Papers* (New York: G. P. Putnam's Sons, 1919 [also University of North Carolina Press]), pp. 19, 20.

"The crucial test of the ability of the University to identify her mission with that of democracy is found in her achievement in the college of liberal arts. For in the college, if anywhere, must emerge the answer to the question whether the ideal of freedom can successfully embody itself in concrete concepts of education and of life. To fail here, under conditions so fitted to the task, is to proclaim that the great underlying principles of democracy can nowhere be attained. Success or failure will spring ultimately from the attitude of the college itself toward what it is about and from no other factor. . . .

"But it is not the ultimate aim of the college to develop men who are only spectators of life, however clear their vision of what in it is ephemeral and what abiding. At this hour of constructive need the college could not more greatly sin against itself and the State than by training men who should hold themselves aloof from the work-a-day life of the world, from participation and leadership in every fine and worthy human cause. The University believes with her whole heart that it is the function of the college to train for citizenship and for service; and she also whole-heartedly believes that citizenship and service proceed from within the man himself, not from external mandate." —President Harry W. Chase, The University of North Carolina, 1920. Inaugural Address, *The State University and the New South.* Chapel Hill, 1920, pp. 63, 64.

"The American college is very much alive today. Its right to live has been challenged, and that challenge calls for answer at a suitable time, but I shall not attempt that answer now. Instead, I shall assume that it has been made, that you agree with me, that there is still a place for the college, and that we are interested in its future and in seeing to it that that future is the best possible. In short, I take it for granted, on the one hand, that the college is to remain, but, on the other hand, that it is not to be stagnant and unchangeable, that it is alive, and is going to remain alive, and therefore to develop."—President E. D. Burton, The University of Chicago, 1923. *Education in a Democratic World* (Chicago: The University of Chicago Press, 1927), p. 57.

"The thesis I desire to maintain about the future of the American College, as thus defined, is that its aim must be educational, and of a cultural rather than a vocational type."—President A. Lawrence Lowell, Harvard University, 1928. *Bulletin of the Association of American Colleges*, February, 1928, p. 13.

"What basic course gives the student the most reasonable opportunity of developing these powers according to their importance, so that the finished product will be the man or woman of investigating, cultural mind and disciplined will? . . .

"The complete course of Liberal Arts, presenting for study

and assimilation the finest thoughts of the greatest minds, tends to knead, to exercise, to energize the various faculties into a mental vigor which fits them to grapple with the more practical problems of life or to concentrate more pointedly and perseveringly upon the specialized problems of the professional or graduate school."—President William M. Magee, S.J., Marquette University, 1928. *Inaugural Address* (Milwaukee: Marquette University Press, 1928), pp. 11, 12, 13.

"The American college is fearfully and wonderfully made. For many years the doctors have been watching it, thumping it and probing into it in the hope of understanding its anatomy and physiology. More recently its psychology and hygiene also have been subject to careful observation.

"Its unaccountable behavior has attracted the attention of the general public, who have been convinced it has a high fever, or a weak heart, or a diseased brain or arteriosclerosis, or all put together. Nearly everybody agrees it must be incurably sick and yet siren-like it draws increasingly thousands of our best youth into its atmosphere and life."—*The Effective College*, ed. Robert Lincoln Kelly, formerly president of Earlham College. New York: The Association of American Colleges, 1928.

"The College of Letters, Arts, and Sciences is basic to the work of all colleges, since it offers the foundation work in science, language, and the humanities. It is not only basic to all other colleges but has largely the responsibility of carrying forward the banner of general culture against the insistent demands for machine-like efficiency of a vocational type, sponsored especially by those who have espoused education as a vocation rather than an intellectual adventure."—President Homer L. Shantz, The University of Arizona, 1930. *Inaugural Bulletin* (Tucson, Arizona, 1930), p. 40.

"The liberal arts college will survive, unchanged in purpose, but with form, curriculum, and method modified to meet the demands of new knowledge and changed conditions. Under wise and progressive guidance the liberal arts college in the years ahead should surpass the achievements of its long past."—President F. W. Johnson, Colby College, 1932. *School and Society*, February 6, 1932.

"The College of Arts and Sciences is an indispensable part of any university organization and as such must set up for its students high standards for intellectual achievement. Its special province is to provide a general and adequate foundation for living in a changing world. The curriculum embracing the physical, mathematical and biological sciences, the social sciences, and the humanities includes those subjects which are considered essential for equipping the individual to understand himself, the world in which he lives, and his place in the universe. The College of Arts and Sciences is also the service department for all the other colleges on the campus and offers the basic preparation necessary for the study of professions such as law, medicine, teaching, and dentistry, and for a wide variety of other occupations."—President Arthur A. Hauck, The University of Maine, 1934. "The University and the State," *The Maine Bulletin* (Orono, Maine), December, 1934, pp. 19, 23.

"There is a general conviction that the college of liberal arts has an even more important contribution to make in the future than in the immediate past."—President John S. Nollen, Grinnell College, 1934. *Bulletin of the Association of American Colleges*, December, 1934, p. 465.

"That which is unique must justify its own unicity. The fact that outside North America other countries, certainly as civilized as ours, have never desired to organize their higher education on our principle may throw some doubt upon its natural perfection. It may suggest that our small four-year college was an admirable issue of expediency under primitive conditions, but is not innately reasonable when circumstances give free choice. It may argue that the attempt to bracket older lads and younger men in one administrative unit gives liberties to youth for which it has not been prepared and prolongs guardianship for those who should be free of it."—President Dixon Ryan Fox, Union College, 1934. Inaugural Address, *School and Society*, October 20, 1934.

"The American college of liberal arts is too complex an organism to yield to easy characterization. A century ago it was the apex of American higher education. Today it is the base. Nevertheless, today the responsibility rests upon it of being the last formal educational process to which the majority of those enrolled within it will ever have easy access, while at the same time the obligation rests upon it to develop within a minority of its membership the stimulus of intellectual enthusiasm and the commitments to precision of thought which shall make those of this group desirable candidates for the graduate schools and the professional schools of the universities. . . .

"Is it to be assumed then that there are no fundamental principles which shall be accepted by the liberal college in determining its role? By no means! This is not to be conceded for a moment. The college is not entitled to be called 'liberal' which does not take its stand and adhere to it upon the fundamental principles that freedom of inquiry, freedom of discussion, and freedom of speech are the inalienable rights of all who would not utilize these rights to destroy the freedom which makes them possible. . . .

"The function of the liberal college then, whether in one role or in another, is to establish within its disciples a habit of mind, eager to know what truth is, persistent in attempt to find it, and loyal to its implications when conviction is acquired that it has been found. . . .

"Formerly the accepted role of the college was to implant in the student's mind that which was authoritatively asserted to be knowledge. Cumulatively down through modern times science has revealed to us into what a blind alley unexamined claims to authority may lead us. Hence it has become indispensable that we revise our conception and restate our objective to be that the desirable role of the college shall be to strive to develop in its students that sense of discrimination and that accuracy of judgment which shall enable them to discern what knowledge really is and how best it may be found.

"Only so may our colleges teach truth and only so through them may knowledge of truth come to mankind."—President Ernest M. Hopkins, Dartmouth College, 1937. "The Role of the Liberal Arts College in American Higher Education," *Proceedings and Addresses at the Inauguration of Edmund Ezra Day, Fifth President of Cornell University* (Ithaca, New York, 1937), pp. 10, 11, 12, 13.

"What of the colleges and schools in our various universities that disclaim any direct vocational or professional aim, as, for example, the college of arts and sciences? It is in these institutions and in our independent liberal arts colleges that we may reasonably look for evidences of the intellectual life at its undergraduate best. What, in fact, do we find? . . .

"Even in these colleges, in which the invading forces of vocationalism have been most effectively checked, the intellectual life is not generally promoted with clear success. Certain defects persistently characterize the scholarly work of these institutions.

"The chief of these defects I venture to enumerate as follows: (1) the work of the student as organized in a series of formal courses tends to be disjointed and atomistic and lacking in cumulative or additive effect; (2) the instructional outcomes are too largely informational in character—not enough attention is devoted to the development of skills; (3) the results to a regrettable extent prove to be ephemeral; (4) the quality of student interest and effort is in general unsatisfactory—a cult of campus indifference tends to stifle student enthusiasm for things intellectual; (5) the undergraduate experiences of the student do not sufficiently induce lasting habits of self-education; and (6) the results of liberal arts education are commonly lacking in social consequence."—President Edmund E. Day, Cornell University, 1937. *Proceedings and Addresses at the Inauguration of Edmund Ezra Day, Fifth President of Cornell University* (Ithaca, New York, 1937), p. 34.

"The liberal arts colleges are still hale and hearty after a century of anxious debate over whether they could survive the competition of vocational schools."—President W. L. Lingle, Davidson College, 1939. Associated Press dispatch from Raleigh, March 17, 1939, reporting address before the North Carolina Education Association.

The Curriculum

"What subject which is now studied here, could be set aside, without evidently marring the system, not to speak particularly in this place of the ancient languages?"—Report of the faculty of Yale College, 1828. *Report on the Course of Instruction in Yale College by a Committee of the Corporation and the Academical Faculty.* New Haven, 1828.

"The endless controversies whether language, philosophy, mathematics or science supply the best mental training, whether general education should be chiefly literary or chiefly scientific, have no practical lesson for us today. This University recognizes no real antagonism between literature and science, and consents to no such narrow alternatives as mathematics or classics, science or metaphysics. We would have them all, and at their best. To observe keenly, to reason soundly and to imagine vividly are operations as essential as that of clear and forcible expression, and to develop one of these faculties, it is not necessary to repress and dwarf the others. A University is not closely concerned with the applications of knowledge, until its general education branches into professional. Poetry and philosophy and science do indeed conspire to promote the material welfare of mankind; but science no more than poetry finds its best warrant in its utility. Truth and right are above utility in all realms of thought and action.

"It were a bitter mockery to suggest that any subject whatever should be taught less than it now is in American colleges. The only conceivable aim of a college government in our day is to broaden, deepen, and invigorate American teaching in all branches of learning. It will be generations before the best of

American institutions of education will get growth enough to bear pruning. The descendants of the Pilgrim Fathers are still very thankful for the parched corn of learning.

"Recent discussions have added pitifully little to the world's stock of wisdom about the staple of education. Who blows today such a ringing trumpet-call to the study of language as Luther blew? Hardly a significant word has been added in two centuries to Milton's description of the unprofitable way to study languages. Would any young American learn how to profit by travel, that foolish beginning but excellent sequel to education, he can find no apter advice than Bacon's. The practice of England and America is literally centuries behind the precept of the best thinkers upon education. A striking illustration may be found in the prevailing neglect of the systematic study of English language. How lamentably true today are these words of Locke: 'If any one among us have a facility or purity more than ordinary in his mother-tongue, it is owing to chance, or his genius, or any thing rather than to his education or any care of his teacher.'

"The best result of the discussion which has raged so long about the relative educational value of the main branches of learning is the conviction that there is room for them all in a sound scheme, provided that right methods of teaching be employed. It is not because of the limitation of their faculties that boys of eighteen come to college, having mastered nothing but a few score pages of Latin and Greek, and the bare elements of mathematics. Not nature, but an unintelligent system of instruction from the primary school through the college, is responsible for the fact that many college graduates have so inadequate a conception of what is meant by scientific observation, reasoning, and proof. It is possible for the young to get actual experience of all the principal methods of thought. There is a method of thought in language, and a method in mathematics, and another of natural and physical science, and another of faith. With wise direction, even a child would drink at all these springs. The actual problem to be solved is not what to teach, but how to teach. The revolutions accomplished in other fields of labor have a lesson for teachers. New England could not cut her hay with scythes, nor the West her wheat with sickles. When millions are to be fed where formerly there were but scores, the single fish line must be replaced by seines and trawls, the human shoulders by steam-elevators, and the wooden-axled ox-cart on a corduroy road by the smooth-running freight train. In education, there is a great hungry multitude to be fed. The great well at Orvieto, up whose spiral paths files of donkeys painfully brought the sweet water in kegs, was an admirable construction in its day; but now we tap Fresh Pond in our chambers. The Orvieto well might remind some persons of educational methods not yet extinct. With good methods, we may confidently hope to give young men of twenty or twenty-five an accurate general knowledge of all the main subjects of human interest, beside a minute and thorough knowledge of the one subject which each may select as his principal occupation in life. To think this impossible is to despair of mankind; for unless a general acquaintance with many branches of knowledge, good as far as it goes, be attainable by great numbers of men, there can be no such thing as an intelligent public opinion; and in the modern world the intelligence of public opinion is the one condition of social progress."—President Charles W. Eliot, Harvard University, 1869. Inaugural Address, in S. E. Morison, *The Development of Harvard University* (Cambridge: Harvard University Press, 1930), pp. lix, lx. Also in *School and Society*, March 22, 1924.

"If it be conceded that the studies which have been usually prescribed in the American colleges are the best fitted to impart a liberal culture, then it follows that the practice of these colleges in making them the ordinary conditions for the first degree is well grounded and ought to be adhered to. If our argument concerning the theory of the curriculum of studies is valid, then these studies ought to be prescribed. There is not a single study that is superfluous. Not one should be displaced, because not one can be spared. The theory of this curriculum has been to provide for all those studies which could properly find a place in a system of liberal culture, or should enter into the scheme of a complete and generous education."—President Noah Porter, Yale College, 1878. *The American College and the American Public* (New Edition. New York: Charles Scribner's Sons, 1878), p. 95.

"The world's progress must be recognized by the universities; and, as they can not impart all knowledge, they must impart the most important knowledge. . . . The method of culture for the human mind may, therefore, properly remain the same from age to age, if any method has been discovered which confessedly is effective. Such a method has been discovered. It is through the discipline of mathematics and the languages."—President Cyrus Northrop, The University of Minnesota, 1885. Inaugural Address. Typescript copy in the library of the University of North Carolina.

"I believe that we offer too wide a range of undergraduate courses, and that this is done at the expense on the one hand of the quality of our collegiate work, and on the other hand at the expense of graduate and research work. . . . When we have detected and dismissed the fads and frills there remains the great circle of science and arts which will not suffer dismissal, and yet for which our long and expensive school system has not yet found enough money nor time enough."—President William L. Bryan, The University of Indiana, 1906. "The Excessive Expansion of the Course of Study in American Universities," *Educational Review*, February, 1906, pp. 135, 140.

"American college students ought also to study a little of everything, for if not there is no certainty that they will be broadly cultivated, especially in view of the omnipresent impulse in the community driving them to devote their chief attention to the subjects bearing upon their future career. The wise policy for them would appear to be that of devoting a considerable portion of their time to some one subject, and taking in addition a number of general courses in wholly unrelated fields. But instruction that imparts a little knowledge of everything is more difficult to provide well than any other. To furnish it there ought to be in every considerable field a general course, designed to give to men who do not intend to pursue the subject further a comprehension of its underlying principles or methods of thought; and this is by no means the same thing as an introductory course, although the two can often be effectively combined."—President A. Lawrence Lowell, Harvard University, 1909. Inaugural Address, in S. E. Morison, *The Development of Harvard University* (Cambridge: Harvard University Press, 1930), p. lxxxv.

"The decline in the number of those American students who study Greek and Latin and who have a reasonable familiarity with the history and literature of Greece and Rome is greatly to be deplored. No educational substitute for Greek and Latin has ever been found, and none will be found so long as our present civilization endures, for the simple reason that to study Greek and Latin under wise and inspiring guidance is to study the embryology of the civilization which we call European and American."—President Nicholas Murray Butler, Columbia University, 1916. *Report for 1915-16*, p. 12.

"It is true that we have been more or less affected by the developments of the last generation in higher education. Our curriculum has given a larger place to modern languages and to the sciences than they once had, while psychology, sociology and political economy have been received hospitably alongside of older disciplines. Radical as we have been in some directions, we have been strangely conservative in the matter of the curriculum. It may be that our limited resources have saved us from the temptations to which a wealthier institution might have succumbed. We have felt that it is no part of our task to give our students a bowing acquaintance with fifty-seven varieties of knowledge. We have never been anxious to have our conspectus of courses look like the *carte du jour* of a metropolitan hostelry. Those students—of whom there seems to be an increasing number—who set more store by *hors d' oeuvres* and French pastry than by meat and potatoes and bread and butter probably find our intellectual menu too restricted. This is neither the time nor the place to enter into the discussion of the merits and demerits of the elective system, but it is a matter of satisfaction to observe that, in these days when the pendulum is swinging away from what a distinguished educator has called *a la carte* education, it is swinging back to the position to which Bates has consistently held for many years."—President Clifton Daggett Gray, Bates College, 1920. Inaugural Address, *Bates College Bulletin*, December 1, 1920, Lewiston, Maine.

"Proposal number one is that we should definitely advise a judicious proportion of our very ablest young men and women to enter the field of the social sciences. I speak as an old teacher of English, reluctant to lose good brains from that field, but convinced that the emergency is such, nationally and internationally, as to demand the drafting of our keenest intellects for economics and political science. . . .

"Proposal number two is for propaganda to combat propaganda. In other words, our courses in colleges and universities should teach our students to resist mass thinking, to search for fallacies in advertising and political presentations, to laugh sham and hokum out of court. Along with this possible cultivation of a healthy skepticism, all of our courses should promote logical thinking in a constructive way. Our propaganda should include the preaching of an idealism which will withstand sophistication and cynicism. We should make clear to our students the obligation we all owe, as educated citizens, to support the right leaders in political life, in the economic and governmental adjustments of the future."—President Raymond Walters, The University of Cincinnati, 1932. In *The Obligation of Universities to the Social Order*, ed. H. P. Fairchild (New York: New York University Press, 1933), pp. 299, 300.

"The meeting ground of our students and our faculty is the curriculum; the course of study. I have received more inquiries from the alumni since my election as to my attitude toward the curriculum than in regard to any other subject. Personally, I think this aspect of college has been over-emphasized. To me teaching is more important than what is taught. A great teacher is more precious than the perfect course of study. . . .

"I have great confidence in the long continued experience of the human race. It is usually assumed that this experience justifies the preponderant position of Latin and Greek which the defenders of that tradition are wont to maintain. . . .

"I cannot myself recognize either as superior. Our students come to us with different tastes, different backgrounds of culture, and different aspirations. In the schools from which they come they have been under the influence of very different teachers. Some have already caught from some great teacher in their preparatory school a spark which has kindled their interest and enthusiasm for one field of learning; some for another. Some, unhappily, have thus far failed to feel the eager devotion to learning which a great teacher may evoke. To prescribe a uniform course of study for freshman year seems to me to have little merit beyond simplicity, and to have positive defects.

"I approach the subject in the spirit of an inquirer. . . . I have long thought that few men had the experience or wisdom to be dogmatic about the curriculum. We shall attempt to make a program for this College, because some program we must have, and our present one seems to lack that flexibility which to me seems essential in a changing world. The second aspect of the course of study to which I invite your attention is the so-called vocational studies. Here my attitude is completely definite. I do not propose that Amherst College shall concern itself with training men for this or that future career, problematic at best. It follows that I would not, if I could, mould the College into a vocational school, nor would I emphasize the so-called pre-professional courses. I would not apply the yardstick of utility to the curriculum. . . . Amherst will continue to be an undergraduate college of the liberal arts. And finally, before we leave the curriculum, let me say a word as to the fine arts. We have long maintained courses in music. Courses in dramatic art and in the fine arts have been instituted in the last decade here and we have been inclined to follow the tradition begun by Charles Eliot Norton a generation ago. I hope we may place even more emphasis on this side of our work. We have always granted the B.A. degree—Bachelor of Arts. I like to think that with a further development of the appreciative and creative side of our students, the degree may come to signify more nearly what its symbols literally have meant. . . ."—President Stanley King, Amherst College, 1932. Inaugural Address, *Amherst Graduates' Quarterly*, February, 1933.

"It is generally understood today that the way out of our difficulties is to bring the social sciences to a place of importance comparable to that of the natural sciences. There is need to develop techniques in the social sciences similar to methods of research in the natural sciences."—President William B. Bizzell, The University of Oklahoma, 1935. "Higher Education in the Southwest," *Higher Education and Society* (Norman: University of Oklahoma Press, 1936), p. 23.

"What constitutes a liberal education at the undergraduate level? There are many answers to this question and almost all stress the need of changing the content of our curricula. Some demand that every college student be required to study philosophy, or courses in general history, or science, or politics or civics. Having listened to many, many such proposals I am convinced that educators today can agree on only one thing, namely, that there can be no agreement on the content of a four-year course in a liberal arts college. Therefore, I start with the assumption that there are many roads to salvation and I look for a solution of the problem through emphasis on the extra-curricular aspect of college life. For the most important single factor in a modern liberal education is the education which students receive from one another.

"The present multiplicity of courses, the plethora of routes for specialists may seem a frightening wilderness to some who seek a general education in our universities. But I am not disheartened by the specialized formal training of our university men, provided as an offset we take pains to secure the basis for an informal liberal education. . . . I am convinced that under favorable circumstances a liberal education can be acquired around the dinner table. Or perhaps I should say, the first step in a liberal education can be so acquired, and more than a first step has never been possible within the academic walls."—President James B. Conant, Harvard University, 1937. "The Role of the Endowed University in American Higher Education," *Proceedings and Addresses at the Inauguration of Edmund Ezra Day, Fifth President of Cornell University* (Ithaca, New York, 1937), pp. 18, 19.

The Elective System

"In education, the individual traits of different minds have not been sufficiently attended to. Through all the period of boyhood the school-studies should be representative; all the main fields of knowledge should be entered upon. But the young man of nineteen or twenty ought to know what he likes best and is most fit for. If his previous training has been sufficiently wide, he will know by that time whether he is most apt at language or philosophy or natural science or mathematics. If he feels no loves, he will at least have his hates. At that age the teacher may wisely abandon the schooldame's practice of giving a copy of nothing but zeros to the child who alleges that he can not make that figure. When the revelation of his own peculiar taste and capacity comes to a young man, let him reverently give it welcome, thank God, and take courage. Thereafter, he knows his way to happy, enthusiastic work, and, God willing, to usefulness and success. The civilization of a people may be inferred from the variety of its tools. There are thousands of years between the stone hatchet and the machine-shop. As tools multiply, each is more ingeniously adapted to its own exclusive purpose. So with the men that make the State. For the individual, concentration, and the highest development of his own peculiar faculty, is the only prudence. But for the State, it is variety, not uniformity, of intellectual product, which is needful.

"These principles are the justification of the system of elective studies which has been gradually developed in this College during the past twenty years. At present, the Freshman year is the only one in which there is a fixed course prescribed for all. In the other three years, more than half the time allotted to study is filled with subjects chosen by each student from lists which comprise six studies in the Sophomore year, nine in the Junior year, and eleven in the Senior year. The range of elective studies is large, though there are some striking deficiencies. The liberty of choice of subject is wide, but yet has very rigid limits. There is a certain framework which must be filled; and about half the material of the filling is prescribed. The choice offered to the student does not lie between liberal studies and professional or utilitarian studies. All the studies which are open to him are liberal and disciplinary, not narrow or special. Under this system the College does not demand, it is true, one invariable set of studies of every candidate for the first degree in Arts; but its requisitions for this degree are nevertheless high and inflexible, being nothing less than four years devoted to liberal culture.

"It has been alleged that the elective system must weaken the bond which unites members of the same class. This is true; but in view of another much more efficient cause of the diminution of class intimacy, the point is not very significant. The increased size of the college classes inevitably works a great change in this respect. One hundred and fifty young men can not be so intimate with each other as fifty used to be. This increase is progressive. Taken in connection with the rising average age of the students, it would compel the adoption of methods of instruction different from the old, if there were no better motive for such change. The elective system fosters scholarship because it gives free play to natural preferences and inborn aptitudes, makes possible enthusiasm for a chosen work, relieves the professor and the ardent disciple of the presence of a body of students who are compelled to do an unwelcome task, and enlarges instruction by substituting many and various lessons given to small, lively classes, for a few lessons many times repeated to different sections of a numerous class. The College therefore proposes to persevere in its efforts to establish, improve, and extend the elective system. Its administrative difficulties, which seem formidable at first, vanish before a brief experience."—President Charles W. Eliot, Harvard University, 1869. Inaugural Address, in S. E. Morison, *The Development of Harvard University* (Cambridge: Harvard University Press, 1930), pp. lxiv-lxvi. Also in *School and Society*, March 22, 1924.

"At present the tendency is more and more toward *university methods*, toward the presentation of various courses, toward giving the student more freedom of choice among these. When carefully carried out, this has been found to yield admirable results; and the fact is now established that large numbers of young men, who under the old system confined rigidly to a single stereotyped course, would have wasted the greater part of their time . . . have become, when allowed to take courses more fitted to their tastes and aims, energetic students."—President Andrew D. White, Cornell University, 1878. "Political Education," *Report of Commissioners to the Paris Universal Exposition, 1878*, p. 371.

"The present state of the higher education in America can be briefly comprehended in one word,—chaos. Thirty years ago there was a college course, simple and distinctive,—the education of the gentleman and the clergyman. The good old classical curriculum has nearly faded from view, though its thread of good still runs along the broad web of scholastic life and work.

"The elective system has come in like a flood. When there is not full election of studies, there is election from numerous courses of study. This election descends into the preparatory schools, and we see youth of fifteen choosing their studies, as they choose their hats and shoes; albeit with somewhat greater independence of fashion. The elective system has been vastly extended through the competition of an excessive number of small denominational colleges, for attracting students. Here we meet the signs of a religious chaos which is chiefly the cause of the confusion in our higher education."—President W. W. Folwell, The University of Minnesota, 1884. *Education*, January, 1884.

"The University is committed to the elective system in the upper classes on the principle that a young man of twenty should know his likes or, at least, his dislikes, and when this revelation comes to him let him welcome it reverently, thank God, and work his way to some sort of usefulness in life."—President Edwin A. Alderman, The University of North Carolina, 1897. *The University Record*, February, 1897.

"Children are being told that they should elect their studies. They cannot elect. They are put to studying things they have never been prepared for and cannot grasp, things which are laborious and unhealthful now, but which they would get easily and naturally enough in time if there should ever be occasion for it. It makes them artificial and concerted.

"We have many of us forced our particular schemes into the work of the elementary school until we have constructed an incoherent and unsymmetrical whole. . . .

"It is hard upon a teacher or child to be manipulated by so many 'experts' who do not agree. There are some things about this modern school system of ours which, as it seems to me, might be very profitably cooled off with a good system of cold water. . . ."—President A. S. Draper, The University of Illinois, 1902. *Educational Review*, May, 1902.

"The faculty should make the assumption when arranging the program of students, and in the class room as well, that the students are in college to give the great body of their time to the work of the curriculum. . . .

"I studied in an institution which had largely a prescribed

course of study. I taught in the same institution after the course of study was, under certain limitations, chiefly elective. I give only the common judgment of all those connected with the institution under both systems when I say that the latter system greatly increased the amount of work done by the average student and to a great extent eliminated the class of students under discussion."—President Joseph Swain, Swarthmore College, 1903. *Transactions and Proceedings of the National Association of State Universities, 1903.*

"Chancellor Andrews did not present a paper, but spoke from brief notes and extemporaneously, giving in the main his experience at the University of Nebraska . . . he expressed the idea that the result of the free elective system was likely to be a one-sidedness in the development of the student. He advocated a change, saying that about forty hours of the required work for graduation should be specifically required, and these forty hours should be in the foundation subjects found in the earlier part of the course. . . ."—Chancellor E. B. Andrews, The University of Nebraska, 1906. *Transactions and Proceedings of the National Association of State Universities, 1906.*

"We must go forward and develop the elective system, making it really systematic. Progress means change, and every time of growth is a transitional era; but in a peculiar degree the present state of the American college bears the marks of a period of transition. This is seen in the comparatively small estimation in which high proficiency in college studies is held, both by undergraduates and by the public at large; for if college education were now closely adapted to the needs of the community, excellence of achievement therein ought to be generally recognized as of great value. The transitional nature of existing conditions is seen again in the absence, among instructors as well as students, of fixed principles by which the choice of courses of study ought to be guided. It is seen, more markedly still, in the lack of any accepted view of the ultimate object of a college education."—President A. Lawrence Lowell, Harvard

University, 1909. Inaugural Address, in S. E. Morison, *The Development of Harvard University* (Cambridge: Harvard University Press, 1930), p. lxxx.

"The system of unrestricted election in college studies, when introduced in America, was intended to promote scholarship by making appeal to particular tastes and capacities. Doubtless in a certain limited number of cases the system succeeded; but experience seems to indicate that in a much larger number of cases it failed of its purpose."—President Nicholas Murray Butler, Columbia University, 1910. *Report for 1909-10*, p. 35.

"A most unhappy result of the elective system introduced a generation ago, and one that was not foreseen, was the destruction of that common body of knowledge which held educated men together in understanding and in sympathy. For more than a thousand years educated men had pursued pretty much the same studies, had read pretty much the same books, and had gained a common stock of information concerning man and nature. The elective system first weakened and then destroyed that common body of knowledge, and as a result brought in its train intellectual, moral, social, and political consequences that are nothing less than grievous."—President Nicholas Murray Butler, Columbia University, 1922. *Report for 1921-22*, p. 16.

"It is a hard saying, but Mr. Eliot [President Charles W., of Harvard], more than any other man, is responsible for the greatest educational crime of the century against American youth—depriving him of his classical heritage."—Professor S. E. Morison, Harvard University, 1936. *Three Centuries of Harvard* (Cambridge: Harvard University Press, 1936), pp. 389, 390.

Discipline

"The first business that I undertook [as President of Brown, 1827] was to frame a new set of laws for the college. . . . It made a vastly greater amount of labor necessary for both officers and students. The design was to render study not a sham, but a reality, and discipline not a form, but a fact."—President Francis Wayland, Brown University, 1827. Quoted in George P. Schmidt, *The Old Time College President* (New York: Columbia University Press, 1930), p. 91.

"By affording the means of pure and attractive social recreations, the students have sought and found their pleasure *at home*, and the high and careless spirits of youth have been regaled with no risk of moral contamination and without a single explosion of unbecoming mirth."—President Francis Wayland, Brown University, 1827. *Report to the Corporation of Brown University, 1827.* Quoted in L. F. Snow, *The College Curriculum in the United States* (New York: Teachers College, Columbia University, 1907), p. 125.

"We are brought into collision with the most capricious and unmanageable part of the student's system—his stomach. . . . The Steward's Hall is a common source of vexation and disturbance at all colleges."—Professor Elisha Mitchell, The University of North Carolina, 1837. Report to the Trustees of the University of North Carolina on a visit to colleges in the North. In K. P. Battle, *History of the University of North Carolina* (Raleigh: Edwards & Broughton Printing Company, 1912), I, 430.

"The son is a high-minded, honorable, brave, generous, good-hearted young gentleman; who scorns all subterfuge and meanness, and who would not lie for the universe! Not he. In this particular at least, he is above suspicion; and, like the Pope, is infallible. While the Faculty are a parcel of paltry pedants, pedagogues, bigots, charlatans—without feeling, spirit, kindness, honesty, or common sense."—President Philip Lindsley, The University of Nashville, 1848. Commencement Address, Nashville, Tennessee, 1848. Quoted in George P. Schmidt, *The Old Time College President* (New York: Columbia University Press, 1930), p. 88.

"Oh, gentlemen, let the boys alone!"—President Jared Sparks, Harvard University, *ca.* 1850. Reported exclamation of President Jared Sparks at a boring faculty meeting at Harvard when trivial rules governing undergraduates were being discussed at great length. Quoted in S. E. Morison, *Three Centuries of Harvard* (Cambridge: Harvard University Press, 1936), p. 281.

"Every applicant should be weighed in the balances of the sanctuary, and dignities fit only for the honorable and the virtuous should be everlastingly withheld from the mean and the profligate."—President Horace Mann, Antioch College, 1858. Second Baccalaureate Address, "Relation of Common Schools and Colleges." Quoted in E. I. F. Williams, *Horace Mann: Educational Statesman* (New York: The Macmillan Company, 1937), p. 320.

"I would recommend . . . the admission of pupils to any department of study, and for any period of time, not less than one term, provided they are found qualified, on examination, to enter, and will conform to regulations—the classification of pupils by their individual studies, and not by any grouping of studies, or by the period of residence; the conferring of all degrees and certificates of proficiency after public examination, conducted by both written and oral questions and answers, and without reference to the institution where candidates have pursued studies; the arrangements of the terms and vacations so as better to accommodate both students and instructors, allowing the former to devote their vacations to such kinds of labor, in the field or school as will enable them to pay the expenses of residence here, and allowing the latter to visit other colleges, and engage by lectures in the educational movements of the states; and the appointment of all professors, hereafter, for specified periods of time, and with salaries to some extent dependent on the amount of time devoted to instruction, and the number of pupils dependent on each."—Chancellor Henry Barnard, The University of Wisconsin, 1859. *Twelfth Annual Report of the University of Wisconsin* (Madison, Wisconsin, 1859), pp. 10-11. Quoted in John S. Brubacher, *Henry Barnard on Edu-*

cation (New York: McGraw-Hill Book Company, Inc., 1931), pp. 104, 105.

"The petty discipline of colleges attracts altogether too much attention from both friends and foes. It is to be remembered that the rules concerning decorum, however necessary to maintain the high standard of manners and conduct which characterizes this College, are nevertheless justly described as petty. What is technically called a quiet term cannot be accepted as the acme of university success. This success is not to be measured by the frequency or rarity of college punishments. The criteria of success or failure in a high place of learning are not the boyish escapades of an insignificant minority, nor the exceptional cases of ruinous vice. Each year must be judged by the added opportunities of instruction, by the prevailing enthusiasm in learning, and by the gathered wealth of culture and character."—President Charles W. Eliot, Harvard University, 1869. Inaugural Address, in S. E. Morison, *Three Centuries of Harvard* (Cambridge: Harvard University Press, 1930), p. lxviii.

"If the mass of undergraduates could be brought to respect, nay, to admire, intellectual achievement on the part of their comrades, in at all the measure that they do athletic victory; if those among them of natural ability could be led to put forth their strength on the objects which the college is supposed to represent; the professional schools would find their tasks lightened, and their success enhanced. A greater solidarity in college, more earnestness of purpose and intellectual enthusiasm, would mean much for our nation. . . ; and if we can increase the intellectual ambition of college students, the whole face of our country would be changed. When the young men shall see visions, the dreams of old men will come true."—A. Lawrence Lowell, Harvard University, 1909, Inaugural Address, *Harvard Graduates' Magazine*, December, 1909. Also in S. E. Morison, *The Development of Harvard University* (Cambridge: Harvard University Press, 1930), p. lxxviii.

"To give the proper oversight to the studies of undergraduates is not enough; their living conditions, their conduct, and their habits must be looked after. The minds need rectifying, but just as often the lives need to be renovated. What profiteth it a man though he speak with the tongues of men and of angels and leave college a dyspeptic; though he understand all knowledge and have the habit of spending money that does not belong to him, or be confirmed in any of the other fatal vices that beset college youth?"—President William P. Few, Trinity College (North Carolina), 1910. *The Inauguration of William Preston Few As President of Trinity College.* Chicago: The University of Chicago Press, 1910.

"The call today upon American schools and colleges of every kind is, I think, to improve the quality of education. We need a united program of education that will consider the interests of the student in his several stages from the primary grades to the university. That is to say, we need what we have talked a good deal about in America, and have never had—a genuine educational ladder. The student, not the subject matter, must become more and more the center of interest and effort. The student must be made more and more to participate in his own education from a creative standpoint rather than take it in like a jug. He must, too, be brought to realize that education is a life-long process. The education that our world so sorely needs will stress the personal, social and moral elements in education, and will expect to be judged by its products—fruits in the soundness of men."—President William P. Few, Trinity College (North Carolina), 1916. *Proceedings of the Southern Association of Colleges and Secondary Schools, 1916.*

"The real guardians of the spiritual treasures which the college passes on from generation to generation are those teachers who impart something more than knowledge to their pupils. It is always easier to make scholars than men. It is through the contagion of personality and character that we are enabled most effectively to transmit these incomparable treasures of the spirit. I am frank to say that the question, 'Has he written anything?' so often employed as a test of a man's fitness for a college position, does not interest me overmuch. Text-books and other contributions through the printed page, invaluable though they be, do not compare in value with those intangible, but not less real, results produced by the true teacher who has been enabled to kindle the fire in another soul because his own soul was first aflame. As some one has put it, a great teacher is worth more to a state though he teach by the roadside than a faculty of mediocrities housed in Gothic piles. It is impossible to overstate the value to society of an educational system that has for its purpose the transmission to succeeding generations of the great moral and spiritual sanctions of the race. On the other hand, it is impossible to exaggerate the menace to the world of a system of education that deifies the state, worships *Weltmacht* as its god and makes a scrap of paper of every moral sanction by declaring that 'necessity knows no law.' "—President Clifton Daggett Gray, Bates College, 1920. Inaugural Address, *Bates College Bulletin* (Lewiston, Maine), December 1, 1920.

"Three primary considerations in college and university administration are provisions for the health, the housing, and the instruction of the student body. Columbia University has in recent years made literally stupendous progress in all these directions."—President Nicholas Murray Butler, Columbia University, 1924. *Report to the Trustees for 1923-24*. Quoted in *The Rise of A University*, Vol. II, ed. Edward C. Elliott (New York: Columbia University Press, 1937), p. 231.

"More attention should be given to exceptional students, and this can be done without neglecting the others. In using the term 'exceptional student,' I do not necessarily mean he who obtains the highest mark in his studies, but the one who is capable of developing into a broad-minded, clear-thinking individual, and who can become a leader instead of a follower."—President

H. S. Boardman, The University of Maine, 1926. *Inaugural Address by Harold Sherburne Boardman, President University of Maine, June 12, 1926* (Pamphlet), pp. 15, 16.

"I put health first because it is fundamental to success and happiness in life. We may garner the wisdom of the ages, but if we have not health, our lives become a curse to ourselves and oftentimes a menace to those of others. Before graduation, therefore, every student should be taught by skilled instructors how to keep in sound physical condition."—President M. Lyle Spencer, The University of Washington, 1928. Inaugural Address, *School and Society*, March 17, 1928.

"The ideals of students and administration are identical in the main: To raise the standard in pure joy of living by improving the intellectual, physical, and moral ability to enjoy life both in the University and in later years. Here the greatest opportunity confronts our fraternities and sororities. An intellectual fellowship can take the place of a driving activity program without in any way decreasing the benefits of activities. By building up an intellectual comradeship, fraternities and sororities can contribute an important element to American education."—President Homer L. Shantz, The University of Arizona, 1930. *Inaugural Bulletin* (Tucson, Arizona, 1930), p. 39.

"What is the responsibility of the university to the students who enter its doors? There are two views, widely divergent, on this question. One view is that the university is essentially interested in the conservation and the transmission of knowledge and in research as an impersonal objective. This view is clearly stated by Dr. Flexner as follows: 'The university professor has an entirely objective responsibility—a responsibility to learning, to his subject and not a psychological or paternal responsibility for his students.' This is typically the attitude of the graduate school and of the professional school in this country. The former, from the very nature of the case, must take an objective, impersonal view of its functions, while the latter must recognize its responsibility to the profession for which it trains and to the public which is to be served by its votaries. But the graduate and the professional schools do not constitute the whole of the university. Should their philosophies then be permitted to permeate the whole institution? The trend in the United States has been decidedly toward a refutation of this theory. Evidence of this may be seen in the tendency to separate undergraduate work into junior and senior colleges; the establishment of personnel organizations for the social, educational and vocational guidance of students and the recent wide-spread interest already referred to, in the problem of improving instruction in the undergraduate college. It is, it seems to me, impossible for an educational institution to refuse to be concerned about the individual welfare of its students. . . ."—President James Monroe Smith, Louisiana State University, 1932. *School and Society*, January 16, 1932.

"The second group in the college family is the students. It is because of them that I have come to Amherst. The trustees would not have drawn me back; the faculty would not have induced me to give up the advantages of freedom from routine which I have been enjoying for five years. But the students are both an enticement and a challenge. An enticement because of the unknown potentialities of youth, its passionate enthusiasms, its exuberant vitality, and its folly. And a challenge because just here in intimate contact with youth lies the possibility of failure for a mature man, and the possibility of failure is the major challenge which life offers."—President Stanley King, Amherst College, 1932. Inaugural Address, *Amherst Graduates' Quarterly*, February, 1933.

"The modern university imposes upon a president duties of such a varied nature that it is of course impossible for him to enjoy the intimate contact with undergraduates which Princeton presidents were able to enjoy in earlier times."—President H. W. Dodds, Princeton University, 1934. *Report of the President for 1933-34*, p. 9.

"I agree that hard work is an excellent thing for the boy who is just turning into a man and I know it is a fatal mistake to make life too easy for our college and university students. I do not believe, however, that it should be a function of our educational system to provide handicaps which are unfairly adjusted so that they affect certain students and not others. I also am inclined to think that in these days we need not worry about life being too easy or not providing a sufficient challenge. If we have any question about our college life tending to soften our students, let us bend our efforts to making our collegiate and professional work even more effective in developing character and moral stamina."—President James B. Conant, Harvard University, 1934. *Harvard Alumni Bulletin*, December 7, 1934.

"Finally, and most important of the president's constituents are the students. They are entering a new and changing world. We do not know enough about this world to train specifically for it. What can we do for the young people who look to us for guidance?

"I think we can serve them best by adhering to the objectives which have always guided the liberal arts college. We can continue to use the liberal arts curriculum, with its mingling of natural science, social science and the humanities, to train minds to analyze and evaluate throughout the whole range of human affairs. Since each of these three disciplines involves different creative attitudes and distinct methods of weighing evidence, they are all necessary to the well-rounded man. There is enough truth in Henry Kingsley's aphorism that he who has learned how to learn can learn anything to justify the liberal arts curriculum as a builder of minds."—President H. W. Dodds, Princeton University, 1936. Address at the inauguration of President W. A. Eddy, Hobart and William Smith Colleges, 1936. Typescript copy in the library of the University of North Carolina.

"The university cannot fail to safeguard by every available means the physical health of its students while they are on the campus. This is elemental, and has long been a recognized policy of Cornell, as of practically all other American institutions of higher learning. The same principle should hold for the mental health of the resident student body. But what of measures that bear constructively upon the later health of the students? It is here that improvements are urgently needed. It is important that young people in their late teens and early twenties acquire habits that will make as far as possible for lifelong health. Thus the acquisition of interest and skill in a form of sport that may be wisely continued in later years is good health insurance. The recent rapid expansion of intramural recreational activities among both men and women on the campus of this University is a development by all means to be encouraged. As soon as possible, facilities should be provided to make such activities an all-the-year-round experience of every able-bodied student in the University. Anything short of this program will fail to discharge the University's obligation to the health and physical development of its student body. . . .

"Toward the moral standards and practices of its students the University must, I think, take a somewhat different attitude. In certain aspects, the moral life of the students is a student responsibility just as is their social life, but there are certain important differences. The laws and regulations of the larger community in which the University is located must be respected. Moreover the University may properly require unvarying observance of certain standards of personal conduct generally expected by the public of its self-respecting citizens. Students failing to meet these requirements should be prepared to sever their local connections. A university cannot wisely undertake to correct fundamental deficiencies of personal character; certain important character traits should have been firmly established in home and school well before the day of college matriculation."—President Edmund E. Day, Inaugural Address, Cornell University, 1937. *Proceedings and Addresses at the Inauguration of Edmund Ezra Day, Fifth President of Cornell University* (Ithaca, New York, 1937), pp. 35, 36.

"The student is usually taken for granted. Statistically that seems entirely reasonable. If one takes the total number of college students and divides it by the number of colleges, it becomes obvious that there are students enough for all. Like many other averages, the figure conceals many more important facts than it reveals. The most important single fact about college students is their maldistribution. Some colleges have the kind of students they need and desire in the numbers they can best serve, but those colleges are very few indeed. Most institutions have either too few or too many; they have students with too wide a range of intellectual capacity to permit the college to handle each student successfully; they do not offer the kind of work the student most needs, or if they do, he does not accept the offering. If the matter is studied from many points of view and without distorting preconceptions, it becomes evident that the student can in no circumstances be taken for granted. One of the most serious problems confronting the educational world is the adequate placement of students in appropriate institutions of higher education. . . .

"Faith in himself must be the chief asset of the student if he is to be successful. . . . Not all the teaching will be inspired; some of it will lack skill, more will be deficient in philosophic grasp; some of it will be painfully trivial. . . .

"When these reflections cross my mind, as they often do, my respect for the student seeking the good life increases. . . .

"The only conceivable objective, in dealing with students, is one which is individual to each. We must seek to help him be a significant person, physically, intellectually, emotionally, and spiritually. That matches his secret ambition; it interprets his dreams. College should be a constantly expanding experience in self-realization. That accords perfectly with all that educational research has learned about individual differences; it is in harmony with all that is known about physiological and biological differences. It probably accounts for the fact that the greatest religious teachers of all times have approached reform, not through the reconstruction of society upon a microscopic scale, but through the regeneration of the hearts and minds of individuals. To the regeneration of the individual student the liberal education is directed."—President Henry M. Wriston, Lawrence College, 1937. *The Nature of a Liberal College*. Appleton, Wisconsin: Lawrence College Press, 1937.

"If public education is to reflect the democratic view of distributed leadership, it must emphasize increasingly the study of individuals and the individualism of instruction. This calls for an enormous program of vocational guidance of the wisest sort. In a multitude of good leaders lies the safety and happiness of the world."—Chancellor Ernest H. Lindley, The University of Kansas, 1937. *Educating for Democracy: A Symposium* (Yellow Springs, Ohio: The Antioch Press, 1937), pp. 19, 20.

"First, know thy subject; second, love thy students; and third, have common sense."—President R. E. Blackwell, Randolph-Macon College (1902-1938). Quoted in *The New York Times* July 8, 1938, the day following his death, as a maxim of President Blackwell.

"Presidents differ in their treatment of students. Eliot said he was too busy to greet every Harvard boy he passed in the Yard, but countless men remember with deep interest his call when they were ill in the Infirmary and his solicitude for their recovery. Everyone who saw Bryan preside at Commencement at Ohio University was impressed with the word of individualized personal greeting he gave to each graduate as he handed out the diploma. Some of us teach: at Bowdoin, Sills gives a largely elected course in literature; nearly every senior for decades took Hyde's course in ethics, which under his teaching magic touched almost every problem the college and its students faced. Baxter (Williams) announces that he plans to teach next semester. My course, held weekly in the 'playroom' in my home, with complete informality prevailing, is one of the most pleasant parts of my job."—President James L. McConaughy, Wesleyan University, 1938. "The College President," *The Educational Forum*, May, 1938.

"College is the greatest place in the world for those who ought to go to college and who go for the right reasons. For those who ought not to go to college or who go for the wrong reasons, college is a waste of time and money."—President Robert M. Hutchins, The University of Chicago, 1938. *The Saturday Evening Post*, January 22, 1938.

"A college president often stands or falls in his handling of two problems—chapel and food."—President James L. McConaughy, Wesleyan University, 1938. Address before the Connecticut Valley Alumni Association of Amherst College, *Springfield Republican*, May 16, 1938.

Religious Life

"Columbia University is a Christian institution, and by its charter and traditions its Christianity is truly catholic and the spirit of St. Paul's Chapel will be as broad and as tolerant as the spirit of the University. Its office will be to preach and to teach Christian religion and Christian morals in the broadest and most fundamental sense of those terms. Since the foundation of the College a daily service has never been omitted, but now that a splendid building is provided for religious worship there is every reason to believe that this service will attract a larger number of students and be a far more important factor in the daily life of the University than ever before. . . ."—President Nicholas Murray Butler, Columbia University, 1906. *Report for 1905-06*, p. 2.

"Many students are indifferent to religious appeals simply because they have never been brought to realize the importance of religion. Home training in religion has in this generation all but disappeared, and that which formerly supplied the foundation on which the college might build is no longer to be relied upon. Compulsory measures to overcome this deficiency are neither wise nor successful. Sensational methods are as objectionable on grounds of principle as of taste, and they produce no permanent results. The students must be reached individually; resourcefulness, sympathy, and determination will succeed in reaching them. . . ."—President Nicholas Murray Butler, Columbia University, 1911. *Report for 1910-11*, p. 40.

"The religious perception of our time in its widest application is the consciousness that our well-being, both material and spiritual, lies in intelligent coöperation. The state university in its sympathetic study of relations that reconcile the divisions of society, while not concerned with differences in religious organization is inevitably and profoundly concerned with religion itself. All of its study of men and things leads through the cooperating channels that connect them beyond the sources of immediate life to the one great unity than binds all together." —President Edward K. Graham, The University of North Carolina, 1915. "Inaugural Address," *Education and Citizenship and Other Papers* (New York: G. P. Putnam's Sons, 1919 [also University of North Carolina Press]), p. 24.

"The college cannot teach about religion in a purely intellectual or scientific spirit. Religion has its intellectual aspect and from that point of view it must be dealt with on the same principles as that on which the college deals with all other matters intellectual. But it is also a life, with the continuance and development of which the college is even more concerned than it is with the discussion of it. And in its aspect as a life it is influenced by many things that are not set down in the curriculum. It is affected by the chapel service, which ought to be simple and yet so beautiful and impressive as to be a precious memory throughout life. It is affected by the physical surroundings of the service. It is for this reason that I greatly hope that ere many years have passed we shall have at the University of Chicago a chapel which by its exterior beauty and dignity will dominate all our quadrangles and symbolize the supreme place of religion in life; the interior of which will incline the soul to prayer, kindle aspiration, and solemnize the mind in view of life's great realities, while it also kindles hope and courage and banishes fear and despondency; where noble Scripture impressively read, and prayer unitedly offered to heaven, and the great hymns of the ages, and fervent but sane words of instruction and exhortation shall lift us out of all that is low and mean and show us the greater possibilities of human life."—President E. D. Burton, The University of Chicago, 1924. *Education in a Democratic World* (Chicago: The University of Chicago Press, 1927), pp. 112, 113.

"During the past ten years, and especially since the World War we have heard much about the decadent moral condition of the young people of the country. If one should take seriously all that has appeared in print on the affirmative side of the argument, he would indeed see a black picture for the future. Every institution has its moral and social questions, and I suppose those of this institution vary but little from those of institutions coming under similar environments. We have had our problems in the past and we expect to have them in the future, but I do not think that we have any reason to worry that our country is 'going to the dogs' on account of our youth.

"One of the much mooted questions is that of alcoholic intemperance. An unbiased investigation made among presidents, deans, professors, and students in colleges and universities in the United States during the early part of this year tends to show emphatically that (1) there is less drinking among college students today than there was prior to the coming of the Eighteenth Amendment; (2) that the spirit of adventure, for the most part, prompts such drinking as remains; (3) that conditions surrounding students in college communities today are more conducive to sobriety than they were previous to prohibition; (4) that an overwhelming majority of college presidents, professors, and students feel that prohibition has justified itself.

"We should hesitate to form general conclusions on premises which are purely local or of an indefinite or isolated character. The youth of today are not taught to be seen and not heard, and are consequently more in view than they were twenty years ago. This more intimate association with their elders, together with greater personal liberties has resulted in an enlarged knowledge at a younger age and a different perspective of life. This in itself creates new problems for the colleges as well as for the preparatory schools.

"Neither do I believe that the problem of the sexes has passed a condition of control. It always has been a social problem, it is now, and so far as one can see it will remain with us for the future. But that the youth of today has degenerated into a condition of immorality as some would have us think I do not for a moment concede. It is true that we of an older generation look askance at some of the doings of youth, but I can well remember that the attitude and actions of the young people of my day were not all that our elders desired. I believe that faith in our young people is justified and that the social problems of the University can be handled as we meet them and that the good sense of the large majority of our boys and girls will in the end prevail over the occasional lapses of the small minority. However, we should not be satisfied with the thesis that mankind has not retrograded. Our customary method of thinking, in such an analysis is likely to first endeavor to make comparisons of equality and then if possible to pass to those of superiority. It is difficult to prove that the world is growing better. We hope and pray that it is, but after passing through such a period of hate and bloodshed as that created by the World War, and the subsequent reconstruction period, one can not help a feeling of doubt and undecision. There are so many variables in the problem that our correlations are difficult to attain.

"It is, however, of considerable encouragement to find, that, notwithstanding the many and sundry attractions which tend to keep people from the churches, actual figures show that church membership has almost doubled in the past 25 years and has increased much faster than the population. Of chapel attendance at educational institutions we can not make this statement. The general tendency during the past few years has been to make chapel attendance optional or to abolish it altogether. It appears that the old dignity and religious atmosphere of the daily chapel service is fast disappearing. If one looks for the reasons they are not hard to find. With us conditions have limited our chapel attendance. The growth of the student body without a corresponding growth in our physical plant has brought about a congestion for which we have found no solution except the discontinuance of chapel until we have a suitable place in which to conduct it. This does not mean, however, that we are suffering from religious anemia, for I am sure that the quiet activities of our Maine Christian Association more than offset any ill effects which may result in the discontinuance of chapel. I wish to emphasize the good work which is being done by this organization under the direction of the M. C. A. Secretary. It is my opinion that the student of the present day has a clearer perception of the relation of religion to life and social service, than at any time in the past."—President H. S. Boardman, The University of Maine, 1926. *Inaugural Address by Harold Sherburne Boardman, President University of Maine, June 12, 1926* (Pamphlet), pp. 10, 11, 12.

"The chapel service should be the culmination of the life of the school. There is something in all of us which we are not quite ready to see die. In public worship may be found elements for the nurture of these priceless values. The chapel should vividly embody the germinal idea of the college, it should be the crowning act in the life of the school, so rich, so reverent, so inspiring that no one would feel it an obligation to attend, but rather a fruitful opportunity."—President A. A. Shaw, Denison University, 1927. Inaugural Address, *Inauguration of President Shaw, Denison University, Granville, Ohio.*

"Alma Mater! A university is supposed to be a benign mother to its students—here and now arises the glorious opportunity for the University to vindicate to its students the right to this title and to extend the saving influence of its mother love to society at large.

"How, you ask, may this be done? By perfecting the hearts as well as the minds of its students by a sound ethical training, by an ethical training not based upon motives of hygiene, convention, popular opinion, but upon the changeless law of God."—President William M. Magee, S.J., Marquette University, 1928. *Inaugural Address* (Milwaukee: Marquette University Press, 1928), p. 16.

"Above and beyond all there stands the element of religion, without which the abundant life is impossible, the religion which, surmounting creeds and doubts and the cynicisms of little men, carries the soul into the central presence. This religion is not to be found so much by youth through preachments as through those opportunities for meditation which in the overcrowded program of university life we so often deny them. The age-old injunction stands true today: 'Be still and know that I am God.' "—President William Mather Lewis, Lafayette College, 1932. In *The Obligation of Universities to the Social Order*, ed. H. P. Fairchild (New York: New York University Press, 1933), pp. 403-404.

"The fact that such discussion as this has taken place in the Conference is significant of much. It indicates that there is a general realization that something is rotten in the state of Denmark. . . .

"Even the universities are realizing that when they have pursued abstract truth to the very limit, there is still something left undone. I, for one, profoundly believe that education is truncated that does not deal, as has already been said, with the whole man; and I am still old-fashioned enough to believe that religion in some form or another is essential to every full, rounded education. The conditions of national and international life today are demonstrative that we do need something beyond the pursuit of abstract truth. . . .

"Happily, I come from a land, Canada, where the habit of going to church has not altogether passed away. I come from a university that, while it is a state university, is made up of many constituent religious elements. It is the result of a federation of a state university, which while nonsectarian is not irreligious, with a Methodist university, an Episcopal university, and a Roman Catholic college.

"The result of this combination is that through the whole university body there are religious influences. These colleges influence the whole university body, and I think that the general university body has in turn a wholesome influence on what might prove denominational narrowness."—President Henry John Cody, The University of Toronto, 1932. In *The Obligation of Universities to the Social Order*, ed. H. P. Fairchild (New York: New York University Press, 1933), pp. 411, 412, 413.

"Yet, the opportunity for group worship seems to me one of the most essential functions or one coördinately essential function of the university of today. . . .

"I think spiritual values do not come to the youth until he stands up and says with a certain learned man of old: 'What shall I do to be saved?' And none of us dares answer through one particular field of knowledge, but it is by finding the issues of that knowledge for those outside ourselves that there comes that definition we seek, I think, rather in vain. . . ."—President Aurelia H. Reinhardt, Mills College, 1932. In *The Obligation of Universities to the Social Order*, ed. H. P. Fairchild (New York: New York University Press, 1933), pp. 421, 422.

"The political purpose of Sovietism has already developed into a matter of serious concern for all other governments of the world.

"The spiritual element of this system, or rather the entire eradication of all things spiritual and religious from the life of the proletariat, is perhaps the most threatening menace to Christianity since the invasion of lower Europe by the Goths, the Huns, and the Vandals.

"The social, industrial, and economic effects of this titantic upheaval in all its protean forms have rendered futile all efforts to restore an economic balance of power and all endeavors to establish a universal league of nations and to return the balance of world peace to its proper equipoise.

"If the American university is to take an interest in the spiritual welfare of the American public, then it should take proper cognizance of a system of education that professes to teach the elimination of religion and of all things spiritual from the life of man."—President L. J. Gallagher, S.J., Boston College, 1932. In *The Obligation of Universities to the Social Order*, ed. H. P. Fairchild (New York: New York University Press, 1933), pp. 435, 436.

"I am wondering whether this sense of values is not caught from those who make certain ideals popular. Knowledge alone is not enough. A man may use mathematics to rob a bank, chemistry to kill. He may use psychology to cheat his fellows. . . .

"Now whenever we get a generation of students to accept this materialistic philosophy of life—that man is an animal and only an animal—he will act like an animal, and we will have a recrudescence of the jungle. But when we can get a man to accept the spiritual conception of life, accept the idea that he is an immortal child of God, he will act as a child of God ought to act, and he will live life with zest."—President Daniel L. Marsh, Boston University, 1932. In *The Obligation of Universities to the Social Order*, ed. H. P. Fairchild (New York: New York University Press, 1933), pp. 428, 429, 430.

"By going back about forty years to those undergraduate days that were my own, I remember that in the colleges generally, there was a large variety of religious exercises; and the layman is inclined to believe that the vitality of spiritual life is reflected, to some extent at least, in the number and the spirit of the religious exercises.

"In particular, in those days in the college which I attended, there were twelve prayer meetings in every week, nine of which every one of us was invited to attend. At the present time there are no prayer meetings at all in most of our colleges.

"There came a feeling of abhorrence on the part of the undergraduate for the cloak of piety. He was very unwilling to make public that which concerned the spiritual life through contact with his fellows. . . ."—President F. C. Ferry, Hamilton College, 1932. In *The Obligation of Universities to the Social Order*, ed. H. P. Fairchild (New York: New York University Press, 1933), p. 405.

"The chapel problem at Amherst is one which has divided both faculty and student body. And in this division of opinion it has seemed to me quite proper to propose my own program. Our chapel is an institutional exercise conducted by the president, at which attendance is required. It enables the students to know their president, it enables him to express something of the corporate unity which inheres in the small college. Our students are of course the alumni of tomorrow. And I am convinced that Amherst's alumni of today owe something of their devotion to the College as an institution, something of their conception of the Amherst tradition, to the fact that day by day during their college course they gathered with their fellow students and their faculty in Johnson Chapel."—President Stanley King, Amherst College, 1932. Inaugural Address, *Amherst Graduates' Quarterly*, February, 1933.

"Until a few years ago, this responsibility of leadership for the college's religious service, whether it was required service or not, was largely delegated to almost any one who was handy. And no wonder the service degenerated on almost every college campus. . . .

"I suppose it is true that the academic world in the last decade has spent ten thousand times as much upon intercollegiate sport equipments as it has upon buildings for religious services for its students; and certainly at least ten thousand times as much every year on the expense budget for coaches and so forth as upon chaplains or religious leaders. I am not sure that that is a fact of which we have a right to be proud.

"And, finally, I am very sure that if the college religious service, the chapel, is to mean anything at all, we ought to realize that the service itself should be made just as reverential and inspiring as possible. I went for four years at a very early hour,

I suppose, to regular morning prayers, at a chapel building that had absolutely no inspirational value to it, and to a service conducted by this, that, or the other member of the faculty, most of whom went through it in a perfunctory way that certainly did not give any element at all of inspiration to those of us who were there."—President James L. McConaughy, Wesleyan University, 1932. In *The Obligation of Universities to the Social Order*, ed. H. P. Fairchild (New York: New York University Press, 1933), pp. 415, 416.

"Is religion itself a legitimate field of learning in the university? Is it a specific experience of the race, a necessity for each growing citizen, and a way of cultural growth for the future, or is it only a vestigal activity, an antiquated prescientific anachronism? For my part, I believe that religion (not the sects) is basic to morals, central in our American culture, unique as a dynamic within the individual, able to save us from ourselves and lead us out into nobility. I believe that without religion we are forced to substitute weak conventions for permanent values and abiding standards; that, without religion, civilization, with an adequate reinforcement for the great strains that come upon it, must yield inevitably to disintegration and decay. Believing these things, I believe also that the university which makes no effort to stimulate in its sons and daughters a sensitiveness to the issues of religion is likely to be a danger rather than a benefit to the state. Certainly it cannot serve its people as fully as it should unless it finds some way, as it has always done, to blend with knowledge and culture the rugged force of character and the spiritual power that give to these life and value. So only may knowledge become wisdom."—President Robert G. Sproul, The University of California, 1932. In *The Obligation of Universities to the Social Order*, ed. H. P. Fairchild (New York: New York University Press, 1933), pp. 382, 383.

"I feel sure we all agree that proper ideals are needed if spiritual values are to have any part in the curriculum of universities—such ideals as will in no way stultify the mind, cramp the faculties, but will produce healthy, manly, self-reliant leaders with initiative, accomplished all-round men—an ideal that embraces the whole man, body and soul; though, of course, this particular session of our Conference, if it has any reason for its existence, is professionally concerned with the latter.

"We deplore the moral evils of the world today but I would wager that a very large percentage of them come from errors of judgment, from wrong-headedness, and not so much from downright malice. It does not seem to be that men hate or despise spiritual values. The vast majority have no grasp of what they are, and many of the remaining minority have rather obscure views. They can't very well respect a thing of which they are totally ignorant. Are we not asking too much when in our courts of justice we expect a man to take an oath to God and to abide by its sanctity, if he has been taught there is no Supreme Being or at least that it is very doubtful. While we know the President-elect of the United States does actually believe in the Bible and his oath of office taken on that traditionally sacred volume will mean something to him, still we can easily imagine that it might be a man for whom the book would mean no more than a stray volume of the Congressional Record. If invocations are spoken in the Senate and House of Representatives and at all official functions of the Government and are to be looked upon as just so many words vainly uttered to carry out formalities, we should much better dispense with them. We should also put away the various pictures that represent the Fathers of the Constitution in prayer, if our universities teach us to consider such portrayals as quite meaningless. I feel sure that much of George Washington's diaries and his several pronouncements should be catalogued under 'fairy tales,' if spiritual values are to be as intangible and unintelligible as some universities would seem to wish to make them."—President Coleman Nevils, S.J., Georgetown University, 1932. In *The Obligation of Universities to the Social Order*, ed. H. P. Fairchild (New York: New York University Press, 1933), pp. 391, 392.

"The educational program of the University would not be

complete if it offered only an opportunity for intellectual development and failed to stress spiritual values. We shall continue to encourage those things which contribute to aesthetic appreciation and to the building of upright character. Our hope is that our graduates, because they have studied here and have participated in the social and cultural activities of this university community, will be numbered among those whose enjoyment of life is increased through the appreciation of fine music, drama, and pictures, and through the reading of good books. We are eager to see developed in our students those qualities of character which are their heritage as sons and daughters of Maine. Honesty, fortitude, initiative, self-reliance, loyalty, and helpfulness—these are the traits which we claim as distinctively ours to cherish and to preserve. As members of the faculty we recognize our responsibility for maintaining in our lives those high principles which we hold up to our students. While the University as a state institution does not teach the religion of a particular creed, we are ready at all times to coöperate with those religious organizations which include students of the University among their members. Our own religious organizations seek to promote an attitude of reverence and to stimulate an interest in religious activity which finds expression in worship, in social service, and in the every-day life of the campus."—President Arthur A. Hauck, The University of Maine, 1934. *The Maine Bulletin* (Orono, Maine), December, 1934, p. 22.

"This University has made provision for religious services for its students from the very beginning. They have always been entirely voluntary. The Sage preachership, endowed shortly after the University opened, has from the start been filled from week to week by leading divines of all denominations. The several churches of Ithaca share effectively in the religious work that is done among the university students. College years are, of course, a period of religious unsettlement for many young men and women. Earlier moorings are often broken as unfamiliar lines of knowledge are pursued. It is a time when not infrequently religious beliefs have to be reconstructed. To an extraordinary extent, our times have lost any sure sense of direction. Civilization is confused partly because it is no longer sure of its own meaning and significance. It is part of the task of our institutions of higher learning to help students fortify and if necessary rebuild the fundamental faith by which men live and work."—President Edmund E. Day, Cornell University, 1937. Inaugural Address, *Proceedings and Addresses at the Inauguration of Edmund Ezra Day, Fifth President of Cornell University* (Ithaca, New York, 1937), pp. 38, 39.

"We do not deny that there are dangerous influences at work in some institutions, but we do wish to affirm that college youth have not lost their faith as some would have us believe.

"It is admitted that going to college causes a radical change in childish views and that during the sophomore year, there is a distinct tendency away from religion in contrast to the situation in the freshman year. On the other hand, during the junior and senior years there appears to be a return to or more interest in religion and religious activities.

"The evidence of this survey abundantly supports the conclusion that, if students are not interested in the services of the church and in religious service, most of the disinterest started before they went to college and university."—Council of Church Boards of Education, 1937. *Christian Education*, October, 1937.

Athletics

"Within the past term a Gymnasium amply provided with apparatus has been erected on the college grounds, and a competent instructor has been engaged in superintending this establishment and in teaching the students a system of safe and invigorating exercise. The importance of having within the college premises facilities for the acquisition of physical education is conclusively evinced by the result of the present experiment. . . . No serious accident has occurred—uncommon health has prevailed."—President Francis Wayland, Brown University, 1827. *Report to the Corporation of Brown University, 1827.* Quoted in L. F. Snow, *The College Curriculum in the United States* (New York: Teachers College, Columbia University, 1907), p. 125.

"Physical exercise has of late years received a large share of public attention, in connection with sedentary pursuits. This is right . . . the subject requires prudent management, or the introduction of the system of exercise now recommended will do as much harm as good. . . . The wise men of antiquity . . . drew the line firmly between gymnastic exercise, for the cultivation of vigor and beauty, as curative processes and gentlemenlike accomplishments, as a part of the education of the boy and the daily recreation of the man, on the one hand, and the training of the athletes on the other. The former they regarded as essential to a sound mind in a sound body; the latter as mischievous and immoral."—President James Felton, Harvard College, 1860. *Report of the President of Harvard College, 1859-60*. Quoted in W. Carson Ryan, Jr., *The Literature of American School and College Athletics* (New York: The Carnegie Foundation for the Advancement of Teaching, Bulletin No. 24, 1929), p. 63.

"The growth of college athletics within very recent years has led to a very general and somewhat heated discussion regarding them. In the last year (1884) especially, the question of their regulation has become a burning one with more than one Faculty. . . . Athletics have been carried to a higher degree of development and specialization at Yale, Harvard, and Princeton, than at any other colleges in the country. . . . Professionalism has done much within the last five years to bring discredit upon college sports; and by professionalism we mean the purpose to win a game by any means, fair or foul. . . . Harvard, . . . has very recently forbidden the football elevens of the University from engaging in any more intercollegiate matches. This action was due to the belief that football had become a 'brutal and dangerous' game."—Edward M. Hartwell, *Physical Training in American Colleges and Universities*. Washington: United States Bureau of Education, 1886. Circular of Information, 1885. No. 5. Quoted in W. Carson Ryan, Jr., *The Literature of American School and College Athletics* (New York: The Carnegie Foundation for the Advancement of Teaching, Bulletin No. 24, 1929), pp. 65, 66.

"In recent years, increasing attention has been continually directed to the importance of physical culture among young men in college. There is reason to believe that, if the importance of this subject has not been exaggerated, at least the methods employed for encouraging it have been more or less mistaken. If vigorous exercise should be practiced by a portion of the young men under instruction in college, the same ought to be the case with all; yet it is doubtful whether the great proportion of the students in any of our colleges participate in the exercise in institutions which are esteemed so important. . . . What is more likely to happen is the selection of a limited number of athletes who are supposed to possess more than usual skill and who are charged with representing the college in their match games with other institutions. . . . Those not thus selected will relapse into sluggishness . . . , and thus the mass of the students will derive very little benefit from the efforts thus made for their physical improvement. . . . Though a very limited number of young men actually participate in these sports, the burden falls more or less on all alike. The expeditions got up to visit sister colleges in these trials of agility or skill involve serious expenditures, . . . though but a limited number engage personally in these games, yet the interest taken in them by the mass of students is general and absorbing. As these contests approach, there is more or less distraction of the minds of the students from their proper pursuits, and, for the time being, a more or less serious neglect of study. This is an evil inevitable while the present system is maintained, and is of sufficient magnitude to justify, in the opinion of the undersigned, an absolute prohibition of intercollegiate games altogether. . . ."—President F. A. P. Barnard, Columbia College, 1888. *Report for 1887-1888.* Quoted in *The Rise of a University*, Vol. I, ed. William F. Russell (New York: Columbia University Press, 1937), pp. 204, 205.

"There is something exquisitely inappropriate in the extravagant expenditure on athletic sports at such institutions as Harvard and Yale, institutions which have been painfully built up by the self-denial, frugality, and public spirit of generations that certainly did not lack physical and moral courage, endurance, and toughness, yet always put the things of the spirit above the things of sense. At these universities there must be constant economy and inadequacy in expenditure for intellectual and spiritual objects; how repulsive, then, must be foolish and pernicious expenditures on sports!"—President Charles W. Eliot, Harvard University, 1893. *Reports of the President and the Treasurer of Harvard College, 1892-93*, p. 14.

"There are, therefore, real abuses connected with these games. But shall we abandon the manly features or reform the abuses? It is a question for the large universities to answer. The smaller colleges will be able to hold their boys within bounds for the present. The small college is still democratic. Its president and faculty and students are still the closely knit fabric of a simpler time. There are no distinctions of rank and wealth. The president relies on the love of the boys, and wins it by seeking to aid them in all right ways. No high wall of affairs shuts him off from them; no intrusive demands of the outside world draw them away from him. The influx and efflux of a great university make the voice of the public more potent."—President E. D. Warfield, Lafayette College, 1894. *The Forum*, January, 1894, pp. 653, 654.

"Interest in the game has, I think, not yet become so general and so absorbing in the West as it is in the East. But it is rapidly growing, and Western colleges and universities are likely to have to deal soon with the same problems respecting foot-ball as are now embarrassing the Eastern. I regard foot-ball as a valuable athletic game. It calls for and cultivates temperate and regular habits of living, vigor and agility of body, quickness of perception, readiness of resource, manly courage, skill in planning, and subordination of the individual will to cooperation of the team. These are all admirable fruits of good athletic training. Unhappily, as now conducted, the game seems to be attended with too much danger, and tempts players who are not thoroughly disciplined to some unworthy tricks and to occasional 'slugging.' I believe that it can be relieved of its objectionable features without depriving it of the interest that it now excites, and I hope that it may be."—President J. B. Angell, The University of Michigan, 1894. *The Forum*, January, 1894, p. 647.

"A rough sport it must always be; but a certain degree of roughness is no bad seasoning for the recreations of those who are conscious of superabundant physical energy. If, on the other hand, the game cannot be purged of its revolting excrescences, its fate is sealed; and foot-ball contests will be remembered only as survivals, in the midst of civilization, of the outrageous sports of barbarians. Until the effort at reform has failed, however, I shall not believe that foot-ball is in itself a coarse or undesirable form of physical recreation."—President J. G. Schurman, Cornell University, 1894. *The Forum*, January, 1894, pp. 643, 644.

"Will athletics live in the Ideal Christian College? Yea, abide and flourish. The monastic idea that the soul belongs to God and the body to the devil is dead; but its results are not. The ideal college will teach each student to aim for bodily strength, vigor, activity, grace, beauty. And, as an end to this, athletics will receive every encouragement. But they are prone to fall from grace and need to be soundly converted. When this happens, intercollegiate football—a brutal game when played by strong men—will leave all Christian colleges and come back no more. Hired professionals or semi-professionals will under no subterfuge or pretexts be found on their teams. The colleges of the future most either relinquish their claim to be considered as Christian institutions, or else they must practice on their athletic grounds the same principles that they teach in their leisure on ethics.

"Yet doubt it not that the Ideal College will win its victories. But its pennants will wave all the more proudly, because in every case they shall have been won by unpaid students in honorable conflict."—President C. E. Taylor, Wake Forest College, 1895. Baccalaureate Address, "An Ideal Christian College," *The Wake Forest Student*, March, 1916.

"The powerlessness of our educational leaders to originate, and their failure to adopt, effectual measures for evolving order out of the athletic and gymnastic chaos over which they nominally preside, constitutes one of the marvels of our time."—Edward M. Hartwell, 1898. *On Physical Training* (Washington: United States Bureau of Education, Annual Report of the Commissioner of Education, 1897-98). Quoted in Howard J. Savage, *American College Athletics* (New York: The Carnegie Foundation for the Advancement of Teaching, Bulletin No. 23, 1929), p. 23.

"There will be a lively meeting of the Intercollegiate Football Association at the Fifth Avenue Hotel next Monday. The question of professionalism will be settled."—News item from New York City, November 2, 1899. Quoted by President John L. Griffith, National Collegiate Athletic Association, 1936. *Proceedings of the National Collegiate Athletic Association, 1936*, pp. 87, 88.

"College life has a side and relation which demand the hardness and endurance of the soldier. It has a side which is built up of mighty *musts*. This side is represented by football. Every member of the eleven must train, must practice, must endure risks, must mingle with his fellows, must keep his temper, and must obey his captain. . . . Life is to be interpreted as sound, wholesome, righteous . . . such an interpretation creates the highest qualities of health and of healthfulness. Football embodies and enforces such an interpretation. It emphasizes the aggressive, the forth-putting, the direct, the positive. . . . It embodies actuality. . . . It teaches one to do . . . it bucks, it pushes, it breaks, it runs, it goes; it goes through the line, it goes around the ends, but it goes. . . . Football develops self-restraint. . . . For it teems with temptations to be mean. . . . The gridiron is a small ethical world, marked all over with the white lines of moral distinctions . . . it is in ethics what the Socratic thinking shop was supposed to be—a training of the individual. It thus helps to make the finest type of gentleman."—President Charles F. Thwing, Western Reserve University, 1901. "The Ethical Functions of Football," *North American Review*, November, 1901.

"On the whole, the advancement of physical education in America has been greater in the past twenty-five years than in any other period in its history. Obviously the most striking and rapid expansion has been in the department of athletics. . . . For the most part the athletic movement owes its characteristic features to its devotees and the public. Faculties and boards of trust have done comparatively little—and much of that little ill—toward shaping and guiding the movement."—Edward M. Hartwell, 1903. *On Physical Training*. United States Bureau of Education, 1903. Quoted in W. Carson Ryan, Jr., *The Literature of American School and College Athletics* (New York : The Carnegie Foundation for the Advancement of Teaching, Bulletin No. 24, 1929), p. 65.

"I think that the two most important questions that have ever been brought before the North Central Association are these : the report yesterday afternoon on accredited schools, and this discussion this morning (athletics). . . .

"Years ago the University of Missouri was guilty of all the low-grade athletic sins that any institution of learning could be guilty of. The sins of higher grade it perhaps avoided. The president, I must say, stood constantly against corruption in athletics, but he happened to be a simple-minded creature that has always been easy to fool and is easy to fool now. He doesn't know how to look a man in the face and question his word until he knows that man to be a liar. . . . I determined to get somebody that had a better head for conducting these things (athletics) than I had, and, following the example of the University of Chicago . . . we scoured the Federal Union for a director of the gymnasium, and under his control we placed all athletics from a croquet mallet and a tennis racket up to the gymnasium and football. We strove to get a man and not a great lump of beastly muscle, and we found a man in a graduate of Stanford University taking post-graduate work at Clark University. The man has cleansed the university boys, and athletics have become with us—forgive my modesty—a means of grace. . . . But in order to keep clean ourselves we must cleanse the northern half of the Mississippi Valley."—President R. H. Jesse, The University of Missouri, 1903. *School Review*, May, 1903.

"I think that we in Stanford University are ready to join with Professor Woodward's scheme of putting the whole matter of athletics in charge of a composite committee. Two years ago in California we abolished the professional coach, and we shall, as soon as we can get around to it, abolish the gate money. The rest of the evils will mostly take care of themselves. . . .

"It seems to me . . . that one very important element rests with the faculty itself. It is the absolute duty of the faculty to see that there is nobody in the institution for football alone. The football player should be compelled to go right on with his work in essentially the same way as the others do. . . .

"I have the permission of the Michigan men here to say a very plain word. We had Walter Camp with us as a coach, and every influence that came from Camp was good. We had two other men from Yale afterward, Cross and Chamberlain; their influence was good, but they did not win any games. And then we had other men who did win a game. Among others we had Yost, and with Yost we won the game of that year; and what I want to get at is simply an illustration.

"A young fellow came in from the mines who wanted to study mining engineering—a tremendously big and strong fellow. He was admitted because of certain symptoms of earnestness he showed—admitted as special student, having no credits whatever. He was not allowed to take part in any athletic sports whatever at Stanford, failed in his studies, and was dropped.

Yost carried him to Michigan, where he has become the center of the strong team which is the pride of Michigan University; and this man, who was not able to pass any examinations when he was not playing, has been playing some ten or fifteen games a year at Michigan. And he is a type of the kind of corruption for which, in its last analysis, the faculties of the universities alone are responsible. It is up to us to see that this kind of man is not used for that kind of purpose.

"There are a great many other illustrations of that sort which I might give, and I know the Michigan men will pardon me for using their particular sins when the rest of us have all been sinners. All of us who have ever had Yost or any Yost-like man about are not to be counted as sinless. . . .

"I feel proud, as a representative of Stanford, where we once had Hetherington, of the work that Hetherington has done in the University of Missouri in cleaning up and purifying the condition which is made by the toleration by the university faculties of all those various evils and by the extension of the methods by which men win at any cost."—President David Starr Jordan, Leland Stanford Junior University, 1903. "Athletics," *School Review*, May, 1903.

"Expenditures for football are steadily increasing. A quarter part of all who take part in this sport are injured enough to lay them up for ten days on the average, and a much larger proportion of those who really play the game for the season are thus injured. The changes in the rules during the past ten years have tended to increase the number of injuries, rather than to diminish it. . . . Moreover, the ethics of the game, which are the imperfect ethics of war, do not improve. . . . Of all the competitive games in which the students are interested, football is the only one against which any serious objections can be raised; but there is increasing objection to the great exaggeration of all athletic sports. . . . But whenever the evils consequent upon this exaggeration are mentioned it should also be mentioned that the outdoor sports on the average and in the mass do more good than harm; for they promote vigorous physical development, and provide invaluable safeguards against effeminacy and vice."—President Charles W. Eliot, Harvard University, 1903. "Athletics," *Harvard Graduates' Magazine*, March, 1903. Quoted in W. Carson Ryan, Jr., *The Literature of American School and College Athletics* (New York: The Carnegie Foundation for the Advancement of Teaching, Bulletin No. 24, 1929), p. 93.

"The widespread public interest in intercollegiate athletic contests, their popularity with the student body, and their manifest dangers if left to develop without responsible control, raise some difficult problems in any large university. These contests are surrounded by moral as well as by physical danger. . . .

"To prohibit intercollegiate athletic contests is, in my opinion, more than unwise; it is unreasonable. To regulate and control them, however, is of the first importance. . . .

"From a theoretical point of view much may be said for the endowment of intercollegiate athletic sports and the abolition of gate receipts, as has often been proposed. But so long as Columbia is in urgent need of large sums for the support of instruction and research and for the erection of buildings, and so long as the present system of financial control is in satisfactory operation, it would be an error of judgment to ask that we be put in possession of the large sum of money necessary to endow our athletic sports."—President Nicholas Murray Butler, Columbia University, 1904. *Report for 1903-04*. Quoted in *The Rise of A University*, Vol. II, ed. Edward C. Elliott (New York: Columbia University Press, 1937), pp. 441, 442, 443.

"The game of football has become seriously injurious to rational academic life in American schools and colleges, and it is time that the public, especially the educated public, should understand and take into consideration the objections to this game."—President Charles W. Eliot, Harvard University, 1904. *Reports of the President and the Treasurer of Harvard College, 1903-04*. Quoted in W. Carson Ryan, Jr., *The Literature of American School and College Athletics* (New York: The Carnegie Foundation for the Advancement of Teaching, Bulletin No. 24, 1929), p. 94.

"All discussion of whether a college or university should or should not concern itself officially about athletics may be avoided by saying that students of higher learning are in athletics to stay. No good institution known to me could possibly get its students out. Athletics, with tremendous power to affect health, morals, and college spirit, are unavoidable. . . . As president I am not called upon to ask whether athletics are worth the outlay. They are inevitable. If not properly regulated, they become a source of degradation; but if properly regulated they become a means of grace."—President R. H. Jesse, The University of Missouri, 1904. "Objects and Methods of Physical Training in Colleges and Universities," *Proceedings of the National Education Association, 1904.* Quoted in W. Carson Ryan, Jr., *The Literature of American School and College Athletics* (New York: The Carnegie Foundation for the Advancement of Teaching, Bulletin No. 24, 1929), p. 31.

"Football, as the most exaggerated form of intercollegiate games, is being widely condemned. As at present played, the game should no doubt be abolished. The entire country has been laid under obligations to Columbia University for its announced determination to banish the game; and Harvard never did the country a better service than it is now doing by the investigations it is making and the action it will no doubt take in due time. . . .

"That this excessive importance attached to athletics is doing harm to American education cannot be questioned. And these evils are more pronounced in the larger and older colleges of the East and North. They are evils that have grown out of mere bigness. They have come from great prosperity, like many of the evils in the business and political life of the country. These larger colleges must do something to lighten the strain that is now upon athletics; and something will doubtless be done before long. Perhaps to abolish the gate receipts would produce the desired results.

"These pronounced evils of athletics in the larger eastern colleges have not threatened the colleges in the South. Our evils are not evils of prosperity, but evils of adversity; and they came from lack of organization, from the chaotic state in which so much of our education finds itself. The country has been too poor, the colleges have been too small, and the communities in which the colleges have been located too sparsely settled to give Southern intercollegiate games the vast crowds and immense gate receipts that have produced the fanaticism and wild enthusiasm in the North. And yet athletic conditions have been no better in the most parts of the South than in the North. But the unfortunate situation here is attributable to the disorganized state of education, and, as a symptom of this disorganization, it is most discouraging. Southern colleges are growing rapidly, and the entire section is becoming prosperous as never before. Prosperity will soon come to intercollegiate athletics; and if to the evils of disorganization, we add the evils that come from bigness and prosperity, we shall have a state of things that will be unendurable. It is absolutely essential that all reputable Southern colleges at once put themselves right in the matter of intercollegiate athletics."—Professor (later President) William P. Few, Trinity College (North Carolina), 1906. "The Excessive Devotion to Athletics," *The South Atlantic Quarterly*, January, 1906.

"No game is fit for college uses in which men are so often knocked or crushed into insensibility or immobility that it is a question whether by the application of water and stimulants they can be brought to and enabled to go on playing. No game is fit for college uses in which recklessness in causing or suffering serious bodily injuries promotes efficiency, and so is taught and held up for admiration. . . . The immoralities or brutalities connected with particular sports are, however, much less injurious to the educational institutions of the country than the gross exaggeration of all competitive sports which is now working incalculable harm to schools, colleges, and universities. . . . From the educational point of view, the value of any sport is to be tested chiefly by the number of persons who habitually take part in it for pleasure during the educational period and enjoy it in after life. Tried by this test, football is the least valuable of all college sports."—President Charles W. Eliot, Harvard University, 1906. *Reports of the President and Treasurer of Harvard College, 1905-06.* Quoted in W. Carson Ryan, Jr., *The Literature of American School and College Athletics* (New York: The Carnegie Foundation for the Advancement of Teaching, Bulletin No. 24, 1929), p. 94.

"Most of its evils have come, it is not necessary to say, with its intensification, with the glorification of the player, with the professionalizing of what was once but a means of recreation. . . . Perhaps those who know more about football than some of the rest of us do can, by processes of elimination, find and correct what has distorted or debased the game in recent years; and we of the teaching body can at least see that it does not have too much sympathy from our curricula,—and inherited savagery."—President John H. Finley, College of the City of New York, 1906. *Review of Reviews,* January, 1906, pp. 73, 74.

"During the autumn of 1905 various occurrences took place which served to focus attention upon the game of football as it had come to be played by American college students. . . . Moreover, the vigor of the more important contests and the excitement attending them had proved most attractive to a large portion of the public outside of the universities, so that they took on more and more the character of a public spectacle instead of a sport. Immense crowds were attracted to witness the contests, and sums equal to the annual income of many an American college were received in gate money in a single day. Football, indeed, threatened to overshadow, and in some institutions did already overshadow, every other academic interest. The example of the colleges had speedily been followed by the secondary schools, . . . and not a few schoolmasters were beginning to complain of the evils which afflicted the colleges. Appreciation of these facts had been growing in the public mind for some years past and the events of the football season of 1905 brought matters to a crisis. . . . That these contests were gladitorial in character, the history of the last few years of the game plainly proves. . . .

"The most serious effects of intercollegiate football were not worked upon the participants but upon the spectators and upon the general public. . . ."—President Nicholas Murray Butler, Columbia University, 1906. *Report for 1905-06*. Quoted in *The Rise of A University*, Vol. II, ed. Edward C. Elliott (New York: Columbia University Press, 1937), pp. 443, 444.

"The last two years have been marked in the history of intercollegiate athletics in the West by some important reforms. Eligibility to intercollegiate teams has been limited to undergraduates and to those who have been at least one year in residence. The number of games has been restricted and close attention has been given to securing a reasonable excellence of work in the classroom from students who are eligible for the teams. . . . It is desired to prevent the undue solicitation of promising athletes in the secondary schools to attend any particular institution. This has been done oftentimes without the knowledge or consent of the authorities and has assumed such form as to be unbecoming the dignity of institutions of learning. Again, it is desired to prevent students from passing from college to college in order to make a market of athletic skill. It is felt, also, that the excitement attending a long series of intercollegiate contests has been excessive and should be held in proper subordination to the other main purpose of college life. . . . Competitive sports have their merits which cannot be ignored. They have also dangers which require constant watchcare to prevent. Above all things such contests should be above suspicion of unworthy methods and motives."—President Harry Pratt Judson, The University of Chicago, 1907. *The President's Report, 1906-1907*, p. 9.

"The exaggeration of athletic sports in schools and colleges remains a crying evil, and there are no clear signs that any effectual remedy is taking effect. . . . The college sport most popular with spectators and newspapers, namely, football, is the least useful of all the games; because a smaller proportional number of students are fit for that sport than for any other. Another objection to all the violent sports is that they cannot be played after the college period. A sport which will be useful to any healthy man until he is sixty is a much more valuable college sport than one that he cannot play after he is 23. . . .

"The number of intercollegiate contests should be reduced to two in each sport during any one season, the rest of the competition in each sport being exclusively home competition. . . . In order to give this policy a chance to succeed, it would be necessary for two or more colleges to agree that they would permit only two intercollegiate contests in a season in each sport."—President Charles W. Eliot, Harvard University, 1908. "Athletics Still Exaggerated," *Harvard Graduates' Magazine*, June, 1908. Quoted in W. Carson Ryan, Jr., *The Literature of American School and College Athletics* (New York: The Carnegie Foundation for the Advancement of Teaching, Bulletin No. 24, 1929), p. 93.

"Hardly had the question of Tulane's right to state appropriations been dropped when another controversy with Tulane, quite as bitter as that over state support, arose concerning the eligibility of Louisiana State University's football players. . . . Charges were made by Tulane that several members of the Louisiana State University squad were paid players—'ringers' —and that Coach Wingard [of L. S. U.] knew that they were being paid. The matter was never settled to the satisfaction of Tulane and for several years athletic relations between the two schools were discontinued. Because of this controversy Louisiana State University's famous championship team of 1908 never played Tulane University."—Marcus W. Wilkerson, *Thomas Duckett Boyd: The Story of a Southern Educator* (Baton Rouge: Louisiana State University Press, 1935), pp. 267, 268.

"I believe strongly in the physical and moral value of athletic sports, and of intercollegiate contests conducted in a spirit of generous rivalry; and I do not believe that their exaggerated prominence at the present day is to be attributed to a conviction on the part of the undergraduates, or of the public, that physical is more valuable than mental force. It is due rather to the fact that such contests offer to students the one common interest, the only striking occasion for a display of college solidarity."—President A. Lawrence Lowell, Harvard University, 1909. Inaugural Address, in S. E. Morison, *The Development of Harvard University* (Cambridge: Harvard University Press, 1930), pp. lxxix, lxxx.

"The athletic policy of the Conference of the Middle West has again proved its value. The important changes in the whole attitude of the student body and the public toward athletics caused by the reforms of the conference can with difficulty be appreciated by those not familiar with the old system. . . . Intercollegiate athletic contests are an interesting feature of student life and an interesting outlet for student enthusiasm. When not permitted to become the principal thing in college these contests have an undoubted value. . . . It must not be thought, however, that nothing remains to be done, or that all possible dangers have disappeared. There continue features, especially in football, which are dangerous to life and health. These must be substantially eliminated if the game is to continue."—President Harry Pratt Judson, The University of Chicago, 1910. *The President's Report, 1909-1910*, p. 17.

"In 1905 the American game of football came under a severe storm of criticism. The academic authorities in many institutions had lost all control of intercollegiate athletics; . . . it was clear that the game must be purified, moderated, reformed, or else abolished. . . .

"Nor was it alone in the colleges that the game was condemned; in the secondary schools conditions were worse. The American game is totally unfit for secondary-school students. . . .

". . . the greater part of the old arrangement still holds true. This is because the evils are inherent in the game . . . the colleges generally would be justified in following the example of Columbia University in abolishing the game outright. . . .

"If the game is abolished, is there any substitute that can be offered to take its place? The writer believes that most of the present evils of the football game would disappear by going back to the British Rugby game of football. . . ."—President David Starr Jordan, Leland Stanford Junior University, 1910. *Proceedings of the National Education Association, 1910*, pp. 357, 358, 359.

"Football, the most significant of all college games, can be defended on the ground of being a training for the brain, a training for the heart, and a training for the will. With all that may be said against athletics—and much may be said—much more, very much more, may be said in their favor. The credit arising from athletics, to be placed to the advantage of the American college, is great."—President Charles F. Thwing, Western Reserve University, 1910. *A History of Education in the United States Since the Civil War* (Boston: Houghton Mifflin Company, 1910), pp. 138-139.

"Training for football means early hours, clean life, constant occupation for body and mind. Breach of training means ostracism. That this game tides many a freshman over a great danger, by keeping him healthily occupied, I have come firmly to believe. It supplies what President Eliot calls a 'new and effective motive for resisting all sins which weaken or corrupt the body'."—Dean Le Baron Russell Briggs, Harvard College, 1913. *College Life.* Boston: Houghton Mifflin Company, 1913. Quoted in W. Carson Ryan, Jr., *The Literature of American School and College Athletics* (New York: The Carnegie Foundation for the Advancement of Teaching, Bulletin No. 24, 1929), p. 11.

"Sportsmanship in American colleges is visibly and constantly changing for the better. . . . Every little we can do to make clean our national game helps our citizens to make clean the greater game of our national life."—Dean Le Baron Russell

Briggs, Harvard University, 1914. Address of the president of the National Collegiate Athletic Association, *American Physical Education Review*, April, 1914. Quoted in W. Carson Ryan, Jr., *The Literature of American School and College Athletics* (New York: The Carnegie Foundation for the Advancement of Teaching, Bulletin No. 24, 1929), p. 258.

"Intercollegiate athletics provide a costly, injurious, and excessive régime of physical training for a few students, especially those who need it least, instead of inexpensive, healthful, and moderate exercise for all students, especially those who need it most. . . .

"Nearly all that may be said on this subject about colleges applies to secondary schools. The lower schools as a rule tend to imitate the worst features of intercollegiate athletics."—President William T. Foster, Reed College, 1915. "An Indictment of Intercollegiate Athletics," *The Atlantic Monthly*, November, 1915, p. 377.

"The evils of intercollegiate athletics are many and great; and of these evils the most comprehensive and the most searching is *mutual distrust.*

"Let our colleges keep at the head of the athletics men who try to be honest, let those men trust each other down to the ground, and half the evils of intercollegiate athletics will die a natural death."—Dean Le Baron Russell Briggs, Harvard University, 1915. President's Address, *Proceedings of the National Collegiate Athletic Association, 1915*. Quoted in W. Carson Ryan, Jr., *The Literature of American School and College Athletics* (New York: The Carnegie Foundation for the Advancement of Teaching, Bulletin No. 24, 1929), p. 86.

"Taken all in all, intercollegiate athletics, even as they are at present, in state universities, on the whole do justify themselves."—President David Kinley, The University of Illinois, 1916. *Proceedings of the National Association of State Universities, 1916*. Quoted in W. Carson Ryan, Jr., *The Literature of American*

School and College Athletics (New York: The Carnegie Foundation for the Advancement of Teaching, Bulletin No. 24, 1929), p. 107.

"There may be reasons why the athletic coach should not receive three times as much salary as the professor of Greek; but there is no inherent reason why he should not hold a position of equal dignity. He can do more good than the professor of Greek, and a great deal more harm."—Dean Le Baron Russell Briggs, Harvard University, 1916. President's Address, *Proceedings of the National Collegiate Athletic Association, 1916.* Quoted in W. Carson Ryan, Jr., *The Literature of American School and College Athletics* (New York: The Carnegie Foundation for the Advancement of Teaching, Bulletin No. 24, 1929), p. 86.

"But if we take a lesson from the camps we shall provide for a more general participation in games by college students. . . . We do not want 'athletics as usual,' because they have usually been abused. But we want all business and all sport, all work and all play, relieved of superfluity and extravagance, stripped for action in the nation's service, and coördinated with the laboratory and the library and the classroom in the endless task of creating men to be citizens of America."—President W. H. P. Faunce, Brown University, 1917. "Athletics for the Service of the Nation," *Proceedings of the National Collegiate Athletic Association, 1917.* Quoted in W. Carson Ryan, Jr., *The Literature of American School and College Athletics* (New York: The Carnegie Foundation for the Advancement of Teaching, Bulletin No. 24, 1929), p. 180.

"The feeling of American college professors towards intercollegiate athletics is one of growing hostility. . . . A great many college teachers are wondering whether, in President Wilson's phrase, the side shows are not crowding out the main performance . . . in regard to the eligibility of players and their methods of playing the games, we have developed in intercollegiate athletics a code of ethics which at their best are shady and at their worst plainly corrupt."—Professor Frank Aydelotte, The Massachusetts Institute of Technology, 1917. "Spectators and Sport," *The Oxford Stamp and Other Essays* (New York: Oxford University Press, 1917), pp. 22, 23, 28, 29.

"The newly acquired property, to which the Trustees have formally given the name of Baker Field, will enable the University not only to fulfill the ambitions and hopes of the students of today and tomorrow, but also to achieve one of the aims and ideals of its educational system. Here physical exercise can be had under almost perfect conditions; here the foundations of health and physical comfort can be firmly laid; here those personal associations that mean so much in after life, can be formed; and here character can be both tested and trained.

"Moreover, through its possession and use of Baker Field, Columbia University can once more show its concern for the interests and satisfactions of the people of New York. To this field they will shortly come in large numbers to enjoy those admirable spectacles of generous rivalry and free competition which stir the emotions and give widespread enjoyment. New York will be the gainer because Columbia is better furnished for its task."—President Nicholas Murray Butler, Columbia University, 1922. *Report for 1921-22.* Quoted in *The Rise of A University*, Vol. II, ed. Edward C. Elliott (New York: Columbia University Press, 1937), pp. 445, 446.

"Quarrel with athletic sport as we will, and regret as we must that in institutions of learning it seems to turn relative values topsy-turvy, no recent observer of young men can deny that in some men's education—in the development of their character—it is a mighty force."—Dean Le Baron Russell Briggs, Harvard College, 1922. *Reports of the President and the Treasurer of Harvard College, 1921-1922.* Quoted in W. Carson Ryan, Jr., *The Literature of American School and College Athletics* (New York: The Carnegie Foundation for the Advancement of Teaching, Bulletin No. 24, 1929), p. 11.

"Surely, as the aim in instruction is to give education to all, that in athletics should be the physical culture of all. . . . Having great intercollegiate games every Saturday throughout the autumn in a stadium filled with many thousand spectators is not well either for members of the team or the student body. It tends to disturb seriously the work of education, and still more to distort in the minds of the public and of the alumni the real object of the college."—President A. Lawrence Lowell, Harvard University, 1926. *President's Report to the Board of Overseers of Harvard University, 1925-26.* Quoted in W. Carson Ryan, Jr., *The Literature of American School and College Athletics* (New York: The Carnegie Foundation for the Advancement of Teaching, Bulletin No. 24, 1929), p. 186.

"We want sports which help to educate, or we do not want them at all. . . . Much of the current criticism of football seems to amount simply to the statement that the game is altogether too interesting to be tolerated. But America will never condemn any kind of work or play because it is of absorbing interest. To find out what are the elements of supreme interest to American youth, and utilize those elements in the various 'projects' of the curriculum, would be the part of wisdom."—President W. H. P. Faunce, Brown University, 1926. *Annual Report.* Quoted in W. Carson Ryan, Jr., *The Literature of American School and College Athletics* (New York: The Carnegie Foundation for the Advancement of Teaching, Bulletin No. 24, 1929), p. 137.

"In a general discussion upon any subject of wide importance we always find the extremist. This is true in questions pertaining to the scope and management of athletics. Some would reduce the sports to their lowest terms, while others advocate the opposite. That it is a serious problem in all institutions must be conceded. This is shown by the many references made by educators and organizations throughout the country. In a recently published bibliography of intercollegiate football, seventy-six major references are given, a large majority of which have been written in the last three years. The Carnegie Foundation for the Advancement of Teaching announced only a few months ago that it was about to undertake at the request of the National Collegiate Athletic Association, a study of intercollegiate athletics. The study will include a complete sketch of conditions with regard to athletics both intercollegiate and intramural in American colleges and universities, including management, eligibility, control, and the relation of sports to the educational process. It is hoped that when completed it will present a sufficient number of facts to give an understanding of the present place of athletics in the institutions of the country. It is estimated that two years will be consumed in the study. . . .

"The athletic situation at Maine has passed through various stages in the past. We should congratulate ourselves, however, that never in its history has it been in such a healthy condition. To be sure it is far from perfect, but if the co-operation of students, faculty, and alumni count for anything, then we should feel that great gains have been made in the past few years."—President H. S. Boardman, The University of Maine, 1926. *Inaugural Address by Harold Sherburne Boardman, President University of Maine, June 12, 1926* (Pamphlet), pp. 12, 13.

"President Eliot talked, but President Butler acted. Football was abolished at Columbia.

"But the pressure was too great. In due time the game was re-established at America's largest university.

"Since then football has been growing by leaps and bounds. Today it is easily the most popular game in the land. It is no longer a sport, but a spectacle. . . .

"The chief trouble with football in our colleges today is not so much in the way the game is taught or played, as in the timidity and laxity of college authorities in enforcing the standards they set."—President Hamilton Holt, Rollins College, 1927. "An Appeal to College Presidents," *American Review of Reviews*. May, 1927, pp. 529, 530.

"There are, I maintain, two ways, and only two, of being honest in athletics. One of these has been propounded by Hamilton Holt, President of Rollins College. . . . Possessing a conscience undulled by long association with the devious ways of intercollegiate athletics, he grew quickly disgusted with the practices carried on under the cover of rules, standards and high pretensions, and proposed in a moment of impatience to drop all sham and pretense, to junk all rules of eligibility, and to go frankly into the open market and buy the best football material to be had for the money to uphold the name and spread the fame of the college. . . .

"Of course Hamilton Holt has not done and will not do what he threatened to do in a mood of exasperation. He would not in that case be the type of man to be the president of Rollins College; the emphasis which he is laying on building up a select faculty and adequate facilities for a liberal education would be out of place. On the contrary, he would be succeeded by a Connie Mack, D.D., LL.D., and the campus of Rollins College would be graced by a million-dollar stadium and a library which could be picked up at any Woolworth emporium.

"The other way of being honest is perhaps more difficult, but it is not, I think, impossible. It is to diffuse throughout the college, its graduates and friends, its governing board, its faculty, its students, its athletic management and coaching staff—it is to diffuse, I say, throughout the institution a vigilant integrity—a conscience which will be active and on the alert to make sure that any football team or any other team which represents the college in any intercollegiate sport is really representative of the college, that it is built up out of a student body which has been attracted to the college by its character, its quality and its reputation as an institution of learning; that it is bone of its bone and flesh of its flesh, and not something extraneous to the college; not something which has been brought into a quasi relationship to it by emoluments, inducements or persuasions which have nothing whatever to do with the drawing power of the college itself; in a word, something which is not foreign, but our own."—President George Norlin, The University of

Colorado, 1929. "Going Straight in Athletics," *School and Society*, February 16, 1929.

"It is a useless enquiry at this day to ask who were responsible for the development in the colleges of commercialized sports. . . .

"But there can be no doubt as to where lies the responsibility to correct this situation. . . . The responsibility to bring athletics into a sincere relation to the intellectual life of the college rests squarely on the shoulders of the president and the faculty.

"What ought to be done?

"The paid coach, the gate receipts, the special training tables, the costly sweaters and extensive journeys in special Pullman cars, the recruiting from the high schools, the demoralizing publicity showered on the players, the devotion of an undue proportion of time to training, the devices for putting a desirable athlete, but a weak scholar, across the hurdles of the examinations—these ought to stop and the inter-college and intramural sports be brought back to a stage in which they can be enjoyed by large numbers of students and where they do not involve an expenditure of time and money wholly at variance with any ideal of honest study. . . . The need today is to reexamine our educational regime with the determination to attain in greater measure the simplicity, sincerity, and thoroughness that is the life blood of a true university in any country at any time."—President Henry S. Pritchett, The Carnegie Foundation for the Advancement of Teaching (formerly president of the Massachusetts Institute of Technology), 1929. In Preface to *American College Athletics*, by Howard J. Savage (New York: The Carnegie Foundation for the Advancement of Teaching, 1929), pp. xx, xxi.

"Not long ago, one of the great foundations undertook an exhaustive survey of the athletic situation in our colleges and emerged with a body of highly interesting and valuable data which seriously disturbed the slumbers of the authorities at a number of institutions and left everyone feeling a little uncomfortable. To be sure a few institutions—among them the one over which I have the honor to preside—were found to be white as the driven snow, while others ranged through various shades of gray down to uncompromising black. It must be admitted, distressing as it is to do so, that those of us who came off unscratched were by the others credited with shrewdness and discretion more often than with unadulterated virtue. It was alleged that we had merely been too clever to be caught and it was remembered to our discredit that we had not ranked very high in the matter of athletic victories—at least not in football, by which the average American still tests collegiate virility. And I may add that it was a little uncomfortable for us to be suddenly confronted with the fact that gentlemen in other institutions whom we had implicitly trusted as upright exponents of the finest ideals of sport were, in point of fact, harboring illicit athletes and supporting them by corrupt practices—apple concessions and the like—in a luxury to which they had not previously been accustomed. Moreover, some of our own household maintained that we had been stupidly, indeed perversely, good, and that the children of Mammon were undoubtedly wiser in their day and generation than were we. Such is the fate of good deeds in a naughty world.

"Whatever judgment may ultimately be passed upon it, the Carnegie Foundation Report conclusively indicated that current judgments upon the health of intercollegiate athletics present an amazing diversity, extending from the opinion of those at one extreme who feel that the patient is suffering with a mortal malady from which he can never recover, and that chloroform should be used as quickly as possible, to those at the other extreme who proclaim the patient thoroughly sound, suffering at worst from a little over-indulgence in high living. Between these two views is a great body of intermediate opinion, reflecting a fairly firm conviction that the patient has no fatal ailment but is afflicted with an appreciable number of minor complaints, some of which probably require the surgeon's aid, and others of which will cure themselves, if the sufferer is put on a simple diet, and required to live a more cloistered life. Far be it from me to dogmatize concerning these several forms of diagnosis. In a certain sense all may be correct, in that each of the pronouncements may be valid as to particular institutions, or regions, or games. Suffice it to say that my personal sympathies are rather with this last intermediate group. I feel quite certain that the patient is not going to die, although in fits of exasperation I have often wished that he would; but I am almost equally certain that in some essential respects he must alter his manner of life, if he is to meet his obligations, improve to the full his opportunities, and deserve the respect of the judicious."—President James R. Angell, Yale University, 1930. "The Familiar Problems of Collegiate Athletics," in *Problems and Procedures in Intercollegiate Sport* (Extracts from addresses and reports at the Convention of the National Collegiate Athletic Association, 1930), pp. 7, 8.

"Only the other day, in a large state university in a state bordering upon our own, a week before a crucial game involving a conference championship, the coaching staff felt the need of stirring up 'spirit' on the campus, and took the necessary steps to do so. 'Pep' societies took up the cry. Students were constrained to enter their class rooms with minds intent on nothing but the impending game. Each day they answered the roll call with the words 'Beat Timbuctoo.' Cumulatively, calculus, psychology, American government, and other academic interests were relegated to the limbo of things to be forgotten. The game crowded out all other thoughts, and on Friday before the game the students 'declared' an all day rally, mobs invaded the classrooms, property was destroyed, and professors who remained at their posts, faithful to the purpose of the University, were shamefully manhandled. But the University won the football game in a blaze of glory, and you will say, 'boys will be boys.' Well, 'boys will be boys,' but can you dismiss the situation with this phrase? Are the 'boys' really to blame? Again, the other day the president of another state university imported a coach at a salary double that of the ablest professor on the faculty. Did he not in doing so say almost in so many words that 'the game's the thing,' and that while the university lends dignity to the stadium, the stadium lends distinction to the university? Perhaps we can dismiss this too with the remark that presidents will be presidents as long as fans are fans.

"It is a serious situation, and the Carnegie report [Bulletin Number Twenty-Three, 1929], cannot be dismissed as lightly and flippantly and cynically as has been done on the sporting page. It does not propose to abolish intercollegiate athletics; it recognizes their value; it proposes only to save them from their own excesses; and I for my part believe that they have their place, but that they have their place only so long and only in so far as they are kept in their place."—President George Norlin, The University of Colorado, 1930. *Athletics in Ancient Greece and Modern America.* Pamphlet. Boulder, Colorado, *ca.* 1930.

"Gentlemen, you are doing something in teaching American intercollegiate football which is absolutely necessary and fundamental in American life. . . .

"I have also noticed this, as an administrator and also as a professor, that the easiest time in the year in which to maintain the morale of the whole student body is in the football season." —President T. C. Knoles, College of the Pacific, 1932. *Proceedings of the Special Convention of the National Collegiate Athletic Association, 1932*, pp. 14, 15.

"The greatest evil in athletics today is subsidizing. When we attempt to discuss this phase of athletics, we seem to be somewhat timid. All know this evil exists in our colleges and universities, to a large extent in some and to a small extent in others. . . .

"We should not continue our *laissez faire* policy, . . ."—President S. V. Sanford, The University of Georgia, 1932. *Proceedings of the National Collegiate Athletic Association, 1932*, pp. 111, 112.

"Without the illusions of the holier than thou attitude, we

hold that the athletes must stand on the same basis as other students in all matters of honor, scholastic work, scholarships, fees, rooms, loans, jobs, and any other financial aid. This simple principle of openness and equality of opportunity for all students in the matter of financial aid will basically decide the issue as to whether intercollegiate football is to be a spectacular racket or a college sport. . . . The sincerity of our intercollegiate conference agreements is tested in the award by representative and responsible faculty committees of all scholarships, loans, jobs, and any other direct and indirect financial aid of the institution on a basis open equally to all students. . . . Is student life to revolve mainly around a circus subsidized and brought into the institutions or is it to center mainly in the teachers, library, classrooms, laboratories, historic buildings, shrines, trees, and flowers which are a part of the soil, the air, and the spirit of the place?

"In this matter of athletics the colleges and universities are all brothers together in aspirations and frustrations. The ground we have gained we will not surrender. We are not yet what we would become, and we need the help of all. With the coöperation of trustees, alumni, faculty, and students, the colleges can preserve and advance themselves as educational centers in which intercollegiate sport will become a more representative by-product of the youthful zest for games and athletic skill, the spirit of sportsmanship, and a community-wide participation in athletic play. The colleges have no greater means of teaching than through their departments of physical education, gymnasiums, intramural and varsity fields, the lessons of the physical basis of intellectual vigor and the spiritually radiant personality, the satisfaction and values of clean living, the sportsmen's code of fair play, courage, self-sacrifice for the team and the college, mayhap to be translated into a social code of the higher loyalties of justice and coöperation among men."—President Frank P. Graham, The University of North Carolina, 1933. "Report of the President," *University of North Carolina Record*, December, 1933, pp. 10, 11.

"Today the main attack is on the conspicuous features of 'bigtime football.' Teams wholly, or in part, hired by methods of subsidy too numerous to list here, but most of them perfectly well recognized, and some of them shabby and disreputable, constitute item one. The next is the existence of the high-salaried coach and the things that go with him. Too often he receives an important part of his salary in undesirable ways and he has to justify himself by a winning team and the top-heavy gate receipts this is supposed to assure. The gate receipts once secured are not infrequently used in large part to perpetuate the system—bigger and better stadia, more coaches at higher salaries, more equipment, more attendants, more luxurious conditions of travel. Then, as a lesser item, there are to be mentioned the barnstorming teams, playing in California one week, in New York the next, and in Chicago the third, accompanied by all the ballyhoo that newspapers can be induced to offer. Needless to say, such trips made in term time reduce to a farce any pretense of serious intellectual discipline on the collegiate level, and betray before the public the whole status of the college as an institution embodying high educational ideals.

"When it comes to remedies, suggestions vary widely. Many are for the complete abolishment of the game, perhaps substituting for it Rugby, which was successfully played on the Pacific Coast for a number of years and which has recently been rejuvenated at a few institutions in the East. Others would keep football, but 'give it back to the boys.' By this phrase some persons mean to proceed by absolutely abolishing the coach. Others, maintaining that boys should be given competent teaching in sports as well as in mathematics or languages, would simply eliminate the coach while a game is in progress, throwing complete responsibility then on the captain and the team. Up to this time, no one, so far as I am aware, has been able to induce the boys to take control of the game on any terms whatever. In view of the huge crowds before which the games are played, and of the passionate excitement often engendered, and especially with the present rules permitting the incessant shuttling of men on and off the field, undergraduate captains are wholly unwilling to assume the necessary responsibility, and the more so in that the physical fitness of the players is often one of the problems involved.

"Now there are certain fundamental questions about the whole issue which must be dealt with by anyone who believes in the paramount worth of our collegiate and university education, and who at the same time appreciates the very real values inherent in football. (1) Is football to be kept a game, or is it to be run frankly as a business and for advertising purposes? (2) If it is to be a game, is it to be played by amateurs, or by hired men? (3) If by amateurs, is the training in it to be given by educated men of high character, who will conduct it with intelligence and understanding as an important disciplinary accessory to the essential educational aims of the institution, or by men whose preponderant interest is in holding their lucrative jobs by producing winning teams at whatever cost? If the former, then the football instructor deserves the same kind of self-respecting position as other teachers enjoy, with the certainty that he will be judged by his employers not in terms of a season of victories, and certainly not in terms of public clamor in case of defeat, but in terms of his total contribution to the morale of the situation in which the skill and inspiration of this teaching are only a part, though a highly important part. Upon the replies made to these questions rests, I am confident, the future of college football, and if the answers are wisely given, I think most of the objectionable features of the game will slowly but certainly fade out."—President James R. Angell, Yale University, 1934. "The Collegiate Sports Complex," *Vanity Fair*, May, 1934. Also in his *American Education* (New Haven: Yale University Press, 1937), pp. 256-258.

"When I went to the University of Florida, I learned that my athletic organization wasn't entirely controlled on the campus. I know that some university presidents think that their athletic organizations are entirely theirs and probably they are but I found that mine was controlled to some extent off the campus. I knew it was a dangerous thing to monkey with because an experienced president told me, 'Now, Tigert, before you get far into this thing of being a university president, I want to tell you one thing: don't get too close to the athletics.' When I found that part of our athletics was not controlled on the campus, it became necessary for me to eliminate a man who had built up a very powerful organization from Pensacola to Key West."—President John J. Tigert, The University of Florida, 1934. *Transactions and Proceedings of the National Association of State Universities, 1934.*

"It is devoutly to be desired that such apparent progressive evolution could be reported in the realm of intercollegiate athletics, notably football. Football can hardly be considered amateur as long as there is pronounced laxity in administering scholastic requirements of admission and promotion, favoritism in distribution of student aid, and extravagance in payment of coaches' salaries and other concomitant expenditures of travel and accoutrements."—President G. E. Snavely, Birmingham-Southern College, 1934. *Bulletin of the Association of American Colleges*, December, 1934, p. 474.

"I wrote to the Carnegie Foundation, suggesting that they might wish to make another study—a report of progress. I had a long letter from the Carnegie Foundation to the effect that that was a very difficult and a very expensive thing to undertake. They had spent very large sums of money on the earlier report, and they found it very difficult to get the truth about these situations in the various institutions. The writer, however, wrote, 'It is our opinion that the conditions, based on a good deal of observation, are worse now than they were in 1929 and that one institution is saying to another institution, by word, "If you leave us alone we will leave you alone." ' "—Chancellor E. H. Lindley, The University of Kansas, 1934. *Transactions and Proceedings of the National Association of State Universities, 1934,* p. 206.

"And now I come to the most important aspect of the whole

matter as far as the persons here assembled are concerned. If we are to train the whole boy, and if the work represented by this group lies at the basis of everything that all the rest of us may attempt, it is of superlative importance that you should yourselves have a sense of unity and a common attitude toward these boys and girls in our schools and colleges. No one in the entire list of college officers, instructors, professors, deans, or presidents, begins to have the opportunity to learn and to influence the attitude and fundamentals of living that are current among students as do the athletic coaches and the teacher of hygiene and physical education and the college doctor. If you yourselves have the quality to do it, your opportunity is boundless. I would rather have an athletic coach of the right kind than almost any other officer of the college. Or perhaps it would be more forcible and no less true to say that an unwholesome athletic coach or teacher of health education can do more harm than almost anyone else."—Dean Herbert E. Hawkes, Columbia College, 1934. *Proceedings of the National Collegiate Athletic Association, 1934*, pp. 94, 95.

"It is a curious thing that the question of subsidization should attract so much attention when it is an insignificant result of far more serious evils which exist in the football world. Were some of these greater evils corrected, the problems attendant upon the subsidization of athletes would disappear. . . .

"The original sin, I believe, in football is ignorance of its significance and consequent disregard of its importance by those who should assume responsibility. . . .

"We have generally assumed that it [football] is a part of the physical education of the college youth. A brief analysis would indicate that it does not qualify as such. . . .

"Another justification which is often made for football is its advertising value to the college. Facts and figures dispute this heartily. . . .

"The true significance of football has at no time in its history been recognized by the educators. They have persisted in looking upon it as a necessary evil. . . . Herein is the crime against football . . . it deserves to be taken back into the colleges and universities as part and parcel of the educational project. It deserves the leadership of the best the university has to offer. . . .

"The second great evil in football is deceit. All other problems of subsidizing, gambling, drinking are small in comparison with this one of academic dishonesty. The subtle development of this dishonesty is amazing. . . .

"The famous Carnegie Foundation report was notable not because of what it revealed, but of what it failed to reveal. That an able foundation could spend so much and get so little is evidence of the silence and concealment in which the whole business is shrouded. . . .

"The third great evil in football is its commercialization. This is again the fault of the colleges."—President R. C. Hutchison, Washington and Jefferson College, 1936. *Proceedings of the National Collegiate Athletic Association, 1936*, pp. 90, 91, 92, 93.

"In taking over the entire financial administration of organized athletic sports and, by the aid of a slight increase in the tuition fees, assuming their costs, the trustees of Union College have taken a step new, if not unprecedented, in this important field of education. . . ."—President Dixon Ryan Fox, Union College, 1936. *School and Society*, February 1, 1936, p. 158.

"My pleasure at being invited to speak here this morning before this group, . . . was somewhat tempered by a thing I read in a sports column of a Philadelphia newspaper the day I arrived. . . : 'two men who never get anywhere : one, the fellow who wants the income tax abolished ; second, a college president who rails about commercialism in football.' . . .

"No college is free from athletic problems, but I have no doubt in my mind that football will continue to be the great game it is so long as we have a substantial number of colleges, and I believe an increasing number of colleges, that are realising the necessity for working out a continuing and permanent policy of sound attitude toward athletic problems within the institution, . . . It is for each college to give the answer for itself."

—President T. J. Davies, Colorado College, 1936. *Proceedings of the National Collegiate Athletic Association, 1936*, p. 112.

"A striking illustration of this dishonesty [covert methods employed by college officials, as President Hutchison charged] occurred in the Middle States Association of Secondary Schools and Colleges. Several years ago this association took action to the effect that colleges awarding athletic scholarships would be removed from accredited standing. From the beginning the committee took the position that they were not a police force, and that certainly the presidents and chancellors could be trusted to be honest. This proved a tragic assumption. The method of the committee was to give each president ample warning that they would, on a certain date, ask him for a simple statement as to whether athletic scholarships existed in his institution. In the meantime it was his business to find out, if 'he did not know.' The first such statement was asked for in October of 1933. Within this area there were notoriously subsidized teams, yet to the amazement of all, every single college and university presented a letter signed by its president or chancellor stating on his honor that, save for certain temporary exceptions allowed by the association, there was neither subsidizing nor athletic scholarships. In 1934 the great travesty was repeated, and the Middle States was pure—not one athletic scholarship east of the Ohio line. The chairman of the committee made his report, and then laying his paper down said, very simply, that despite this report the committee was convinced that there was more subsidizing than ever before. The effort of the Middle States Association was finally abandoned, and I was informed that it was because of the obvious dishonesty of the statements of some of the college presidents which made impossible any progress by the association."—President Ralph C. Hutchison, Washington and Jefferson College, 1936. *Proceedings of the National Collegiate Athletic Association, 1936*, p. 93.

"I am sorry that the gentlemen who attended this meeting [Intercollegiate Football Association, 1899] failed to settle the question, but the fact is I do not expect to live to see it settled. It is surprising, however, how many men each year suddenly discover that our college athletics are not 100 per cent amateur. A nationally known university president sometime ago suggested that perhaps college athletics were about 85 per cent all right. I think I called attention last year to the fact that we cannot measure scientifically the honesty and integrity of the legal or medical profession, of the men at the heads of some 400,000 business corporations, of the politicians, or in fact of the school teachers, college professors, or newspaper writers. I am sure, however, we will all agree that none of these groups are 100 per cent perfect. Further, I am sure that no one can with any accuracy maintain that college athletics are more or less professional today than they were, let us say, fifty years ago. My own opinion, and it is only an opinion, is that there are fewer boys per thousand today being illegitimately subsidized in our colleges than was true twenty-five or fifty years ago."—President John L. Griffith, National Collegiate Athletic Association, 1936. *Proceedings of the Association for 1936*, p. 88.

"I feel that college presidents are the ones who are responsible for the athletic standards of their institutions. Almost any president may have in his institution the type of athletics that he and the trustees decide they want. If he has 'professionalism' it is because that is what he believes is desirable. A policy of special favors for athletes does not creep into an institution unbeknownst. No president in the country, who is on the job, can avoid being held responsible for the athletic program and policies of his college. . . .

"I believe in football. I believe it is our greatest American college game. . . . We have two seasons in football; first, September through November, for scoring; second, December, for scorning; during the first period we play the game, and during the second some of us pan the game; forward passes are the thing during the first three months, and dirty digs thereafter. . . .

"I trust I am not being impudent or imprudent if I say that I hope the Carnegie Foundation will not again investigate college athletic standards, . . . I am not unappreciative of the earlier Report, when I say that I do not think that a second would do any good. Indeed, it is my own impression that the first resulted in a tremendous lot of publicity and talk, and very little positive action. . . .

"As for me, I should like to be recorded as in favor of a *laissez faire*, let well enough alone, policy on these matters. . . .

"Let's let football alone, and let's let each institution work out its own standards of eligibility frankly, openly, without any censoriousness on the part of the rest of us. . . ."—President James L. McConaughy, Wesleyan University, 1936. *Proceedings of the National Collegiate Athletic Association, 1936*, pp. 98, 99, 100, 104.

"I have come here today to make an appeal to the National Collegiate Athletic Association to use its great influence to preserve athletics as an integral and important element in American higher education. The educational and spiritual values of participation in sport are being threatened and destroyed by the widespread corruption of college and university teams. The evils are apparent and widely discussed. In a recent number of a popular magazine there is an article which treats, in the form of a debate, the question whether intercollegiate football should be abolished. The article is an amazing illustration of the perversion of popular thought on this subject, in that all the arguments urged for the retention of football would seem, to a believer in the traditional values of athletic sports, to be reasons for its abolition. I do not myself believe in the abolition of football or of any other intercollegiate sport, but I am convinced that the conception of the function of college athletics must be altered if they are to survive. . . .

"I know a college in which all the varsity athletes are required to state each season that they are not in receipt of any subsidy given primarily on athletic grounds. One of the best athletes and best students in the institution had signed these statements regularly throughout his course. In his Senior year the Student Government discovered that he had received regularly and secretly an athletic scholarship subscribed by a group of alumni in violation of the regulations and the wishes of the college authorities. The boy had lied about this on the assurance of the alumni that the statement was merely a formality and that everybody else did the same thing everywhere. The Student Government Committee felt reluctantly compelled to expel him. The boy himself had been increasingly uncomfortable about the whole situation and took his punishment like a man. He had been a good student and was about to be nominated as a candidate from the institution for a Rhodes Scholarship. His college career was wrecked and his prospects destroyed because of the fact that he was misled by older men whose first duty should have been to set him straight. . . .

"The younger generation of the present day hates nothing so much as hypocrisy. Youth is traditionally deficient in humor, and our young men and women may in some instances carry this feeling to extremes and tend too easily to suspect the motives of those in authority over them. But when they see each autumn, in the intervals between sermons in the college chapel and lofty discussions in their course in ethics and the Bible, the spectacle of college officials winking at the system of hired players and blandly putting a hypocritical front on plain dishonesty, they inevitably lose faith in the moral standards upon which our education is supposedly based. These young men are not all heroes. Many of them learn speedily enough to become hypocritical and dishonest themselves. The athletes take the money, and the thousands who are not athletes enjoy the spectacle, and so the evil system is continued, through lack of courage and leadership on the part of college officials and alumni."
—President Frank Aydelotte, Swarthmore College, 1937. *Proceedings of the National Collegiate Athletic Association, 1937.*

"It is my personal conviction that only in the measure in which our colleges are willing to have faith in each other, to rely upon the athletic integrity of their opponents, free from suspicion and rancor—only in that measure shall we preserve the spirit of amateurism in American athletics. And unless we who are in charge of athletics in our educational institutions rise to the ability to maintain athletics on this plane of good faith, then I submit to you that we have proved unworthy of the charge which has been committed to us.

"There is one more thing I would like to say. There is need for a frank and sensible attitude toward eligibility. Whether or not a student is a bona-fide student, and so is qualified to represent his college on the athletic field, depends primarily upon whether he is seriously in search of an education in coming to college and upon whether he is maintaining in full measure satisfactory performance in his academic work. Like many other college presidents, I have the personal conviction that we can depend upon the good faith of our opponents in deciding the eligibility of their players and I like to think that they can depend in the same way upon us."—President Robert C. Clothier, Rutgers University, 1936. *School and Society*, April 10, 1937, pp. 505, 506.

"In the realm of sports American mass manners leave much to be desired. The behavior of spectators at professional athletic contests is frequently deplorable, but for the most painful exhibitions of bad manners one must turn to intercollegiate football games and the flask-toters and alcoholic partisans who attend them. Yet the blame for lack of sportsmanship cannot be shifted to the intoxicated or ignorant alone. The behavior of alumni and undergraduates at college contests has called forth deserved criticism of our national system of higher education. Obviously universities cannot afford to ignore such criticism or to fail to take steps to correct the conditions which lie behind it.

"Believing that the time had come to call attention to a situation all too general throughout the nation, the University Council on Athletics distributed with the football tickets last fall the following statement over my signature:

" 'Indulgence in alcoholic beverages at football games has assumed proportions which seriously menace the future of the sport as an intercollegiate activity. On behalf of the friendly rivals of the day who strive to maintain high standards of sportsmanship on the field, and in the interest of the vast majority of spectators to whom such drinking is an offense, Princeton University requests that all persons refrain from the use of alcoholic liquors while attending athletic contests under its auspices.'

"The request met with virtually unanimous approval and attracted public attention far beyond my expectations, justifying the opinion that the root difficulty was thoughtless custom which had developed in recent years, and which was generally recognized as not peculiar to Princeton. So generously was my request received and so sympathetic was the response as evidenced by the conduct at subsequent games that I felt constrained to issue at the end of the season the following statement of thanks through the pages of the *Alumni Weekly:*

" 'The sympathetic and responsive reception accorded Princeton's request that all persons refrain from the use of alcoholic liquors while attending football games under its auspices was gratifying to those responsible for the administration of the University and to all who have the best interests of the game at heart.

" 'The general atmosphere in which our football games were played this year harmonized with the fine sportsmanship exhibited on the field. May I, through the columns of the *Weekly*, convey most sincere thanks to the alumni for their loyal cooperation in this delicate and difficult matter? May I also express to our visitors and to the supporters of opposing teams the University's gratitude for their understanding of the spirit and purpose of the request and for their generous response to it?

" 'I should be less than human if I did not add to this official expression of thanks a word of personal appreciation to the alumni and friends for the evidence which they have conveyed to me of a determination that the ideals of the sport must be maintained.' "—President H. W. Dodds, Princeton University, 1937. "Report of the President" for 1936-37, *The Official Register of Princeton University*, October, 1937, pp. 26-28.

"Athletic problems, chiefly football, often hamper a president's success. Knox's record-breaking string of football defeats certainly did not help Britt with his alumni; at Iowa Jessup found that the university's expulsion from the 'Big Ten' reflected on him throughout the State; at Centre the alumni and community insistence on a nationally successful team contributed to the resignations of Ganfield and Turck; Lewis (Lafayette) has lost much alumni support by his demand for a 'clean-up' of football; Clothier (Rutgers) is bothered by a 'big-time' athletic tradition in a small-sized university; Ward (Western Maryland) was a leader among the more religiously inclined colleges of the country, although his football team achieved success which made his colleagues suspicious of the methods used to attract and hold players; Wilkins (Oberlin) having tried with little success to change the athletic standards of the Ohio colleges, is now encouraging the organization of an informal national group of institutions 'like-minded athletically'; the chief criticism of Graham (North Carolina) throughout the State is based on his valiant but probably unsuccessful effort to eliminate subsidies to football players in the Southern Conference. The presidents of women's colleges—and Reed with no intercollegiate sports—may congratulate themselves that they are spared!

"King at Amherst has used athletics skillfully to revive undergraduate morale and alumni support. Amherst's athletic record was low when Pease resigned; some alumni felt that the undergraduates had become blasé, content with defeats. King, who boasts he has never played any outdoor game except croquet, became an ardent fan, following the team to all its games, backing the new coach wholeheartedly, pleased when boys with athletic promise were admitted. Victories followed; the campus became more athletic-minded than any other similar New England college; gifts for a new athletic plant costing three quarters of a million were soon secured. Jordan, the coach, became Athletic Director; his name is prominent in the catalogue list of administrative officers. Few, in building the new Duke, saw to it that a stadium became one of the most striking parts of the new campus and that the football team became nationally known and successful. Tucker's wise use of athletics did much to nationalize Dartmouth."—"Prexy," by a college president, 1938. An anonymous article in *Harper's Monthly Magazine*, January, 1938, p. 196.

"My concern is over impressions repeatedly implanted in the public mind regarding the sincerity and motives of the colleges in their administration of athletics, particularly football; by the careless or deliberate bandying of sweeping generalities in public writings and speeches; the blanketing of all institutions under broad indictments of particular abuses; the use of slogans and catch phrases with vivid implications which cannot fail to make a deep impression on the public mind, and which are used without qualifications. Examples of these generalities can be found in almost any national magazine in the fall of the year. Here are a few picked at random from the current crop:—

"(1) 'The "A. A." is the Athletic Association in each college to which the institution turns over football, basketball, baseball, etc., much as the proprietor of a carnival turns over the "hit the nigger in the head" privilege to an individual concessionaire.'

"Thus does the public get its impression of the principle of institutional control in operation.

"(2) 'Every little while the Carnegie Foundation throws a fit about all this, *but nobody does anything about it, and nobody will.*'

"(3) 'There is not a college in the United States, excepting Johns Hopkins and one or two others, that does not subsidize athletes.'

"(4) 'The athletic situation is a mess. Conferences are printing one rule, but actually obeying another.'

"While examples of any of the abuses referred to may undoubtedly be found, such statements, I submit, would not stand up against a presentation of the facts, in a substantial majority of institutions at least; but the dismaying fact is that they get over to the public and at one stroke obliterate or obscure from the public perception the constructive progress that has been made through years of earnest endeavor by associations such as are meeting here today, and by many institutions and conferences."—Professor W. B. Owens, Leland Stanford Junior University, 1938. President's Address, *Proceedings of the National Collegiate Athletic Association, 1938*, pp. 70, 71.

"Indeed intercollegiate football, as it is conducted today before crowds running as high as 102,000 people who pay in as much as $300,000 at a single game, is big business. Its management is in the hands of men of proved executive ability, some of whom have served with great industrial enterprises.

"Almost every sizable college in the country has a director or graduate manager of athletics. It is his job to provide and direct athletic activities for the entire undergraduate body, to engage coaches, to arrange games and to let contracts for the buildings and improvement of the stadium and other sports properties.

"The chief concern of this executive is to run football at a handsome profit, for it is the revenues accruing from football that support the whole athletic structure in the majority of colleges. He hires the best coach available at the price he can offer. He purchases the latest equipment as recommended by the coach—jerseys, pants, head guards, shoulder harness, hip pads, knee braces, shoes, mud cleats, tackling dummies, pushing machines and scrimmage machines.

"He engages a team physician and a trainer to supervise the conditioning and health of the players. He makes the arrangements for the training camp and for hotel and Pullman accommodations when the team travels. He contracts for games that draw the crowd. He sells radio rights for broadcasting the home games and he sells his team to the public through his director of sports publicity."—Allison Danzig, 1938. *The New York Times Magazine*, October 2, 1938.

Finance

"I have already remarked that probably somewhat more than a million and a half of dollars have been invested in New England for the support and maintenance of collegiate education . . . probably twelve hundred thousand dollars of this sum has been expended upon bricks and mortar. If this is a necessary expense, no reasonable objection to it can be made, but, if otherwise, it is a most unfortunate misapplication of property. That it is not necessary, is I think evident from the fact that by far the greater number of institutions of learning throughout the world do without it. . . . Suppose . . . that the funds thus expended had been appropriated to the partial (and I would have it no more than partial) endowment of professorships, to the purchase of libraries and instruments of philosophical investigation and illustration. . . . I think that every one must be convinced that our Colleges and Universities would have attained to a rank very different from that which they now hold. . . . It would not be difficult to show among us Colleges which have expended a hundred thousand dollars in buildings, and yet are almost entirely destitute of even the rudiments of a library or philosophical apparatus. . . . As it is, we have in this country scarcely anything that can be called a library. The means do not exist among us for writing a book, which in Europe would be called learned, on almost any subject whatever. I cannot but believe that our destitution in this respect is to be ascribed in a great degree to this part of our Collegiate system. . . ."—President Francis Wayland, Brown University, 1842. *Thoughts on the Present Collegiate System in the United States* (Boston: Gould, Kendall and Lincoln, 1842), pp. 127, 128.

"A college is like a lighthouse. If the light at the top is dim it is good for nothing. So the value of a college depends on its teaching and formative power, and these will depend more on right methods of instruction, including the arrangement of studies, and on having the right men, than on anything money can buy. Money *can* buy teaching power, which many, with knowledge enough, have not, but common sense, and weight of character, and the power of inspiration and unselfish devotion to the highest interest of the young men, these money cannot buy."—President Mark Hopkins, Williams College, *ca.* 1872. Quoted in J. H. Denison, *Mark Hopkins* (New York: Charles Scribner's Sons, 1935), p. 227. One of the ablest and most successful of the "old time" college presidents, Mark Hopkins is probably best known for his emphasis upon the development of the individual student.

"Not a few of our theorizers contend that the ideal American university can only be realized by *the aid and direction of the State.* They look to the few State universities which have maintained a respectable existence amid the wrecks of so many—preëminent among which is the University of Michigan—as the germs of the Universities which alone promise to be permanent and great, and as the yet unchartered and unendowed University of the Nation, as the protector and nurse of them all, contending that in the future development and perfection of our educational system no other can survive in the struggle for existence. Their reasons are the following: As society advances, the State will more and more liberally provide for the education of all its citizens. As the lower schools improve, so must the higher. . . . It will follow, . . . that the universities of the State will surpass in resources and appliances every institution of an individual or corporate character. . . .

"Against these arguments it is enough to reply that experience has proved that it is difficult, if not impracticable, to preserve a State university from interference by popular and political critics and leaders . . . the Regents of a State university can never be wholly removed from public and private demands and remonstrances on the part of men who have the ear of the people for the hour. Places will be sought for by unworthy aspirants and their friends; the teachings of the university will be called in question on every point where they bear upon current questions of science, or religion, or finance, or health, or education. Whatever theory of culture the university may adopt will now and then be assailed by an organization of honest or dishonest demagogues, either educational or political."—President Noah Porter, Yale College, 1878. *The American College and the American Public* (New Edition. New York : Charles Scribner's Sons, 1878), pp. 388, 389, 390.

"Aversion to taxation has been the greatest obstacle to the schools in the Southern States. Taxes are simply money paid for civilized government. The savage alone is exempt from taxation."—President Charles D. McIver, Normal and Industrial Institute (later Women's College of the University of North Carolina), *ca.* 1890. Quoted in Charles W. Dabney, *Universal Education in the South* (Chapel Hill: The University of North Carolina Press, 1936), I, 204.

"The Ideal College will not be hampered by lack of means with which to do its work. The more clearly its high mission and destiny are recognized, the more generous will be the streams of consecrated wealth which will flow into its treasuries. Men will rejoice to know that there is a way to transmute gold and silver into spiritual and intellectual force, and will be glad through permanent endowments to perpetuate their own influence into unborn centuries. . . ."—President C. E. Taylor, Wake Forest College, 1895. Baccalaureate Address, "The Ideal Christian College," *The Wake Forest Student*, March, 1916.

"The president and trustees as they now exist have their chief justification in financial conditions. We know that the lack of money is the root of all evil. Our private educational corporations, dependent on the generosity of millionaires, are in a remarkable and almost anomalous position. Yet it is evident that this unique phase of development has not only kept the university in advance of popular appreciation, but has also tended to maintain the stability of society. At a time when large fortunes and monopolistic corporations are needed for the material development of the country, the generous gifts of a few men of great wealth have done much to allay popular clamor."—

J. McKeen Cattell, Columbia University, 1902. "Concerning the American University," Phi Beta Kappa Address at the Johns Hopkins University, May 2, 1902, *Popular Science Monthly*, June, 1902, pp. 180-181.

"So much has been said, and so often said, in previous reports concerning the need of new endowment, that there is little use in repeating those statements here. It is desirable, however, that once more the fact be placed on record that the endowment of Columbia University is too small, by several millions of dollars, to enable it to meet its educational obligations, to say nothing of extending those obligations in ways and by methods that are commendable and desirable."—President Nicholas Murray Butler, Columbia University, 1907. *Report for 1906-07*, p. 9.

"These problems and these needs [increases in salaries and new buildings] are the stuff of which a university's life and a university's business are made up. If the University was truly described in 1902 as a giant in bonds, then in 1916 it is a whole company of giants bound hand and foot by financial impotence. This is the situation with which the Trustees are day by day confronted, and it will remain to confront them, in one form or another, until the time when their capital funds are increased by about $30,000,000.

"The simple fact is that Columbia University is under-capitalized. If it is possible for a great industrial enterprise to procure all the capital it needs when the return is but 20, or 10, or even 5 per cent, why should a university be held back from accomplishment, through lack of sufficient capital, when the returns are everlasting and are to be measured in terms of human life, human satisfaction, and human achievements?"—President Nicholas Murray Butler, Columbia University, 1916. *Report for 1915-16*, p. 9.

"May I presume to suggest the lesson to be drawn from the fact that it now costs the taxpayers of the state two dollars for the care of the unfortunates in state penitentiary and state asylum as compared to one dollar for the education of the students in the university colleges and schools.

"It may not be expected that the people of Montana will contribute more freely than they now do merely upon the argument of presumed or intangible benefits. One of my principal aims will be to keep the state as fully informed as I am able concerning the tangible results of the educational and scientific work undertaken within the university. It may not be possible for us to do all that you tell us to do. We shall, however, try to tell you all that we do. For my part, I am satisfied to trust the cause of the proper support of the work of the university to the court of public opinion that has had a fair chance to be informed of the facts in the case."—Chancellor E. C. Elliott, The University of Montana, 1916. *School and Society*, June, 1916.

"We will strive to use economically, effectively and gratefully all the material resources which the state has given to us. It is true that the enrollment in the institution and the demands made upon it by the state have already run far beyond its resources, but this is an incident of growth and although inconvenient for the time being has no power of permanent injury. We have absolute confidence that when the state realizes our faithfulness in the few things that we have, it will gladly increase its appropriations and support."—President E. O. Sisson, The University of Montana, 1917. *School and Society*, November 17, 1917.

"The amount which the Government will receive in revenue from these provisions [of the War Revenue Act, taxing inheritances and bequests], if they are kept upon the statute book, will be very small in comparison with the grave damage thereby inflicted upon the educational, philanthropic, and religious institutions of the country. It would be indeed disastrous if the many and far-reaching changes that are to accompany the war and the new forms of taxation which the war will compel, took such a form as to imperil the effectiveness and even the existence of the great philanthropic and educational institutions of the country."—President Nicholas Murray Butler, Columbia University, 1917. *Report for 1916-17*, p. 9.

"It goes without saying that unless the State supports the University that it must close its doors, for our endowment, like that of most Land Grant colleges and state universities, is very small. I am thoroughly convinced that the time has come when a careful survey of the aims and purposes of this institution should be made by some agency. This survey should include an investigation of the higher educational needs of the State, together with the way that the four colleges in the State are meeting the demands. A careful study of this kind will be infinitely better than the way we have been drifting with the tide from year to year, and will give data which may be used to predict future demands. At the same time an honest study should be made to determine how much the State of Maine can afford to spend for higher education. I am sure no one, and least of all, the Trustees of the University, desires to see the State go beyond its financial resources, to support any State institution, but it should be remembered that there is no greater asset of the State than the boys and girls of Maine, and they should be given the opportunity of the privileges of higher education in so far as it is within our power as citizens of the State to provide it."—President H. S. Boardman, The University of Maine, 1926. *Inaugural Address by Harold Sherburne Boardman, President University of Maine, June 12, 1926* (Pamphlet), p. 7.

"Frankly I have a good deal of sympathy for a big corporation whose income has been cut and cut until its very life is at stake and I can understand why they want to reduce taxes. I think that in many cases the men who are in charge of the operations are very sympathetic with schools and higher education, but they are compelled by the necessity of the case to conserve their funds. I do not agree with them in what they are doing, but I can sympathize with them, and I can sympathize very sincerely with the church schools. They are fine, sincere people and they too need money. Their income has been cut badly and some of them are just about on the brink. Some have already gone over."—President R. A. Pearson, The University of Maryland, 1934. *Transactions and Proceedings of the National Association of State Universities, 1934.*

"The American college is not a monument; it is a living institution; born of great labor and nurtured through sacrifice. Its continued growth depends now, as always, upon large gifts from a few, small gifts from many, and faith and hard work on the part of all believers in education."—President C. W. Chamberlain, Denison University, 1934. *Bulletin of The Association of American Colleges*, December, 1934, p. 467.

"One of the things which strikes me about this whole question of revenue, as we have learned particularly in our own state recently, is that educators are constantly asking for money, particularly in the school districts."—President F. L. McVey, The University of Kentucky, 1934. *Transactions and Proceedings of the National Association of State Universities, 1934.*

"I have had a good many years' experience in attempting to encourage the state to do as well as it could in connection with the maintenance of public education. I am very much convinced that it is a much easier road for all persons concerned if there is full coöperation and recognition of the fact that all persons engaged in education of any kind whatsoever have a stake in this problem."—President Walter A. Jessup, Carnegie Foundation for the Advancement of Teaching (President of the State University of Iowa, 1916-1934), 1934. *Transactions and Proceedings of the National Association of State Universities, 1934.*

"Something more than a log with a Mark Hopkins on one end and a youth on the other, is needed to make a modern university. 'Brick and mortar do not make a university,' the unsympathetic critic declares, but every college faculty knows that no university has ever been adequately equipped without brick and mortar. The picture of university teachers pursuing learning without books, searching for new truth without scientific equipment, dwelling congenially in the open air under the shade of some friendly tree while the learners sit nearby gathering in the pearls of intellectual wisdom that drop from the dialectical discourses of the staff, is too romantic to be true.

"Now and then you hear someone talk about universities as if the only things they needed were piety, hope, and charity. You will, I am sure, not misunderstand me, when I say that some of them lived too long on piety, dwelt too exclusively in the realm of hope, and appeared too frequently as seekers of alms. A university whose moral and religious conceptions are high, may be intellectually stagnant and reactionary; a university that feeds on hope without having the necessary equipment for the advancement of human learning, may deceive its student for the time being, but in later life they learn that they were gold-bricked by clever salesmen; a university that depends on charity from day to day, with no clear margin of resources to venture into untouched realms of inquiry, may exist, but it cannot grow."—President Lotus D. Coffman, The University of Minnesota, 1935. "Building a University," *Higher Education and Society* (Norman: University of Oklahoma Press, 1936), p. 309.

"If the effect of high taxes is gradually to confiscate wealth, privately supported colleges and universities must acquire their endowments before such destruction takes place. Those who do not get adequate endowments within the next twenty years may never get them."—President William P. Tolley, Allegheny College, 1936. *Second Annual Conference of Trustees of Colleges and Universities*. Lafayette College, 1936.

"Now, I haven't the slightest doubt that as far as bricks and mortar are concerned all the colleges and universities, private and public, are going to survive for many, many years. But I am sure you will agree that bricks and mortar do not make universities and that they might survive in that form and still die."—President James B. Conant, Harvard University, 1936. Address at the Harvard Club in New York June 9, 1936, *The Mission of the Endowed Universities*. (Pamphlet.)

"If the advanced work in a university is to be made available on a broader scale than hitherto, a great extension of financial assistance will be necessary. If the selection of the group to receive this aid is made on graduation from high school, the junior college can then be left to perform its special task. Each locality will decide what type of education it wishes to provide at public expense. In making this decision the relatively few university students can be disregarded, for under the plan I am suggesting they will have left the local community at the end of the high-school course and have proceeded to a liberal arts college *en route* to advanced work."—President James B. Conant, Harvard University, 1938. "The Future of Our Higher Education," *Harper's Monthly Magazine*, May, 1938.

"Colleges need all the money they can get. This is true of all institutions of higher education, but especially true of those that provide graduate and professional instruction. The spokesmen for all these institutions, publicly and privately supported, are doing, and should do, what they can to get each for his own institution the funds that he thinks are necessary to carry it forward with the causes it is set to serve. But there is only so much money to be had either by taxes or direct gifts. Extravagant expenditure of money at Washington in recent years and the excessive taxes that have been laid make it difficult for the several states to get the funds they need for all their operating purposes including education, and even more difficult for privately supported institutions to secure gifts from tax-burdened supporters and friends. It becomes an acute problem, and it is now an acute problem here in North Carolina, to adjust all our institutions of higher education to their appropriate tasks so that they may have resources with which to do their work."—President William P. Few, Duke University, 1939. Address before The North Carolina Education Association, Raleigh,

March 17, 1939. Typescript copy published in part in the Raleigh *News and Observer*, March 18, 1939.

Changes in Two Decades

"There was a great interest in Latin and some in Greek, and the courses in the colleges were rationally articulated to actual work done in the high school [in 1914]. . . .

"In matters of religion the colleges today have evidenced a very fine social spirit in defining religion in terms of human relations, but in matters of doctrine, modern colleges are quite uncertain."—President Irving Maurer, Beloit College, 1934. *Bulletin of the Association of American Colleges*, December, 1934, pp. 475, 476, 477.

"In comparison with the undergraduate of 1934, the undergraduate of 1914 was a conservative. Radical sentiment is much stronger in our colleges today—encouraged not seldom by professors of sociology and economics. Many students are wondering what kind of a social order this is that encourages education but offers no employment to the man it has educated. . . . The intellectual life of the campus is more vigorous than in 1914. Standards are higher. Wider opportunities are offered to the gifted students. The bone-head and the idler no longer sets the pace for the class. The time may come when he is eliminated altogether."—President Emeritus C. A. Richmond, Union College, 1934. *Bulletin of The Association of American Colleges*, December, 1934, p. 478.

"College, to me, has come to be the scene of normal, numerous and mutually enlightening encounters between the old and the young by which we have been able to move forward, feet upon the earth and heads in the clouds. Two conclusions seem evident to me. Church constituencies are more and more inclined to endow their colleges with independence as well-reared children are so endowed. Colleges today are more free to perform the true functions of liberal arts institutions, the functions of 'fact finding, fact recording and fact facing.' Censorship of education and the use of education to preserve the *status quo* have more and more come to be considered improper. The college, of course, will continue to feel the impact of contending forces. In the past evolutionists and anti-evolutionists have gone to battle on the campus. More recently, fundamentalists and modernists have been in controversy. Quite certainly the next few years will prove economics to be the sensitive point. Liberals and conservatives will view the college with alarm. But the college, secure in the independence of its position, will go about its business of giving exact information on social and economic questions. Because that position is secure, 'government of the people, by the people, and for the people shall not perish from the earth'."—President H. M. Gage, Coe College, 1934. *Bulletin of The Association of American Colleges*, December, 1934, p. 469.

"We in this country are in the midst of the greatest experiment in higher education ever attempted at any time or anywhere. Can higher education really be democratized? I am not sure. We have not gone far enough to know what results will be forthcoming. At any rate, an education in some kind of college is looked upon by almost everyone in America as the door of opportunity and as the gateway to success. . . .

"I find that today there is far more participation on the part of students in the affairs of the institution. This is true not only in extra-curricular activities but in more important matters such as that of the curriculum. The advice and counsel of students is being sought and acted upon as was never true in the past."—President E. D. Soper, Ohio Wesleyan University, 1934. *Bulletin of The Association of American Colleges*, December, 1934, p. 478.

"The four year college of liberal arts is more firmly rooted in the soil of American life than it was twenty years ago. The blasts of criticism it has endured have deepened its roots, with the promise of better and more distinctive fruit in the years ahead."—President D. J. Cowling, Carleton College, 1934.

Bulletin of The Association of American Colleges, December, 1934, p. 465.

"The American college, during the past two decades, has experienced a great expansion in curricular offerings and a much greater proportionate increase in enrollment. Aside from the increase of courses in the social studies there has been an enrichment in many colleges by the addition of courses in the history and appreciation of the fine arts and music.

"Many colleges through separation into upper and lower divisions, or otherwise, have permitted an elasticity in curricular requirements in the last two years of college, while maintaining a fairly rigid requirement of the completion of subjects of a tool nature in the first two years. Comprehensive examinations and honors courses, and similar devices, have put more and more the responsibility of learning on the student himself. The accumulation of grades, units, and courses as the chief aim of the student is becoming quite taboo."—President G. E. Snavely, Birmingham Southern College, 1934. *Bulletin of The Association of American Colleges*, December, 1934, pp. 473, 474.

"In comparing the conditions in American colleges in 1934 with those which prevailed in 1914, several points of difference are found. . . . The first is the progress which has been made in placing greater responsibility upon the student for securing the education which is suited to his abilities and purposes in life, and in developing his own initiative and methods of study; in teaching him that the acquisition of facts is not sufficient, but that with it must go the power to use the facts to arrive at logical conclusions. This change of emphasis from a cut and dried curriculum to an elastic one has brought with it changes in admission requirements, in college credits, and in methods of measuring intellectual growth. Greater freedom is now given to the student to select the method of study which will best enable him to reach his objective. These changes are by no means yet complete. The second point is the improvement which has taken place in college financial and business administration.

In the period prior to 1914 it was not at all unusual to find responsibility for accounting and business operation lodged in the hands of persons not experienced in such matters. The results were as might have been expected. In many instances adequate records of trust funds were not made, endowment funds and current funds were not kept separate, and clear and explicit financial reports were the exception. During the past twenty years successful efforts have been made to place college accounting and business procedure on a sound basis. The importance of having competent and experienced business officers is recognized, and today the financial affairs of the colleges, with few exceptions, are managed efficiently and intelligently. These improvements are of special importance now that colleges are finding it necessary to examine their expenditures carefully in order to maintain balanced budgets. They have also strengthened the confidence of donors regarding the use of their gifts."—Vice President Trevor Arnett (1924-26), The University of Chicago, 1934. *Bulletin of the Association of American Colleges*, December, 1934, pp. 472, 473.

"Most important advance in American higher education during the last twenty years seems to me to be the progress which has been made in providing better training for our best students. The regimentation which has for a generation been the greatest drawback to the attainment of excellence in college and university work in this country is gradually being abandoned. Faculties are realizing more and more everywhere that the ablest and most ambitious of our undergraduates need to be held up to more severe standards and to be given more freedom in their work than would be possible or desirable for the average.

"The checks and the prodding, the daily problems and exercises, the whole machinery of secondary school methods so widely applied in college teaching in order to make sure that the lazy and indifferent attain at least to a mediocre standard in their academic work—all this elaborate academic routine developed by our professors and deans is not merely superfluous in the case of the best students but is a positive hindrance to them in their work. . . .

"In the wide-spread experimentation to which this movement has given rise, doubtless many false starts have been made, many different schemes have been tried, some of which will inevitably fail, but even the failures will not represent a total loss. They testify also to the change which is taking place in American higher education, the search for quality rather than for numbers, the substitution of real for fictitious values."—President Frank Aydelotte, Swarthmore College, 1934. *Bulletin of The Association of American Colleges*, December, 1934, pp. 471, 472.

"The last twenty years have seen in most of the colleges and universities of this country great increases in endowment, in income, in material equipment, in the size of their faculties and their scale of faculty salaries, in undergraduate registration, in the number of books in their libraries and the use made of them, and in educational experiments of all sorts.

"The faculties include higher percentages of well-trained men, but the percentages of great teachers and of productive scholars are probably no larger now than then. Great figures in the college world are rare today.

"The cultural ideals still live in many old-fashioned colleges, but the teaching of the affairs of the bank, the factory, and the market has come to fill a large place in many a 'modern' curriculum. Here and there 'how to earn a living' seems more important than 'how to live.'

"While the multitude of poorly prepared youths admitted to college contains an increasing number who are moved chiefly by social aims and prove unfitted for any intellectual task; yet the code of undergraduate honor has greatly improved, college morale has become definitely better, respect for scholarship and desire for membership in Phi Beta Kappa have grown markedly, the winning of intercollegiate games has lost much of its unwarranted glory on the campus, and the benefits of athletics are no longer limited to the overtrained few but are shared by nearly all."—President F. C. Ferry, Hamilton College, 1934. *Bulletin of The Association of American Colleges,* December, 1934, pp. 466, 467.

"During the past twenty-one years a major shift has occured in the center of gravity of many American colleges in so far as their educational program is concerned. It is one of two such major shifts since Harvard was established in 1636. This shift has been made in response to the pressure of two theories of education which, operating together, have tended toward a synthesis. The movement away from primary interest in subject matter toward primary interest in the education of the student had already made some progress. This movement, accentuated in an increasing number of institutions, is tempered by the conviction that the freedom of the student after all is best attained as he becomes a Social Person.

"To this end colleges have revivified numerous educational implements long in use—the libraries, the laboratories, the museums, honor systems, seminars—and they have brought into existence numerous other implements characteristic of current practice—free reading periods, independent or self-directive study, tutorial and personnel guidance, achievement tests and other measures of individual advancement, the divisional organization of the educational program into upper and lower divisions and also into a relatively few subject groups, more effective types of final examinations."—Executive Secretary Robert L. Kelly (formerly, President of Earlham College), The Association of American Colleges, 1934. *Bulletin of the Association of American Colleges,* December, 1934, pp. 463, 464.

"The Association of American Colleges has come of age! For twenty-one years it has rendered increasingly effective service to the cause of higher education. What about the progress, during the same period, of the colleges it represents. They too have matured. The infantile undergraduate pranks of an earlier period have well nigh disappeared. The students in great numbers have put away childish things, and have begun to realize their opportunities; thus honors courses, reading periods, and various other plans for creative and independent work have developed during the past twenty years. Thus the give and take of the class room has become more vigorous and stimulating than ever before. Thus students individually and through their college publications have shown a mental curiosity and courage quite unknown in days gone by. This maturing process has been particularly rapid since the fall of 1929.

"Colleges and students facing financial problems have assumed a serious attitude toward things of the mind and spirit. Because of this change in attitude, we may look forward to the next twenty years in college development with confidence and high hope."—President William Mather Lewis, Lafayette College, 1934. *Bulletin of the Association of American Colleges*, December, 1934, p. 463.

"Salaries were not what they should have been even for those days [1914] but the faculties in those times had a fine faith in the supremacy of the spiritual over physical facts, and the inadequate physical housing of colleges was made up for by faith in the value of the mind and heart and faith in good teaching.

"In 1934-35 the colleges find themselves much more efficiently managed from the financial point of view, having developed a high morale in the matter of student loans and the payment of student bills; in financial management of college affairs; having much clearer ideas as to what makes a college library valuable; having great improvement in the buildings, laboratory equipment, health, social life, and recreation generally. In 1934-35 the colleges are not quite so sure that what they have to give is what the people want. The curriculum is still expanding and there is little articulation between the work in high school and that of college, the modern college being interested primarily in evidence on the student's part of intellectual proficiency. The interest has turned from the classics and fundamental sciences to social sciences. . . .

"The colleges of 1934-35, in spite of the depression, have shown a financial stability which would have done credit to many of our commercial concerns, and are fully alive to the importance of the contribution which they have to offer to the American people."—President Irving Maurer, Beloit College, 1934. *Bulletin of The Association of American Colleges*, December, 1934, pp. 476, 477.

"Taking Grinnell College as a typical example of a Mid-Western college, the changes of the past twenty years have been briefly as follows: A notable increase and improvement in physical plant and endowment; a recession in the classics (which I regret); a continuation of the trend toward the laboratory sciences; a phenomenal development in courses leading to a business career; most recently an encouraging interest in the new departments of Art and Drama. New major departments set up during the period: Art, Business Administration, Drama, Education, Physical Education, Psychology, and Speech. So far as the student body is concerned there has been a great growth of interest in public affairs, especially in international relations, and a promising development of student self-government. The attitude of the faculty is less dogmatic and more experimental with reference to problems of education, while the devotion to the ideals of liberal culture remains as strong as ever."—President John S. Nollen, Grinnell College, 1934. *Bulletin of The Association of American Colleges*, December, 1934, pp. 464, 465.

5

FACULTY RELATIONS

The subject of academic freedom does not down. For many years the alarums have been fairly constant. There was little question of academic freedom in this country so long as the higher educational institutions were spending most of their energies upon the classics and mathematics. Few people showed concern about what was taught on these subjects. "No one cared to interfere with the liberty of a professor to translate a passage of Virgil, to solve an equation or to demonstrate a proposition in any way he might please," as President William D. Hyde, of Bowdoin College, said in 1906. He pointed out that interference with academic liberty "comes only when the subjects taught are those for which the people care." He noted that academic freedom was involved in theological questions and then in political opinions and that more recently economic and social questions had come to the front. President Nicholas Murray Butler, in an address at New York University in November, 1932, pointed out that there had been "4 or 5 different centers of gravity about which the problem of university freedom, and therefore of university service, have revolved since universities began": theological and philosophical controversies, and scientific, economic, social, and political questions.

Statements by higher educational leaders concerning academic freedom have been very numerous. But presidents of state universities and of the larger endowed institutions have discussed the subject far more fully than it has been discussed by the presidents of small denominational and privately endowed colleges.

Similarly, and perhaps naturally, the subject of research is not widely discussed by the presidents of the smaller institutions. These tend to emphasize teaching rather than research. "After all, the primary concern of a college is to produce not learned books but able men." This statement by President Dixon Ryan Fox, of Union College, in his inaugural address in 1934, seems to represent the views of the presidents of many of the smaller institutions. Presidents of the larger institutions generally applaud research, although not everybody seems to be agreed on what constitutes research. The dean of a graduate school was heard to say that there was not even complete agreement on the proper pronunciation of the word. President Nicholas Murray Butler, of Columbia University, in his report for 1924-25, said that "between 75 and 90 per cent of what is called research . . . is not properly research at all, . . ." President Daniel C. Gilman, of the Johns Hopkins University, had said in 1903 that "counting the threads of a carpet and the grains in a bushel of sand, may add iotas to knowledge, but it will be to the domain of useless knowledge." Chancellor H. W. Chase, of New York University, said in 1938 that "In too many instances research has been research in name only . . . all departments have sinned. . . ."

On the subject of the importance of teaching, college presidents seem to be in closer agreement. There appears to be a division of opinion, however, concerning methods of teaching. President David Starr Jordan, of Leland Stanford Junior University, in 1902 said that the log in Garfield's conception of a college was not even essential. "The earnest teacher is all in all." President R. E. Blackwell, of Randolph-Macon College, was quoted in 1938 as having said that at his institution "we teach as thoroughly as the athletic rules will allow."

Academic Freedom

"The duty of considering science and learning as an independent interest of the community, begins to be very generally felt and acknowledged. Both in Europe and in America attempts are making to rescue the general mind from the vassalage in which it has been held by sects in the church, and by parties in the state; giving to that interest, as far as possible, a vitality of its own, having no precarious dependence for existence on subserviency to particular views in politics or religion; and, for this purpose, to place it like a fountain opened in regions far above those in which the passions of the day struggle for ascendency,—to which all may come to gain strength and be refreshed, but whose waters none shall be permitted to disturb by their disputes, or exclusively to preoccupy for purposes of ambition."—President Josiah Quincy, Harvard College, 1840. Quoted in S. E. Morison, *Three Centuries of Harvard* (Cambridge: Harvard University Press, 1936), p. 256.

"A university must be indigenous; it must be rich; but, above all, it must be free. The winnowing breeze of freedom must blow through all its chambers. It takes a hurricane to blow wheat away. An atmosphere of intellectual freedom is the native air of literature and science. This University aspires to serve the nation by training men to intellectual honesty and independence of mind. The Corporation demands of all its teachers that they be grave, reverent, and high-minded; but it leaves them, like their pupils, free."—President Charles W. Eliot, Harvard University, 1869. Inaugural Address, in S. E. Morison, *The Development of Harvard University* (Cambridge: Harvard University Press, 1930), p. lxxiv.

"This is an age in which scientific atheism, having divested itself of the habiliments that most adorn and dignify humanity, walks abroad in shameless denudation. The arrogant and impertinent claims of this 'science, falsely so-called,' have been so boisterous and persistent, that the unthinking mass have been sadly deluded; but our university [Vanderbilt] alone has had the courage to lay its young but vigorous hand upon the mane of untamed Speculation and say: 'We will have no more of this'."—Statement of The Tennessee Conference of the Southern Methodist Church (under which Vanderbilt University was in part directed), concerning the case of Professor Winchell of Vanderbilt University, about 1878. Quoted in Virginius Dabney, *Liberalism in the South* (Chapel Hill: University of North Carolina Press, 1932), p. 193.

"I am moved to make a statement of fact and opinion concerning two related subjects which quite recently have attracted some attention in the public mind. The first of these is the freedom of opinion enjoyed in these days by members of the University. The second is the use and abuse of this right by professors of the University Faculty. Concerning the first, I may be permitted to present a statement adopted unanimously by the members of the Congregation of the University on June 30, 1887:

" 'Resolved, 1. That the principle of complete freedom of speech on all subjects has from the beginning been regarded as fundamental in the University of Chicago, as has been shown both by the attitude of the President and the Board of Trustees and by the actual practice of the President and the professors.

" '2. That this principle can neither now nor at any future time be called in question.

" '3. That it is desirable to have it clearly understood that the University, as such, does not appear as a disputant on either side upon any public question; and that the utterances which any professor may make in public are to be regarded as representing his opinions only.'

"To this statement of the Congregation I wish to add, first, that whatever may or may not have happened in other universities, in the University of Chicago neither the Trustees, nor the President, nor anyone in official position has at any time called an instructor to account for any public utterances which he may have made. Still further, in no single case has a donor to the University called the attention of the Trustees to the teaching of any officer of the University as being distasteful or objectionable. Still further, it is my opinion that no donor of money to a university, whether that donor be an individual or the state, has any right, before God or man, to interfere with the teaching of officers appointed to give instruction in a university. . . .

"If an officer on permanent appointment abuses his privilege as a professor, the University must suffer and it is proper that it should suffer. This is only the direct and inevitable consequence of the lack of foresight and wisdom involved in the original appointment."—President William Rainey Harper, The University of Chicago, 1902. *The President's Report, July, 1892-July, 1902*, pp. xxi-xxii.

"But gentlemen, if the worst must come to the worst, I have no hesitancy in saying that it were better that Trinity College should work with ten students than it should repudiate and violate every principle of the Christian religion, the high virtues of this commonwealth, and the foundation spirit of this nation. . . . Personally, I should deem it an honor to teach ten men who love truth and believe in tolerance, and I should deem it a shame to teach a thousand men who believed in intolerance and regarded intellectual bondage a commendable virtue. . . .

"I should prefer to see a wild hurricane break out of some awful fastness and sweep from the face of the earth every rock and brick and piece of timber, than to see Trinity College committed to the policies of the inquisition, and the note of liberty forever stricken from her tongue. . . .You cannot hurt this institution more fatally, you cannot deal it a severer blow, you cannot bring upon it more fully the suspicions of just and honorable men than by enthroning coercion and intolerance. Bury liberty here, and with it the college is buried."—President John C. Kilgo, Trinity College (North Carolina), 1903. Address to Board of Trustees of Trinity College in behalf of Professor John Spencer Bassett. Quoted in Paul N. Garber, *John Carlisle Kilgo* (Durham: Duke University Press, 1938), p. 271.

"This question of academic freedom did not arise so long as the colleges were content to teach Latin, Greek, mathematics, and a little science and philosophy, for the simple reason that nobody cared much, one way or the other, what was taught about these things. . . .

"Social and economic questions, however, are destined to divide the public more sharply than ever before. Unless we can come to a clear understanding as to the mutual duties and rights of the several partners in college administration, professorships of economics and sociology will be as perilous positions in a democracy as chairs of politics ever were under an absolute monarchy, or chairs of theology in the palmy days of papal power.

"Who, then, are the partners in college administration? The parties to this partnership are six. First, the founders, donors, and benefactors. Second, the State. Third, the trustees, regents, or overseers. Fourth, professors and instructors. Fifth, the students. Sixth, the constituency of the college, that portion of the public from which money and students come, and to whom the institution must look for interest, guidance, and support. The most important element in this portion of the public, which I have called the constituency of the institution, is the institution's own alumni."—President W. D. Hyde, Bowdoin College, 1906. *The College Man and the College Woman* (Boston : Houghton Mifflin Company, 1906), pp. 275, 277.

"Freedom of the spirit is the essence of a university's life. Whatever else is done or left undone, that freedom must be made secure.

"But freedom imposes responsibility, and there are distinct limitations, which ought to be self-imposed, upon that academic freedom which was won at so great a cost, and which has produced such noble results. These are the limitations imposed by common morality, common sense, common loyalty, and a decent respect for the opinions of mankind. A teacher or investigator who offends against common morality has destroyed his academic usefulness, whatever may be his intellectual attainments. . . .

"It ought not to escape notice, however, that most of the increasingly numerous abuses of academic freedom are due simply to bad manners and to lack of ordinary tact and judgment."—President Nicholas Murray Butler, Columbia University, 1910. *Report for 1909-10*, p. 23.

"The notion which is sedulously cultivated in some quarters that there are powerful interests, financial, economic and social which wish to curb the proper freedom of speech of university professors in America, probably has little or no justification anywhere. So far as Columbia University is concerned it has no justification whatever. That there are large elements in the population which do desire to curb the proper freedom of speech of university professors, is however indisputable. . . . Genuine cases of the invasion of academic freedom are so rare as to be almost nonexistent. It may be doubted whether more than two such cases have occurred in the United States in the past forty years. It is a misnomer to apply the high and splendid term 'Academic freedom' to exhibitions of bad taste and bad manners. . . ."—President Nicholas Murray Butler, Columbia University, 1914. *Report for 1914-15*, p. 21.

"Certain professors have been refused reëlection lately, apparently because they set their students to thinking in ways objectionable to the trustees. It would be well if more teachers were dismissed because they fail to stimulate thinking of any kind. We can afford to forgive a college professor what we regard as the occasional error of his doctrine, especially as we may be wrong, provided he is a contagious center of intellectual enthusiasm. It is better for students to think about heresies than not to think at all; . . . It is a primary duty of a teacher to make a student take an honest account of his stock of ideas, throw out the dead matter, place revised price marks on what is left, and try to fill his empty shelves with new goods."—President William T. Foster, Reed College, 1915. *The Nation*, November 11, 1915.

"Experience has proved, and probably no one would now deny, that knowledge can advance, or at least can advance most rapidly, only by means of an unfettered search for truth on the part of those who devote their lives to seeking it in their respective fields, and by complete freedom in imparting to their pupils the truth that they have found. . . . One must distinguish between the matters that fall within and those that lie outside of the professor's field of study; when there is a difference in the professor's position in his class-room and beyond it. . . .

"The teaching by the professor in his class-room on the subjects within the scope of his chair ought to be absolutely free. He must teach the truth as he has found it and sees it. This is the primary condition of academic freedom, and any violation of it endangers intellectual progress. . . .

"Every professor must, therefore, be wholly unrestrained in publishing the results of his study in the field of his professorship. It is needless to add that for the dignity of his profession, for the maintenance of its privileges, as well as for his own reputation among his fellows, whatever he writes or says on his own subject should be uttered as a scholar, in a scholarly tone and form. This is a matter of decorum, not of discipline; to be remedied by a suggestion, not by a penalty.

"In troublous times much more serious difficulty, and much more confusion of thought, arise from the . . . right of a professor to express his views without restraint on matters lying outside the sphere of his professorship. This is not a question of academic freedom in its true sense, but of the personal liberty of the citizen. . . . The fact that a man fills a chair of astronomy, for example, confers on him no special knowledge of, and no peculiar right to speak upon, the protective tariff. . . .

"The gravest questions, and the strongest feelings, arise from action by a professor beyond his chosen field and outside of his classroom. Here he speaks only as citizen. . . .

"If a university or college censors what its professors may say, if it restrains them from uttering something that it does not approve, it thereby assumes responsibility for that which it permits them to say. . . ."—President A. Lawrence Lowell, Harvard University, 1917. *Report for 1916-17*, pp. 19, 20.

"Without freedom there can be no university. . . . Freedom of the university means the freedom to study not only the biological implications of the physical structure of a fish but also the human implications of the economic structure of society. It means freedom from the prejudices of section, race, or creed; it means a free compassion of her sons for all people in need of justice and brotherhood. . . .

"But this freedom of the university should not be mistaken for approval of those who are merely sophisticated or who superficially exploit the passing currents or great human causes, or who fundamentally debase the deep human passions and poison the springs from which flow the waters of life. Such an abuse of freedom has the scorn of scholars whose intellectual integrity and wholesome life are a source of freedom. . . . No abuse of freedom, however, should cause us to strike down freedom of speech or publication, the fresh resources of a free university, a free religion, and a free state. . . .

"Finally freedom of the university means freedom of the scholar to find and report the truth honestly, without interference by the university, the state, or any interests whatever."—President Frank P. Graham, The University of North Carolina, 1931. *The Alumni Review*, December, 1931.

"Now, there is a subject which I approach with some hesitation because it is a delicate subject. It is one which, in my opinion, depends for its solution upon faculty members themselves, and not upon the public press or the board of trustees. I refer to the important subject of academic freedom.

"Speaking for myself, I have no quarrel with the tenets of academic freedom as laid down by the American Association of University Professors. I have no quarrel with the chairman's statement of the situation. I subscribe to it in every detail. To try to put the university professor in a class by himself as against the other learned professions, or outside of the rights of American citizenship, seems to me stupid and ridiculous. I think the platform of the American Association of University Professors is all right as far as it goes, but I think there is more to be said on the subject, and that the Association should have incorporated in its platform the idea of responsibility to the university, and prevention of misunderstanding by the public, as forcefully as it has proclaimed the rights of free speech.

"There is a difference between liberalism and license. I would not say that there has been an overemphasis on rights, but I would say that there has been an under-emphasis on responsibilities, and the abuses of academic freedom are not guarded as zealously as the rights are upheld.

"We hear a great deal about a professor's right to free utterance, but on the other hand there exists in our universities a slackness, on the part of the faculty people of differing points of view, which allows the radical and the aggressive member of a faculty to shout from the housetops without contrary expression from those who disagree.

"I must maintain that all sides of a question are a part of education but, if a university is a place of free thought and expression, the conservative should be heard as well as the radical, and the public should realize that both points of view exist; otherwise the position of the faculty group is misunderstood and the university is misjudged.

"If it is contended that faculty utterances are not subject to trustee censorship, certainly this duty and the necessity for such explanation should not devolve upon the trustees. For the trustee to articulate a contrary point of view raises questions as to his attitude on the whole subject of academic freedom. Rather the situation seems to me to rest upon the shoulders of individual faculty members and, if they don't do more about it, I think they will be considered as failing in their duty."—Harold W. Swift, President of the Board of Trustees, The University of Chicago, 1932. In *The Obligation of Universities to the Social Order*, ed. H. P. Fairchild (New York: New York University Press, 1933), pp. 77, 78.

"The essence of a university's method is search for truth, and in order that that search may be prosecuted in a changing world the university must be free. It must make itself free, and it must protect itself in its freedom. It must be protected in its freedom, and it must so exercise its freedom as to increase and not diminish its authority. . . .

"The university in the exercise of its Lehrfreiheit, and because of that privilege, owes a high obligation to society. Every system of education and every educational institution, as Aristotle pointed out with that unfailing wisdom of his so long ago, naturally expounds and defends the system of thought and practice in which it exists. We complain of the Russian Communist because he makes his schools teach Communism. We complain of the Italian Fascist because he makes his schools teach Fascism. But what do we do with our schools? Are they not teaching, and properly, as we think, an understanding and appreciation of these fundamental principles of free democratic institutions in which we believe? Why are the Communist and the Fascist wrong, if we are right? No, the question is not as to whether either of them may be wrong in an attitude towards education, but which of the three theories is right; and there is the point of attack for the scholar. There is the point of interpretation for the thinker. There is the avenue of progress opening before the man who knows history, who understands human nature, who can appraise the great successes and the great failures of the past and point to a path of progress which makes use of human experience but does not hide its face to what may be simply because it has not been. . . .

"The university's freedom is its instrument for knowing the changing world, for aiding the changing world, for shaping the changing world; but it must be liberty, true liberty, and that is something which mankind in his history has been teaching us to understand for now two thousand five hundred years."—President Nicholas Murray Butler, Columbia University, 1932. "Academic Freedom in a Changing World." In *The Obligation of Universities to the Social Order* (New York: New York University Press, 1933), pp. 469, 471, 472, 473.

"There is another consequence of the public tendency to confuse college with university that is still more serious. I mean the constant threat to academic freedom. Freedom of inquiry, freedom to choose without let or hindrance the subjects into which one will inquire, freedom to publish the results of inquiry, freedom to teach what one has found out and what any one else has found and proved, freedom of opinion and of utterance—academic freedom in this all-inclusive sense has not yet been surely won by American universities. A few institutions—the number is tragically small—have a nearly perfect record as defenders of this citadel of scholarship. But, in many universities, the scholar whose specialty includes matters that are subjects of public controversy runs the risk of suppression or dismissal. His security lies in what is grossly miscalled discretion. The areas of danger are not the same in all parts of the country and in all types of institutions. Moreover, as time has passed they have in general shifted from theology and philosophy to the natural and then to the social sciences. They shift, but they do not disappear. In this company it is unnecessary to say that, wherever freedom of inquiry and of teaching are circumscribed at all, the university is emasculated."—Chancellor Samuel P. Capen, The University of Buffalo, 1933. In *The Obligation of Universities to the Social Order*, ed. H. P. Fairchild (New York: New York University Press, 1933), pp. 63-64.

"A university, and especially a university supported from public funds, functions best if it remains aloof from the field of immediate political activity. This is true of the individual professor. While the university must function with due regard to the prevailing social philosophy of the day and should train men for leadership, it cannot, without endangering its larger usefulness, assume direct responsibility for social reform and reconstruction. It should not become an instrument of indoctrination and propaganda. It should be permitted to remain dispassionate and detached. It should not be brought too close to the scene of immediate political action. Its great function is that of investigation and research. It is dedicated to the pursuit of truth."—President E. A. Gilmore, The State University of Iowa, 1934. *Transactions and Proceedings of the National Association of State Universities, 1934.*

"There is only one freedom that we have and that is the freedom that we have as citizens guaranteed under our Constitution. There was a time when we needed academic freedom.

Galileo ought to have had it. In the early days of Harvard they needed it because professors didn't have the right to say what they found or to publish what they found in their own fields. I think that the original need for academic freedom has almost passed out and the tradition stands on, and it has come to be academic license rather than freedom."—President L. P. Seig, The University of Washington, 1934. *Transactions and Proceedings of the National Association of State Universities, 1934.*

"Never to fetter truth, never to straightjacket progress, never to prostitute knowledge, but ever and only to know and to release truth among men—that is a university. . . .

"On specific proposals men differ honestly and should differ tolerantly, each recognizing both the right and the sincerity of the other. Flinging epithets, bogey words, 'Fascist,' 'Communist,' at those who differ on method or tempo of change is as decidedly unacademic as either inquisition or boycott are un-American. . . ."—Chancellor C. W. Flint, Syracuse University, 1935. *Syracuse University Bulletin,* July 1, 1935.

"In addition to the oath of allegiance bills, there has been much consideration of academic freedom in the college world today; a great deal of this was the result of agitation by the Hearst papers. If American institutions of higher learning and their professors are denied the freedom of thought and activity which has always characterized our higher education, it will be a tragedy. Germany is an illustration of a nation with an eminent record in scholarship in the past, whose universities are now entirely subservient to the Government's will. College teachers never had a greater obligation than today to think carefully and fearlessly and to express themselves upon matters in which they can justly be considered authorities. Most of the difficulty about academic freedom comes from the ill-advised statements of teachers in fields where they have no greater competency than the layman; because they are professors, their utterances are given undue credence."—President James L. McConaughy, Wesleyan University, 1935. "The Annual Report of the President," *The Wesleyan University Bulletin*, October, 1935.

"An intelligent, impartial and independent university is the only assurance against ignorance, prejudice, demagoguery, and propaganda. No free social order can dispense with such an institution. No real university can survive the loss of this function. . . .

"Complete academic freedom may be merely an ideal, never fully realized; but it is the only ideal with which liberalism can hope to survive and to attain a reasonable measure of development and security. No university can compromise or surrender it. . . ."—President E. A. Gilmore, the State University of Iowa, 1935. *Bulletin of the American Association of University Professors*, April, 1935.

"How shall universities defend American democracy? By suppressing discussion? By disciplining non-conformists? By dismissing professors whose views are unpopular with some important group of people? By prohibiting students from having contact with any ideas except those sanctioned by some one authority? By indoctrinating students with some kind of social or political dogma? Not in any of these ways. Every one of them is diametrically opposed to the principles to which this democracy is dedicated. Universities can best defend American democracy by tenaciously upholding those rights which American democracy guarantees. They can best interpret American democracy by giving an example of it."—Chancellor Samuel P. Capen, The University of Buffalo, 1935. *School and Society*, June 22, 1935.

"If you have thought that the cry of freedom that has been raised by scientific men and institutions is but a minor issue of the times, I venture to say that you will not long be so persuaded. The high sounding phrase 'the oath of allegiance' is but the forerunner of other seductive phrases that represent an assault on freedom and the debasement of democratic idealism in the very terms of the charter of democracy. Confident of their strength, forces are gathering to push still further the intolerance against which Jefferson warned the people of his day. A victory for intolerance is but the signal for a fresh assault. The assault is upon one of the principles of which we should be proudest: essential freedom within the framework of public good."—President Isaiah Bowman, The Johns Hopkins University, 1935. *A Design for Scholarship* (Baltimore: The Johns Hopkins Press, 1936), pp. 131, 132.

"Academic freedom, in other words, lays a responsibility on the instructor as well as on the university. That responsibility, in a word, is that he should approach his task not as a propagandist, not as a partisan, but as a person of an open mind, regardful of facts, whether or not they support preconceived theories. We need within the sphere of the social sciences more realists and fewer romantics; more objective and less wishful thinking.

"It is, on the other hand, essential that the university should maintain the position that a man at work in the true spirit of science must suffer no interference. Universities are the carriers and the promoters of truth. It is not their business either to maintain the status quo or to serve as agencies for social reform. . . .

"University teachers take upon themselves no obligation which abridges their right as citizens. Outside their classrooms they are subject to no abridgments save those which apply in general to the whole body of citizens. . . .

"Any university worthy the name will fight for its intellectual freedom against all assaults. . . . It must do this, or lose its self, respect. With the example before our eyes of the subordination of universities in so much of the European world to communistic or fascist propaganda, it is singularly tragic that in America there should exist at the moment so many pressure groups waging a guerrilla warfare against the principle which lies at the heart of true university life. That principle we must maintain, and with this attitude there must be no compromise.

"Its maintenance, on the other hand, imposes on members

of university faculties the obligation to be clear about the responsibilities which the right to freedom imposes. Propaganda of any sort is not to be met by declaring that the university exists in order to parade propaganda of another sort—a university exists for truth. . . ."—Chancellor Harry W. Chase, New York University, 1935. *Report for 1934-35*, pp. 8, 9, 10.

"Academic freedom is not academic license. It does not guarantee to any individual the right to teach whatever he pleases nor to impose on the immature, the uncritical, the unwary, his own untested intellectual idiosyncrasies. . . .

"Academic freedom is freedom to teach what is true and to receive instruction in what is true. When it comes to defining what is true, Catholic education seeks the guidance not only of the natural law but of the supernatural revelation that has come to us from God through Jesus Christ, our Lord, and which is interpreted for us by the church. This truth we insist on our right to teach. . . .

"The state has no authority to determine what is and what is not true. . . ."—National Catholic Educational Association, 1936. *Bulletin of the American Association of University Professors*, October, 1936, p. 366.

"Academic freedom is simply a way of saying that we get the best results in education and research if we leave their management to people who know something about them. Attempts on the part of the public to regulate the methods and content of education and to determine the objects of research are encroachments on academic freedom. Attempts to control private lives and public expressions of professors are of another order. They are attempts to interfere with the liberty of the citizen. The democratic view that the state may determine the amount of money to be spent on education and may regulate education and educators by law has nothing to do with the wholly undemocratic notion that citizens may tell educators how to conduct education and still less with the fanatic position that they may tell them how to live, vote, think, and speak."—President

Robert M. Hutchins, The University of Chicago, 1936. *The Higher Learning in America* (New Haven : Yale University Press, 1936), p. 21.

"Temple University adheres to the principle of freedom of discussion on all subjects within law, by students and faculty. . . .

"The administration of Temple University reserves the sole right to express the University's opinion on any or all social, political, or economic questions. At no time shall any group act as though it were representing the University. As a safeguard against misunderstanding, the opening paragraph of any resolutions adopted by such groups and descriptions of the meetings shall carefully indicate the name of the organization, the number attending, and the number voting for and against such resolutions."—President C. E. Beury, Temple University, 1937. Quoted in *Bulletin of the American Association of University Professors*, March, 1937, pp. 252, 253.

"A teacher has as much right to engage in outside activities, and to express his views on public questions, as any other professional man. That his views may not coincide with those of a governing board, or do violence to the convictions of the great body of graduates, may be unfortunate, but to ask him to remain silent unless his opinions conform to theirs, would be to limit his right as a citizen, to deprive him of part of his liberty and to impose humiliating restrictions unacceptable to independent and high-minded men.

"Any University attempting to enforce such a censorship would soon cease to attract preëminent men who combine independence of mind with sound scholarship, the very men who bring it strength and vitality. It would thus pay a penalty so heavy as to make any temporary embarrassment or irritation occasioned by the words or activities of an individual, however imprudent, seem comparatively trivial."—Ogden L. Mills, 1936. *Bulletin of the American Association of University Professors*, December, 1937, p. 671.

"I believe that the tendencies to curtail freedom and impose regimentation in teaching arise from fear, on the one hand, or ambition, on the other. However camouflaged, it is certainly fear that has led large groups to attempt not only the suppression of teaching, but even the suppression of any information at all concerning certain economic and political systems differing fundamentally from our own. To such groups the spirit of Science would reply: 'If our own doctrines cannot stand the light of comparison with these foreign doctrines, the sooner they are discarded the earlier and more painlessly will the ultimate transition to the newer doctrines be made. If, on the other hand, we have real faith in our own system we should have no cause to fear a fair and open study and discussion of all systems. In the end, our own position should be far stronger.' "—President Karl T. Compton, Massachusetts Institute of Technology, 1937. *Educating for Democracy: A Symposium* (Yellow Springs, Ohio: The Antioch Press, 1937), p. 83.

"Most of us speak our minds frankly on public affairs, often even on matters in which we have no competency. I think there is much to be said for the attitude of King (Amherst), who believes his job is to run a college, not to speak out on matters which do not directly concern the campus. He was almost the only one of the Northern presidents who did not publicly denounce Roosevelt's Supreme Court proposals; even when pressed by his trustees, he maintained that this was no concern of Amherst's and refused to be counted, for or against. Most of us are conservatives, as are our bosses, the trustees, in general; and radical economic changes worry us by threatening adversely our endowment income. For many years before being a Democrat became so popular, Sills was the only member of that party heading a college in the Northeast. Even today MacCracken's (Vassar) vigorous support of Roosevelt differentiates him from most of the rest of us. Some of us may be too critical of modern trends at Washington; probably our faculties and students show a higher percentage of approval. In this 'new day' it would be most unfortunate if the proletariat considered college presidents as unresponsive to modern tendencies. We may 'view with alarm' too often; some of us regret that Angell made such a large part of his valedictory at Yale a denunciation of Roosevelt. After all, our job is chiefly academic.

"Presidents of State-supported institutions are under much more of a curb on public matters than those of us who preside over independent colleges; few of the heads of independent colleges, even those which have close denominational ties, are prevented from speaking publicly the truth as they see it. Cowling, at Carleton College, today has much greater freedom than Coffman at Minnesota. Probably this group of presidents can do more than those in institutions under public control to fight for freedom of speech; we can publicly oppose Oath Bills, we can urge freedom for the teacher. There are many signs of impending interference with academic freedom in American colleges; here we have a large responsibility.

"The president's freedom of speech often gets him into trouble. . . ."—"Prexy," by a college president, 1938, An anonymous article in *Harper's Monthly Magazine*, January, 1938.

"They [the universities] have not been, they must not become, instruments of political propaganda. They have been, they must continue to be, sanctuaries for intellectual integrity. . . . Since that memorable day more than seven hundred years ago, when the mother of universities, the University of Paris, came into being . . . it has been the primary purpose of the university to cultivate that variety of mind which, specialized as it may be, sees its own specialty in relation to the whole field of thought and knowledge and experience; which insists on examining every premise, which is not satisfied with the *status quo* merely because it is the *status quo*, which has no disposition to follow the new merely because it is the new, which follows the truth wherever it may lead, which cherishes restraint above license, and worships honour above expediency.

"Today, more than ever before, the universities are challenged to continue in this tradition. The future of the democratic process, of liberty itself, depends upon the way in which they meet this challenge."—Principal and Vice-Chancellor Lewis W. Douglas, McGill University, 1938. *The Installation of Lewis Williams Douglas as the Principal and Vice-Chancellor of McGill University* (Montreal, January, 1938), pp. 17, 18.

"The problem of freedom for teachers and academic freedom in general bids fair to become more acute than at present. There are many indications of increasing interference with reasonable freedom of teaching; in many institutions teachers will, I fear, lose their positions because of an honest, forthright attitude on controversial subjects. College professors in many States are much less secure in tenure than they were. Furthermore, college professors are divided on the question of affiliation with a union, probably the C. I. O., to protect their rights. The American Association of University Professors and the Association of American Colleges face grave difficulties in 1938 along these lines. Many teachers and some administrators are likely to be sacrificed in the effort to preserve academic freedom."—President James L. McConaughy, Wesleyan University, 1938, *The New York Times*, January 2, 1938.

Research

"I have said that the object of a university was partly to educate the young—the picked and chosen youth of the country, but it is also in part the duty of professors to add to the literature and science of their respective departments. The university that fails to do this fails in an essential portion of its proper business."—President C. C. Felton, Harvard College, 1860. Inaugural Address, *American Journal of Education*, ed. Henry Barnard, September, 1860.

"Experience teaches that the strongest and most devoted professors will contribute something to the patrimony of knowledge; or if they invent little themselves, they will do something toward defending, interpreting, or diffusing the contributions of others. Nevertheless, the prime business of American professors in this generation must be regular and assiduous class teaching. With the exception of the endowments of the Observatory, the University does not hold a single fund primarily intended to secure to men of learning the leisure and means to prosecute original researches."—President Charles W. Eliot, Harvard University, 1869. Inaugural Address, in S. E. Morison, *The Development of Harvard University* (Cambridge: Harvard University Press, 1930), p. lxxii.

"Side by side with these men of a general culture and a professional training Columbia aims to contribute in increasing numbers still another precious type to the scholarship and citizenship of the times. She has always been doing something, she aims to do systematically more and more of the original work which belongs especially to our conception of a university in philosophy, in law, in science, and in every branch of learning. She aims to develop the patient student whose controlling desire it will be to add something to the sum of human knowledge. She aims to do her part to make return to Europe, for the benefits of research which Europe has bestowed with such lavish hand upon America. She looks assuredly for the day when European students shall come to New York and Columbia, where now our American youth go to Oxford and Paris and Berlin. No less a result than this, will satisfy Columbia's conception of what is within her power, if New York will sustain her in the work she seeks to do."—President Seth Low, Columbia University, 1890. *Installation of President Low, February 3, 1890.*

"The laboratory is an institution altogether modern. Today, it occupies the position of honor next to the library. . . . It will be necessary to provide distinct laboratories, though not in every case separate buildings, for each of the departments of natural science, physics, chemistry, zoölogy, geology, mineralogy, palaeontology, anatomy, physiology, anthropology, and the rest. . . ."—William Rainey Harper, The University of Chicago, 1902. "The Trend of University and College Education in the United States," *North American Review*, April, 1902.

"The crowning function of a university is that of original research. On this rests the advance of civilization. From the application of scientific knowledge most of the successes of the nineteenth century have arisen. It is the first era of science. . . .

"It is fair to judge a university by the character of its advanced work."—President David Starr Jordan, Leland Stanford Junior University, 1902. "University Building," *Popular Science Monthly*, August, 1902.

"The best teacher is a constant student, and the constant student sooner or later tends to become an investigator. The terms investigation and original research have been so parodied and abused of late, that their real significance is not understood and valued as it should be. Yet these terms stand for the idea which differentiates the university from the college. We shall not reach an ideal condition until every department in the University, without exception, regards itself as charged with the duty of investigating as well as with that of teaching."—President Nicholas Murray Butler, Columbia University, 1902. *Report for 1901-02*, p. 25.

"Counting the threads of a carpet, or the grains in a bushel of sand, may add iotas to knowledge, but it will be to the domain of useless knowledge. Doing what has already been well done is a waste of energy, though we call it research. Time given to isolated and unrelated inquiries is a bad investment. . . .

"The size of a college has nothing to do with the progress of investigation . . . the facts are so obvious that a false exaggeration declares that the progress of science varies inversely as the size of the laboratory; the larger the place and the more the students, the more arduous the administration and the more frequent the interruptions . . . so I would say: Research depends upon a state of mind, and not on the laboratory or the instruments."—President Daniel Coit Gilman, The Johns Hopkins University, 1903. "Research," *The Launching of A University* (New York: Dodd, Mead and Company, 1906), pp. 243, 246.

"America has not yet contributed her share to scholarly creation, and the fault lies in part at the doors of our universities. They do not strive enough in the impressionable years of early manhood to stimulate intellectual appetite and ambition; nor do they foster productive scholarship enough among those members of their staffs who are capable thereof. Too often a professor of original power explains to docile pupils the process of mining intellectual gold, without seeking nuggets himself, or when found showing them to mankind. Productive scholarship is the shyest of all flowers. It cometh not with observation, and may not bloom even under the most careful nurture. American universities must do their utmost to cultivate it, by planting the best seed, letting the sun shine upon it, and taking care that in our land of rank growth it is not choked by the thorns of administrative routine."—President A. Lawrence Lowell, Harvard University, 1909. Inaugural Address, in S. E. Morison, *The Development of Harvard University* (Cambridge: Harvard University Press, 1930), p. lxxxviii.

"It is this organic relation to the democratic state that puts the southern state university at the vital center of the state's formative material prosperity. 'What are southern universities doing,' asks a great industrial leader, 'to give economic independence to southern industry?' It is a fair challenge, and the state university joyfully acknowledges its obligation fully to meet it. It is a part of the business of laboratories to function in the productive state by solving the problems of embarrassed industry. Science has so faithfully performed this obligation that the main arch of modern industry rests on the laboratory. Applied science no less truly rests on pure science and the liberating currents of the spirit of inquiry and investigation that is the vital spark of modern life."—President Edward K. Graham, The University of North Carolina, 1915. "Inaugural Address," in *Education and Citizenship and Other Papers* (New York: G. P. Putnam's Sons, 1919 [also University of North Carolina Press]), pp. 15, 16.

"As the University grows and extends its activities and as its service to the public is so richly multiplied, it is of vital importance that it lay increased and steadily increasing emphasis upon the work of research. It is this which marks off the true university from the *polytechnicum* or from the merely philanthropic organization of higher education. So long as the spirit of research dominates the university and is its major interest, just so long will its teaching be kept fully alive and just so long will its public service be real and vitalizing. To organize and to stimulate research, therefore, is the university's chief business."—President Nicholas Murray Butler, Columbia University, 1915. *Report for 1914-15*, p. 31.

"Another fault of the mechanical spirit in our system of education is the superstitious veneration for degrees as such. This again is a good thing in itself, but it is often carried too far. We tend in America, particularly in small colleges, to appoint to teaching only men with a Ph.D. degree. That degree is good, but it is never the only available measure of intellectual attainment. Many of our most eminent scholars of the present day have never taken it, but are nevertheless both scholars and eminent; while the Ph.D. degree, though no doubt a proof of scholarship, does not necessarily import eminence. The late William James made merry over 'the Ph.D. Octopus,' and used to tell of a man who returned to Cambridge to complete his work in philosophy for that degree. On inquiry, it turned out that he wanted a position to teach English in a certain college and could not get it without the doctorate; but the intelligent officials of that college were not exacting as to his subject, and as he was more nearly prepared for the examinations in philosophy, he found that a ready means of dazzling the eyes of the college into allowing him to teach English. To appoint to the instructing staff only persons with a Ph.D. degree saves some trouble to the appointing power, and provides at least a minimum security. It looks well in the catalogue, and requires no apology. But as a fetish, it is like any other fetish,—more awe-inspiring when not too closely investigated."—President A. Lawrence Lowell, Harvard University, 1920. At the inauguration of President Harry W. Chase, of the University of North Carolina, 1920. *The State University and the New South* (Chapel Hill, N. C., 1920), pp. 32, 33.

"An institution whose concern is truth must find one very real test of its vigor in whether it seeks to contribute new truths to the world's existing store. The impulse toward research springs from the same conditions which insure the vitality of its teaching, and reacts in turn upon its whole inner life. The supreme question here is not whether research is of practical value to the State. To that question the whole history of Western civilization gives eloquent answer. Truth must indeed be sought upon the mountain top, but with him whose passion to look upon her face wins him access to her high abode, she walks hand in hand down into the common haunts of men, and with her touch men's labors lighten, their bodies strengthen, and their souls grow great. In all that men may do there is assuredly nothing more practical than to seek for truth. The real question is rather that of the spirit in which they go about their quest. Research may sink to the level of mere mechanical and lifeless routine, which kills the spirit while it preserves the letter, or it may become such a liberating power that the mind which comes under its spell is caught up forever into a higher and a clearer air. Men with such a vision the State must surely count among its most precious possessions."—President Harry W. Chase, University of North Carolina, 1920. *The State University and the New South* (Chapel Hill, N. C., 1920), p. 66.

"I am frank to say that the question, 'Has he written anything?' so often employed as a test of a man's fitness for a college position, does not interest me overmuch."—President Clifton Daggett Gray, Bates College, *Bates College Bulletin* (Lewiston, Maine), December 1, 1920.

"A university is an institution where students adequately trained by previous study of the liberal arts and sciences are led into special fields of learning and research by teachers of high excellence and originality, and where by the agency of libraries, museums, laboratories, and publications, knowledge is conserved, advanced and disseminated. Teaching is only one function of a university. Its chief function is the conservation, the advancement of knowledge, the pushing out of that borderline between the known and the unknown which constitutes the human horizon."—President Nicholas Murray Butler, Columbia University, 1921. "The Service of a University," *Scholarship and Service* (New York: Charles Scribner's Sons, 1921), p. 62.

"It was Garrick, a great admirer of George Whitefield's preaching, who said that Whitefield's eloquence was so persuasive that he could reduce his hearers to tears merely by uttering the word Mesopotamia. The word research has come to be something like the blessed word Mesopotamia. It is used to reduce everyone to silence, acquiescence and appropriation. The fact of the matter is that something between 75 per cent and 90 per cent of what is called research in the various universities and institutions of the land is not properly research at all, but simply the rearrangement or reclassification of existing data or well-known phenomena. This rearrangement and reclassification are important, no doubt, and sometimes highly significant, but it is an error to confuse them with a genuinely new contribution to the sum total of human knowledge or human understanding. Not many persons in any one generation are capable of real research."—President Nicholas Murray Butler, Columbia University, 1925. *Report for 1924-25*, p. 37.

"The University of Maine, in its present financial status, must exist primarily for its undergraduate students. It is not necessary to argue, however, that graduate and research work should form an important part of the activities of any institution. They give a healthy incentive to the undergraduate work and create an atmosphere which in itself tends to raise scholastic standards. A certain proportion of graduate students has a wholesome effect not only on the undergraduate student body but upon the faculty, and the members of the faculty who can have time to devote to graduate work are keeping themselves more alive and abreast of the times. I only wish that it could be made possible to allow more of our faculty time for this purpose. In the pure sciences, research, and in the applied sciences, experimentation, which amounts to the same thing, become very essential if we are to make any advances. Maine must foster these valuable attributes if we expect to stand for high ideals of service to the State."—President H. S. Boardman, The University of Maine, 1926. *Inaugural address by Harold Sherburne Boardman, President University of Maine, June 12, 1926* (Pamphlet), p. 16.

"There is little place in the Liberal College for technical experts, for research, for what is commonly known as 'productive scholarship'—just enough of all this to keep the teacher mentally alert and up-to-date in his knowledge of facts. The chief function of the teacher is teaching; teaching that inspires the student to self-education, that helps him to find himself, that shows him how to read and creates taste for good reading, how to study and to find in study not a grind but an opportunity to develop mental discipline. The Liberal College might get along without specialists, but teachers whose lives reveal the essentials of genuine culture and profound wisdom, teachers who are evidently the daily disciples and companions of the Master Teacher, the Christian College of Liberal Arts must have at any cost. For teachers such as these enter upon their task as a solemn and joyous vocation. . . ."—President A. A. Shaw, Denison University, 1927. Inaugural Address, *Inauguration of President Shaw, Denison University, Granville, Ohio.*

"In graduate work only those who are themselves productive scholars should be recognized as major professors, and we should never fall below, but not try to rise too far above, standard institutions in our requirements for the master's degree. The Ph.D. degree should rarely be given, and then only to exceptionally capable men if it is to retain its standing as a research degree, rather than fall to a merely teaching degree. Research is one of the important functions of any state university and land grant college."—President Homer L. Shantz, The University of Arizona, 1930. *Inaugural Bulletin* (Tucson, Arizona, 1930), p. 42.

"It seems to me that if research is the great adventure we believe it to be, we can not introduce good students to its inspiring difficulties too soon. The interest thus aroused would make better students of all who are capable of being students at all. It would dispose of the morons quickly and quietly and in a way convincing to them, as units, grade points and mechanisms can never hope to be.

"Conversely, the products of such a system would do much to bring to an end the incessant debate between teaching and research, because men trained under such a system would know that you can not keep the two apart, that while one man may elect to teach and another to investigate, the teacher must keep abreast of his subject and the investigator must transmit what he has learned. Research is merely a search for knowledge and no man belongs on a university faculty who is not engaged in that search. But this does not mean to me that all faculty men must be productive scholars in the narrow sense of the term. There will always be some good men who are primarily teachers, and some good men who are primarily investigators, and some extraordinary men who are both. As to the first two classes, the investigator should be allowed to investigate and the teacher should be allowed to teach, and the reward for good service in either case should be the same.

"Under present conditions we have the strange anomaly of teachers being judged not on their ability to teach but on their research output, and investigators being forced to devote valuable time to teaching that might be given to advancing the frontiers of knowledge. As a result men who might be good teachers if they were encouraged by the hope of future advancement are drifting about in laboratories with a couple of test tubes in their hands making themselves useless in a most arduous and time-consuming way, and men who might be good investigators are wearing out their patience and their students in a vain effort to expound and to inspire. The criterion of the teacher should be ability to teach, and of the investigator, ability to investigate, and neither should look down upon the other so long as he is doing his job well. As it is, the good teacher, looked down upon by his colleagues because he is not producing each year a certain amount of scholarly pap, is frequently made so miserable that he gets out of academic life. That, so long as the largest task of an American university is to teach undergraduate students—and whatever it should be that is what it is—is a distinct loss from every point of view."—President Robert G. Sproul, The University of California, 1930. "The Educational System of California," *School and Society*, November 8, 1930.

"The Universities have facilities for research which we shall never attempt to duplicate. There scholars may push out here and there the boundaries of knowledge. I have profound respect for the research scholar, and for his work. But at Amherst our prime interest is in teaching."—President Stanley King, Amherst College, 1932. Inaugural Address, *Amherst Graduates' Quarterly*, February, 1933.

"It is the duty (if I may presume to speak from the faculty point of view here for a moment) of the university to maintain conditions under which men of distinction and quality can live and work freely in teaching and in research. Given such men, free to stimulate students and to discover truth, and a university exists, whatever else, in response to the needs of a particular social order, may be added unto it. Without such men, no matter what one's theory may be, there is no university."—President Samuel P. Capen, the University of Buffalo, 1932. In *The Obligation of Universities to the Social Order*, ed. H. P. Fairchild (New York: New York University Press, 1933), p. 67.

"If the privately endowed university must choose between its college department and its university as typified by graduate work and research, there is no question in my mind that the decision should be for the university, but I have not seen a situation where the alternative presented itself, nor do I expect to." —Harold W. Swift, President of the Board of Trustees, The University of Chicago, 1932. In *The Obligation of Universities to the Social Order*, ed. H. P. Fairchild (New York: New York University Press, 1933), p. 75.

"The most imperious challenge which confronts humanity today, second only to our moral chaos, lies in the broad field of economics. We cannot meet this challenge by the mere repetition of formulas, however venerable they may be. What is required is not merely a demonstration that this or that detail is wrong but a constructive philosophy of economics which candidly faces all of the new factors that enter into our integrated life to make it both more delicate and more complex. The task is to find an answer which must in its very essence be creative. No mere traditionalism or allegiance to ancient standards as such will serve, nor will political platforms of contending factions. . . .

"By analogy with other fields of learning I have hoped to develop the inference that the economic field stands waiting for the best thought of humanity upon newer and more adequate lines. In a large sense it must interpret the world of today in the light of a new language. While it should take care to preserve those ideas which have been developed by earlier thinkers which will help in finding the solution of today's problems, the new philosophy of economics must be built up inductively as well as deductively, and we must recognize that we have gone only a little way along the paths of economic understanding. Viewed in this light, economics is a science which has a world for its clinic, and the searcher after truth can find myriad avenues to be explored, evaluating in their appropriate ratios many factors which are obviously temporary and incidental in the effort to find the way, step by step, to basic, underlying causes."—President Thomas S. Gates, The University of Pennsylvania, 1932. In *The Obligation of Universities to the Social Order*, ed. H. P. Fairchild (New York: New York University Press, 1933), pp. 184, 189, 190.

"An article in the spring number of the Phi Beta Kappa magazine has caused much comment on many an American college campus; the author describes the college as a place where no scholarly research accomplishments can be expected. We do not believe that the indictment is fair; there are, I think, at least half a dozen colleges with a record in faculty research comparable with that of most universities. . . . Approximately $30,000 is being expended annually at Wesleyan for the encouragement of research; I should like to see this figure increased to at least $50,000."—President James L. McConaughy, Wesleyan University, 1934. "The Annual Report of the President," *The Wesleyan University Bulletin*, October, 1934.

"After all, the primary purpose of a college is to produce not learned books but able men."—President Dixon Ryan Fox, Union College, 1934. Inaugural Address, *School and Society*, October 20, 1934.

"Despite this tremendous expenditure we are open to the charge frequently made that in no country in the world are scholarship and the fruits of education so lightly regarded as in the United States. The reason for this apparent discrepancy between the high price we are willing to pay and the low regard in which we hold the service which we could reasonably expect in return for such an expenditure is our excessive emphasis upon formal education. We mistake form for substance and fondly hope that democracy is to be saved by the mass production of thousands of units of education, certified by diplomas and degrees."—President H. W. Dodds, Princeton University, 1935. *Report for 1934-35*, p. 2.

"In a university where true freedom to learn exists, both the teaching and the research should be of the highest order. The staff should be composed of men of superior ability and training, drawn from every corner of the earth, catholic in their sympathies, cosmopolitan in outlook, and dedicated to the profession they have chosen. They should be paid well enough to insure them a comfortable living, to enable them to attend professional meetings and to travel in foreign countries, and security in their old age should be guaranteed. . . .

"A university does not confine its activities to teaching; it is even more an institution of inquiry. The scientific spirit should pervade and activate its atmosphere. Within the limits of its resources it should carry on researches in every field."—President Lotus D. Coffman, The University of Minnesota, 1935. "Building a University," *Higher Education and Society* (Norman: University of Oklahoma Press, 1936), pp. 313, 314.

"To make teaching most effective, scholarship should be encouraged and time and facilities provided for faculty research. Lest you charge me at once with confusing the small college and the university let me remind you that scholarship and inspirational teaching are not incompatible but complementary. The true teacher is a man of inquiring mind, not satisfied with a parasitical intellectual life but eager to discover truth as yet unknown. The college teacher who views knowledge as something in a dish to pass around among his students without spilling any of it is promptly exposed by undergraduates quick to detect the bluffer. I do not mean that the college should repeat the error of the universities which have placed such heavy premiums on research without distinguishing between that which is commonplace and trivial and that which is significant and creative. The cause of scholarship has been retarded by indiscriminating pressure upon scholarly production and by measuring the results in column inches of articles in professional magazines."—President H. W. Dodds, Princeton University, 1936. Address at the inauguration of President W. A. Eddy, Hobart and William Smith Colleges, 1936. Typescript copy in the library of the University of North Carolina.

"This principle (the application of scholarship to vital human interests) should apply to some extent in all fields of learning, but particularly in the social sciences. A concrete example will serve to illustrate. In the southeastern region of the United

States there are great social, economic, and political problems which concern the welfare of a vast population. . . .

"Land waste represented by the fact that in that region with 17 per cent of the cultivated area of the country there is 60 per cent of the eroded land, human waste represented by woefully inadequate educational facilities and two million tenants changing farms on the average every two years, and economic dislocation due to the crumbling of the cotton economy and the precarious position of export types of tobacco are elements in the picture.

"It is not difficult to visualize the depth of interest which the student must feel as he comes to grips with these problems, upon the solution of which depends the future of the region. His attitude and outlook, his interest in current problems, and his desire to do something about them would surely be more vital than those of the student whose studies had been concerned merely with abstract principles and metaphysical truths.

"After all, if the universities are to ignore, in both teaching and research, the needs of the regions they serve, how will they be met? The conclusion is inescapable that the university has a responsibility not only for research in the fundamental current problems, but for bringing students into contact with professors who are grappling with these problems. This will not lower the tone of the university, but will give it a creative atmosphere, so important in the education of youth, which would be lacking in the university devoted merely to abstract learning.

"Since the answers to the questions raised depend upon one's conception of education, it might not be inappropriate, in conclusion, to essay a definition of higher learning, the issues of which have been the subject of our discussion.

"It does not consist in acquiring facts or techniques and skills. It is not merely the mastery of the tools of learning and of the inherited wisdom of the race, nor the understanding of the principles of metaphysics. It is something more than intellectual discipline, the capacity for scientific abstraction, or mere philosophical perspective. It involves more than books or theories or abstract speculation. It is not the product of any special intellectual regimen. It includes the interpretation of facts and the search for truth in their application. In its most effective form it is derived from dealing with real situations, from the effort to solve difficult intellectual problems that impinge upon life's needs. It does not end with merely discovering the truth. Its effectiveness is determined largely by the extent to which truth finds expression in attitudes, both social and intellectual, in actions, and in motivating purposes."—Chancellor O. C. Carmichael, Vanderbilt University, 1938. "Some Issues in the Higher Learning," *Educational Record*, July, 1938.

"In too many instances research has been research in name only. . . . All departments have sinned. . . ."—Chancellor Harry W. Chase, New York University, 1938. *The Inauguration of Oliver C. Carmichael As Chancellor of Vanderbilt University*. Nashville: Vanderbilt University, 1938.

Teaching

"Goodwin, there is no more comparison between the pleasure of being professor and being president than there is between heaven and hell."—President Cornelius C. Felton, Harvard College, *ca.* 1860-1862. Quoted in S. E. Morison, *Three Centuries of Harvard* (Cambridge: Harvard University Press, 1936), p. 301.

"There has been much discussion about the comparative merits of lectures and recitations. Both are useful—lectures for inspiration, guidance, and the comprehensive methodizing, which only one who has a view of the whole field can rightly contrive; recitations for securing and testifying a thorough mastery on the part of the pupil of the treatise or author in hand, for conversational comment and amplification, for emulation and competition. Recitations alone readily degenerate into dusty repetitions, and lectures alone are too often a useless expenditure of force. The lecturer pumps laboriously into sieves. The water may be wholesome but it runs through. A mind must work to grow. Just as far, however, as the student can be relied on to master and appreciate his author without the aid of frequent questioning and repetitions, so far is it possible to dispense with recitations. Accordingly, in the later college years there is a decided tendency to diminish the number of recitations, the faithfulness of the student being tested by periodical examinations. This tendency is in a right direction, if prudently controlled.

"The discussion about lectures and recitations has brought out some strong opinions about text-books and their use. Impatience with text-books and manuals is very natural both in teachers and taught. These books are indeed, for the most part, very imperfect, and stand in constant need of correction by the well-informed teacher. Stereotyping, in its present undeveloped condition, is in part to blame for their most exasperating defects. To make the metal plates keep pace with the progress of learning is costly. The manifest deficiencies of text-books must not, however, drive us into a too sweeping condemnation of their use. It is a rare teacher who is superior to all manuals in his subject. Scientific manuals are, as a rule, much worse than those upon language, literature, or philosophy; yet the main improvement in medical education in this country during the last twenty years has been the addition of systematic recitations from text-books to the lectures which were formerly the principal means of theoretical instruction. The training of a medical student, inadequate as it is, offers the best example we have of the methods and fruits of an education mainly scientific. The transformation which the average student of a good medical school undergoes in three years is strong testimony to the efficiency of the training he receives."—President Charles W. Eliot, Harvard University, 1869. Inaugural Address, in S. E. Morison, *The Development of Harvard University* (Cambridge: Harvard University Press, 1930), pp. lxvi, lxvii. Also in *School and Society*, March 22, 1924.

"But however attractive this method of instruction [lectures] may be, in relations to the dignity, the ease, the irresponsibility, or the pocket of the instructor . . . it is not the most profitable to the student, unless he is far advanced in knowledge and is animated with an ardent zeal for learning."—President Noah Porter, Yale College, 1878. *The American College and the American Public* (New Edition. New York: Charles Scribner's Sons, 1878), pp. 123, 124.

"Teachers are the seed corn of civilization. We cannot afford any but the best. They are civilization's most powerful agents and we ought to set apart and consecrate to this great work our bravest, best and strongest men and women."—President Charles D. McIver, Normal and Industrial Institute (later Women's College of the University of North Carolina), *ca.* 1890. Quoted in Charles W. Dabney, *Universal Education in the South* (Chapel Hill: The University of North Carolina Press, 1936), I, 202.

"We teach as thoroughly as the athletic rules will allow us." —President R. E. Blackwell, Randolph-Macon College, 1902-1938. Quoted in *The New York Times*, July 8, 1938, upon the death of President Blackwell.

"A log with Mark Hopkins on one end of it and himself on the other was Garfield's conception of such [a school for personal culture] a college. Even the log is not essential. The earnest teacher is all in all."—President David Starr Jordan, Leland Stanford Junior University, 1902. "University Building," *Popular Science Monthly*, August, 1902, p. 330.

"The business of university faculties is teaching. It is not legislation, and it is not administration—certainly not beyond the absolute necessities. There is just complaint because the necessities of administration take much time from teaching. It lessens the most expert and essential work which the world is doing. It seldoms enlarges opportunity or enhances reputation. It is true that teachers have great fun legislating, but it is not quite certain that, outside of their specialties, they will ever come to conclusions, or that, if they do, their conclusions will stand. The main advantage of it is the relaxation and dissipation they get out of it. That is great. And, in a way, it may be as necessary as it is great. Of course teachers could not endure it if they were always to conduct themselves out of the classroom as they do in it. Perhaps others would also have difficulty in enduring it. They are given to disorderliness and argumentation beyond any other class who stands so thoroughly for doing things in regular order. It is not strange. It is the inevitable reaction,—what some of them would call the *psychological antithesis*. Nor is it to be repressed or regretted, for it adds to the effectiveness and attractiveness of the most effective and attractive people in the world. All this is often particularly true of the past masters in the art. No wonder that Professor North, who taught Greek for sixty years at Hamilton College,—'Old Greek' as many generations of students fondly called him,—wrote in his diary that it would have to be cut in the granite of his tombstone that he 'died of faculty meetings,' for he was sure that some day he would drop off before one would come to an end."—President A. S. Draper, The University of Illinois, 1909. *American Education.* Boston: Houghton Mifflin Company, 1909.

"Good teaching is so important in a small college, because a liberal training frees the mind, and the way in which a course is given is as important as the subject matter."—President K. C. M. Sills, Bowdoin College, 1918. *Addresses at the Inauguration of Kenneth Charles Morton Sills, President of Bowdoin College, June 20, 1918* (Brunswick, Maine, 1918), p. 19.

"Our conservatism is discoverable not only in the subjects taught but in our methods of teaching. I have yet to find among our faculty an advocate of painless education. While it is true that to some extent we have made use of the lecture methods in the class room, we have not believed in keeping students too long on diets of predigested food. The methods of the German university, however desirable for mature investigators, have never seemed to us to be adequate for the training of young minds still in the plastic state and needing the more rigorous regimen that is possible through other and older-fashioned methods."—President Clifton Daggett Gray, Bates College, 1920. Inaugural Address, *Bates College Bulletin* (Lewiston, Maine), December 1, 1920.

"If we are to maintain American civilization it can only be done through a policy of sound public education, taking into account the end to be attained—a wholesome American citizenry. . . . With the new emphasis upon university citizenship, paralleling suffrage for all, comes a renewed consciousness of the importance of *reaching* every child. Every child must remain in educational 'quarantine' until there is evidence that the 'test is positive,' evidence that education has 'taken.' This can only be done by effective teaching. . . . The effectiveness of our service will be determined by our ability to teach, our ability to teach will be conditioned by our skill in analyzing the job to be accomplished—the status of the child and the end desired—and modifying our technique in such a way as to accomplish the end. . . . The greatest single need in public education is better teaching. This can best be secured and the public faith in education justified only by recognizing the importance of even slight variations in teaching technique."—President Walter A. Jessup, The State University of Iowa, 1921. "The Greatest Need of the Schools—Better Teaching," *Addresses and Proceedings of the National Education Association, 1921*, pp. 779-782.

"The lecture system is probably the worst scheme ever devised for imparting knowledge. It assumes that what one man has taken perhaps a life time to acquire by the most painstaking observation, hard thinking and long continued reflection, can be relayed or spoon fed to another man who has not gone through a like process."—President Hamilton Holt, Rollins College, 1927. "Ideals for the Development of Rollins College," *School and Society*, August 6, 1927.

"Duke University will not recommend for positions in college teaching even the men who hold the Ph.D. degree unless they have availed themselves of opportunities provided here or elsewhere to test and develop their teaching ability, and have shown that they have some fitness for college teaching. Duke University will provide these opportunities in connection with its own college classes. For underclassmen, that is especially for freshmen and sophomores, our teachers are chosen on account of their personal qualities and teaching power as well as for knowledge of their subjects, and excellence in teaching wins promotion as surely as so-called productive scholarship. . . ."—President William P. Few, Duke University, 1929. *Bulletin of the Association of American Colleges*, March, 1929, p. 47.

"The present system in the university is based upon lectures. Now, despite the low esteem in which these are held by many critics of higher education, they serve a useful purpose by making possible the presentation of knowledge not yet in books, by aiding students in getting started on a new subject in which listening is more helpful than reading, and by setting up nuclei of interest in young minds. On the other hand, lectures admittedly have their evils. They overemphasize the 'general' and tend to defer direct acquaintance with the 'particular'; they engender the habit of passive receptivity on the part of the student and continued repetition on the part of the teacher; they repress initiative by creating the impression that the subject dealt with is complete and that nothing remains to be done; and worst of all, they lead, as so many things in our present system do, to the conclusion that the end of knowledge is to pass an examination and that this may best be done by repeating, verbatim if possible, the words of the professor or the text-book. Under this system the student coming from the high school to the university is likely to be disappointed and lose his zest for learning. He finds that the work he is called upon to do is no different essentially from what he has been doing, that it is the same old grind and can be handled by the same pro-forma efforts and the same subterfuges. . . ."—President Robert G. Sproul, The University of California, 1930. "The Educational System of California," *School and Society*, November 8, 1930.

"Amherst has a great heritage. For one hundred years it has maintained in its faculty the teaching tradition. It has sought out men who in scholarship and character were suitable for its faculty, but it has prized above every other quality the ability to teach. . . . But at Amherst our prime interest is in teaching. The alumni of the College look back to Tuckerman and Hitchcock, to Seelye and Garman in philosophy, Morse in history, Emerson in geology, John Tyler in biology, or William Esty and George Olds in mathematics. Some of us caught a spark of inspiration from one, some from another. They are our common heritage. Teaching to me is the greatest profession in the world. I should like to make Amherst a college which no great teacher would ever wish to leave, and to which great teachers in other institutions would welcome an appointment. Great teachers make great men. And I do not doubt that the secret of our Amherst heritage of distinguished sons is due not to our curriculum, not to the air of the Connecticut Valley, not to any advantage in the type of student that has come to us, but directly to the great tradition of Amherst teachers.

"And great teaching, I think, produces teachers. One of my friends, who is a president of a sister college, comments to me on the number of Amherst men who have gone into teaching and the number who have attained distinction in teaching. He says that on lists of candidates for college presidents in the past score of years the proportion of Amherst names is greater than could possibly be expected from our size and the size of the alumni body. This tradition I shall do everything in my power to continue. It will be my responsibility to provide as far as possible the best environment, both physical and spiritual, for the joyous and fruitful work of my colleagues on the faculty. I shall give every possible encouragement to good teaching and to good teachers."—President Stanley King, Amherst College, 1932. *Amherst Graduates' Quarterly*, February, 1933.

"The art of teaching, which depends for its success upon quick and understanding communication between mind and mind, has deplorably suffered, not gained, by the phenomenal amount of detailed analysis to which it has been subjected during the past forty years. . . . The super-analysis and hyper-dissection of the teaching process have pretty well destroyed much of its power and are responsible in no small degree for the decline of true education during the past generation. The lecture system as a means of communicating facts should have been dispensed with when the art of printing was invented. . . ."—President Nicholas Murray Butler, Columbia University, 1933. *Report for 1932-33*, p. 30.

"One of the greatest crimes committed by the colleges and universities of today is too much exercise of the lecture method for the classroom, making the students passive recipients instead of active participants."—Newspaper report of speech of President Frank P. Graham, The University of North Carolina, 1937. *Greensboro Daily News*, November 4, 1937.

6

OBLIGATIONS TO SOCIETY

Apparently the heads of higher educational institutions are aware of the obligations of higher education to the world about it. President A. Lawrence Lowell, in his inaugural address at Harvard, in 1909, said that one purpose of the university was "to counteract rather than copy the defects of the civilization of the day." President C. R. Van Hise, of the University of Wisconsin, said in a commencement address the following year that the "strength of the state university lies in its close relations to the State." President Harry W. Chase, of the University of North Carolina, said in his inaugural address there in 1920, that the challenge of the South to state universities in that section of the country was a challenge which these institutions could meet "by no merely perfunctory response."

Presidential statements on obligations to the social order reveal concern for the lower schools, for the education of women, for the education of the Negroes in the Southern States, for patriotic duty during the World War, for adult education and extension services, and on federal relations in education.

Higher educational leaders in the East and West seem to have urged the improvement of the schools below the college somewhat earlier than did those in the Southern States, where public high schools were slow to develop. The attitude of the presidents of colleges for men, on the education of women and especially on co-education, appears in statements given in this section. President Charles W. Eliot, of Harvard, in his inaugural in 1869, urged "a cautious and expectant policy" ; President F. A. P. Barnard, of Columbia, as early as 1879, was an energetic advocate of co-education at that institution, and so was

President J. B. Angell, of the University of Michigan, as early as 1880. President John C. Kilgo, of Trinity College (North Carolina), was a strong advocate of co-education in the early 1890's. In 1902, President Nicholas Murray Butler, of Columbia, said that the question was "a dead issue. The American people have settled the matter. . . ."

Statements of Southern college presidents on the subject of the education of the Negro are quite significant in the years that followed the "tragic era" of Congressional Reconstruction when it was easy and also dangerous to stir up the fires of race antipathies. On this subject developed some interesting cases involving academic freedom, the most dramatic and significant case being that of Professor John Spencer Bassett, of Trinity College, in North Carolina. In this section also are presented presidential statements concerning the duty of the colleges during the World War and on the obligation of the higher institutions for adult education and for other services of extension. The subject of federal aid to education has provoked some discussion by the presidents of colleges and universities.

Concern for the problems of society is also expressed in commencement addresses. What college presidents say to graduating classes constitutes an interesting part of their views on higher education. When "fear and apprehension are in the air," the dread of tomorrow seems to color the views of higher educational leaders as they send out fresh crops of graduates. Here may be revealed, through baccalaureateers and pulpiteers, the causes of most of the woes of the world.

General Principles

"A College, in order to succeed well, must be governed by its own principles. Its object is the intellectual cultivation of the community. So long as this is made the governing principle of all its arrangements, it will prosper; for it will accomplish the object which men of sense desire to see accomplished, and its works will speak for it. But if it be made subservient to any other end, it will and it ought to fail."—President Francis Wayland, Brown University, 1842. *Thoughts on the Present Collegiate System in the United States* (Boston: Gould, Kendall and Lincoln, 1842), p. 50.

"Scarcely anything in America is more distinctly American than the relation between the colleges and the common people. The people have made the colleges what they are, and the colleges have, in no small measure, made the people what they are. All classes have contributed to the establishment and the support of the colleges and all classes have reaped the benefit." —President W. S. Tyler, Amherst College, 1857. *Colleges: Their Place Among American Institutions*. New York, 1857 (Pamphlet). Quoted in D. G. Tewksbury, *The Founding of American Colleges and Universities Before the Civil War* (New York: Bureau of Publications, Teachers College, Columbia University, 1932), p. 5.

"Columbia College, college and university both, as she really is, . . . is profoundly conscious that what she is doing is but the earnest of what she yet may do, if New York will but make common cause with her, and enlarge and broaden and deepen her work on every side. She aims today to turn out three different types of men. Her historic work, that which she did for a half a century before she did anything else, she is still doing. She aims to develop the cultivated man, the educated gentleman; the man who, without being specialist in any thing, has been educated enough in all directions to be in sympathy with all learning; the man who knows enough about the past to recognize the value of it and of all experience, but who is not bound down by the past; the man who knows enough about the present to glory in its achievement and its promise, but who never forgets what it means of indebtedness to those who have gone before, to be "in the foremost files of time." In a word, she aims to develop the thoughtful and well-informed citizen, and to fill him with her own high aspirations as to his citizenship and his life. The splendid products of this work adorn the history of the city and the nation from the beginning of our career. We want to do, not less of it, but more, according as we have opportunity."—President Seth Low, Columbia University, 1890. *Installation of President Low, February 3, 1890.*

"As the head of the system of public education, the University stands for the education of the whole people. And it is a truism of educational history that no state has ever developed a complete and efficient system of public schools without making liberal provision for her colleges and universities."—President Thomas D. Boyd, Louisiana State University, 1898. *Report of the Board of Supervisors, 1896-1897 and 1897-1898*, p. 15. Quoted in Marcus W. Wilkerson, *Thomas Duckett Boyd: The Story of a Southern Educator* (Baton Rouge: Louisiana State University Press, 1935), pp. 181, 182.

"It will, no doubt, be argued that a university must reflect the state of the world about it; and that the tendency of the times is toward specialization of functions, and social segregation on the basis of wealth. But this is not wholly true, because there is happily in the country a tendency toward social solidarity and social service. A still more conclusive answer is that one object of a university is to counteract rather than copy the defects in the civilization of the day. Would a prevalence of spoils, favoritism or corruption in the politics of the country be a reason for their adoption by universities?"—A. Lawrence Lowell, Harvard University, 1909. *Harvard Graduates' Magazine*, December, 1909. Also in S. E. Morison, *The Development of Harvard University*. Cambridge: Harvard University Press, 1930.

"The strength of the state university lies in its close relations to the State. The State demands of it service; the university feels a peculiar obligation to the State in which it is situated. It is the duty of the state university to instruct young men and women; it is its duty to advance knowledge, and especially those lines of knowledge which concern the development of the State. It is the duty of the staff of the state university to be at the service of the State along all lines in which their expert knowledge will be helpful; it is their duty to assist in carrying knowledge to the people."—President C. R. Van Hise, The

University of Wisconsin, 1910. Commencement Address. Quoted in E. P. Cubberley, *Readings in Public Education in the United States* (Boston: Houghton Mifflin Company, 1934), p. 480.

"Not many years ago, even in America, the direct benefits of higher education were supposed to be for those who actually attended college. Others shared the benefits only indirectly if at all. But in the state supported institutions a new day has dawned. The state university conceives it to be its duty to carry university instruction to all its people who may be able to profit by it; to discover men and women of talent and to develop that talent; to arouse the people of all communities to the need of civic betterment, of public health and sanitation, of conservation of natural resources—indeed the ways in which the university may serve its people through extension work are endless."—President John C. Futrall, The University of Arkansas, 1914. *University of Arkansas Bulletin.* Inaugural Number, February, 1915, p. 26.

"Whatever may be the particular form of organization, the fact remains that the modern state is coming to recognize that the university is the centralized agency through which much of the state's sentiment and action may be expressed."—President W. O. Thompson, Ohio State University, 1914. *University of Arkansas Bulletin.* Inaugural Number, February, 1915, p. 33.

"The state university is the instrument of democracy for realizing all of these high and healthful aspirations of the state. Creating and procreated by the state it has no immediate part, however, in a specific social program. Its service is deeper and more pervasive. It sees its problem as positive, not negative; as one of fundamental health, not of superficial disease. It looks on the state as a producer; not as a policeman. It is not so much concerned with doing a certain set of things, as infusing the way of doing all things with a certain ideal. Not by spasmodic reform, nor by sentiment, nor by the expiations of philanthropy; but by understanding, criticism, research and applied knowledge it would reveal the unity of the channels through which life flows, and minister to the purification of its currents. It would conceive the present state and all of its practical problems as the field of its service, but it would free the term service from the narrowing construction of immediate practice. The whole function of education is to make straight and clear the way for the liberation of the spirit of men from the tyranny of place and time, not by running away from the world, but by mastering it."—President Edward K. Graham, The University of North Carolina, 1915. "Inaugural Address," in *Education and Citizenship and Other Papers* (New York: G. P. Putnam's Sons, 1919 [also University of North Carolina Press]), pp. 13, 14.

"Among all the problems which we face none is more important than that of improving the institutional spirit and mechanism by which an educated American leadership is to emerge from the colleges and universities into the service of an aspiring and troubled world. The higher institutions have carried many splendid traditions, the products of centuries of trial and error. One after another they have been superimposed as insight and necessity have determined their coming. Often they have fallen into accidental relationships not thought-determined. Some ideals and methods fitted to a previous century's needs carry an academic respectability not consistent with the requirements of our own time. A new estimate of college functions and their relations is required if education for leadership is to be a tidy and effective process."—President Henry Suzzallo, The University of Washington, 1920. "Foreword" to Jay W. Hudson, *The College and New America*. New York: D. Appleton and Company, 1920.

"The laws passed recently in almost all of our mountain states, enforcing free education for all children, compulsory attendance for all children, a lengthened period of schooling each year, a sweeping advance in the requirements of teachers in the public schools, the erection of Smith-Hughes high schools in our county seats—these are prophetic of a new world rounding into form. . . .

"Now these changes—economic, legal, and educational—mean that we who work in Berea today inhabit a world and minister to a world radically different from that in which our predecessors lived, even a score of years ago. Adaptation, which has been the very watchword of Berea, will force upon us changes of emphasis and possible changes of method. . . .

"But, grant all that has been said regarding the changing times, Berea's essential task is changeless. It is this: Within the bounds of our enlarging equipment, to put within the reach of each of those mountain boys and girls who need it most, the opportunity of finding and forming friendships with the best that is in the world; the opportunity of finding one's self in one's work; the opportunity of binding one's self in friendship and in toil to the friendly power behind the world.

"As I understand it, our task is to place the opportunities of which I speak within the reach of the mountain boys and girls of the Southern Appalachians. It is to this work that most of our endowment has been given, and it is to this work that the great majority of our friends and co-workers have dedicated themselves. It would, doubtless, be unwise rigidly and absolutely to exclude from our student body those elements which would help us to cosmopolitanism, but our task concerns primarily and dominantly the mountain people."—President William J. Hutchins, Berea College, 1920. Inaugural Address. Typescript copy in the library of the University of North Carolina.

"The challenge of the South to the Southern State University today is that she show herself worthy of leadership in this great constructive enterprise, this the world's latest attempt to evolve a new and higher civilization. Such a challenge she can meet by no merely perfunctory response. It is for her passionately and reverently to dedicate herself and all of her self to this great task, to set about it, not in the spirit which would discipline men into obedient and unthinking servants of some rigidly preconceived mechanical and authoritative state, which holds the lives and souls of men as mere instruments to its calculated ends;

but in the spirit of the democracy she serves, that spirit which sets men truly free to embody in ever higher and nobler forms the best that is in their hopes and dreams and prayers."—President Harry W. Chase, The University of North Carolina, 1920. *The State University and the New South* (Chapel Hill, N. C., 1920), pp. 57, 58.

"The university is an integral part of the society it serves and it could not, if it would, be oblivious to the necessities of that social order. This is only more obviously and compellingly true of universities which are beholden to the public purse for their financial support than of those which rely largely for their maintenance upon the usufruct of an established economic order. It is in the last analysis essentially true of all. The university must constantly face, and honestly deal with, the changing obligations which arise from shifting circumstance, and it must be particularly sensitive to those requirements of a given era which are especially urgent, as is in our day a more thorough and scientific understanding of the social and economic fundaments of civilization. Society has a right to look to the university for intellectual leadership in all that affects a basic knowledge of man and the university in which he dwells."—President James Rowland Angell, Yale University, 1932. In *The Obligation of Universities to the Social Order*, ed. H. P. Fairchild (New York: New York University Press, 1933), pp. 12, 13.

"Universities have a responsibility to their social order. That responsibility varies from generation to generation, and it varies with the sort of social order they serve. That is, it varies from nation to nation. I am not sure but that it varies regionally within a nation like the United States in very marked and definite ways.

"I cannot resist an illustration of our common lack of realization of this fact. I heard the other day, for example, of the newly elected dean of a graduate school in a State university, located in a poor State confused about its economic life, with a not very intelligent record in government, with a high rate of illiteracy, who announced that it was his conception of the function of that university that it should make itself the last stronghold of the classical learning in America!"—President Samuel P. Capen, The University of Buffalo, 1932. In *The Obligation of Universities to the Social Order*, ed. H. P. Fairchild (New York: New York University Press, 1933), p. 71.

"Persons of high intellectuality and with college training are to be found among those imprisoned for attempts to prey upon society.

"In view of such a situation, . . . the question arises, what can justly be expected from higher education to aid in curing the present ills that afflict the social order. . . . The first approach will have to be made in the field of economics and sociology. . . . The second approach, character education of students, appears to be the task of the faculty collectively and individually."—President George Thomas, The University of Utah, 1934. *Transactions and Proceedings of the National Association of State Universities, 1934.*

"I should be guilty of blindness or cowardice were I not to make some remarks concerning troubles which the University has experienced from so-called political interference. . . . We do not want our institutions to be the spoils of this or that group of self-seeking individuals. I do not need to tell you that many things which have happened out here in the name of politics, have harmed the good name of this University. Those things travel fast and far, growing no less sharp with time or distance. But even so, if all the facts were but known, we should find that other universities have suffered even more than we, from misguided or even malicious political interference. Perhaps in many of these difficulties those operating our universities have themselves been largely to blame, in that they have gone too far away from their primary responsibility for education."—President Lee Paul Sieg, The University of Washington, 1934. Inaugural Address, *Addresses at the Inauguration of Lee Paul Sieg, President of the University of Washington, October 5, 1934.*

"The people of the United States have now entered upon a vast program of social welfare. Social security has become the dominating thought in the minds of our political leaders. In the enthusiasm of the moment, there is danger of much misdirected effort and wasteful expenditure of public funds. The institutions of higher learning have an opportunity that they have never had before in giving the right direction to the whole program of social legislation. Educational administrators everywhere must face this problem squarely and coöperate with the social scientist in the task of making his work rigidly scientific, and institutions of higher learning in the Southwest should take the lead in this movement."—President William B. Bizzell, The University of Oklahoma, 1935. "Higher Education in the Southwest," *Higher Education and Society* (Norman: University of Oklahoma Press, 1936), p. 24.

The Lower Schools
In the East and West

"When so many Professorships have been established in all the other sciences, as well as in literature and the arts; it is truly wonderful to us, that so little attention has been bestowed upon the science of mental culture, and that there is not (as we believe there is not) and never has been, a single Professor of Education on this side of the Atlantic. Will it not be an honor to that college, which shall be the first to supply this deficiency and open a department for the thorough education of teachers?" —The Faculty of Amherst College, 1827. *Two Reports of the Faculty of Amherst College to the Board of Trustees, 1827.* Quoted in L. F. Snow, *The College Curriculum in the United States* (New York: Teachers College, Columbia University, 1907), p. 156.

"It is too obvious to require extended remark that the universal diffusion of the means of common education cannot be accomplished without creating a great demand for education of a higher grade. If a population of five millions of children and young persons are to be taught, we shall need more than an hundred thousand teachers to instruct them. Our common schools will also be almost worthless unless they be well taught. If teachers are ignorant, the office of teacher will soon sink into contempt. Our schools, instead of being filled with every class of society, as they ought to be, will contain only the children of vagrants and mendicants. . . . It is manifest then, that if a system of general education be adopted, it can only be sustained by providing a competent supply of well instructed teachers. . . .

"Such a [common school] system therefore, in order to be in any eminent degree successful, involves the necessity of a class of higher seminaries, seminaries capable of teaching teachers, in other words institutions for professional education."—President Francis Wayland, BrownUniv ersity, 1842. *Thoughts on the Present Collegiate System in the United States* (Boston : Gould, Kendall and Lincoln, 1842), pp. 4, 5.

"What then can the university do for the state? First of all she can form the head and crown of our system of schools, sending her life-giving influence to its remotest fibres. The university should be the great normal school for teachers of high schools, academies and colleges. The university by refusing its degrees and honors to illiterate and unworthy candidates, can not only raise the standard of scholarship in all the schools, but can elevate the professions from the low condition into which they have confessedly fallen. . . . The university in organizing colleges of medicine and law, owes it to the people not merely to instruct the few to heal diseases, and manage suits at law, but to teach the many how to keep well and out of litigation. . . .

"The time is not distant when a Department of Public Health will be established in all universities, which will teach all that can be known as to the causes of epidemics, the sanitary conditions and control of cities, hospitals, asylums, prisons, school buildings, dwellings and all constructions and enclosures. . . ." —President W. W. Folwell, The University of Minnesota, 1869. Inaugural Address. Typescript copy in the library of the University of North Carolina.

"Do not think, because you see the Presidents of Rutgers and

Princeton, and a Professor from Yale, here tonight, that we are come to ask for money for our colleges. I might give you some strong reasons why you should help us, but I forbear. . . . I have come here to ask you to do yourselves the honor to elevate education all through the State of New Jersey; not only to improve your elementary schools, but to establish middle schools and devise a plan to institute High Schools all over the State."—President James McCosh, Princeton University, 1871. Addresses delivered in reference to Free High Schools before the legislature of New Jersey, March 1, 1871. Typescript copy in the library of the University of North Carolina.

"What has been said of needed reformation in methods of teaching the subjects which have already been nominally admitted to the American curriculum applies not only to the University, but to the preparatory schools of every grade down to the primary. The American college is obliged to supplement the American school. Whatever elementary instruction the schools fail to give, the college must supply. The improvement of the schools has of late years permitted the college to advance the grade of its teaching, and adapt the methods of its later years to men instead of boys. This improvement of the college reacts upon the schools to their advantage; and this action and reaction will be continuous. A university is not built in the air, but on social and literary foundations which preceding generations have bequeathed. If the whole structure needs rebuilding, it must be rebuilt from the foundation. Hence, sudden reconstruction is impossible in our high places of education. Such inducements as the College can offer for enriching and enlarging the course of study pursued in preparatory schools, the Faculty has recently decided to give. The requirements in Latin and Greek grammar are to be set at a thorough knowledge of forms and general principles; the lists of classical authors accepted as equivalents for the regular standards are to be enlarged; an acquaintance with physical geography is to be required; the study of elementary mechanics is to be recommended, and prizes are to be offered for reading aloud, and for the critical analysis of passages from English authors. At the same time the University will take to heart the counsel which it gives to others.

"In every department of learning, the University would search out by trial and reflection the best methods of instruction. The University believes in the thorough study of language. It contends for all languages—Oriental, Greek, Latin, Romance, German, and especially for the mother tongue; seeing in them all one institution, one history, one means of discipline, one department of learning. In teaching languages, it is for this American generation to invent, or to accept from abroad, better tools than the old; to devise or to transplant from Europe, prompter and more comprehensive methods than the prevailing, and to command more intelligent labor, in order to gather rapidly and surely the best fruit of that culture and have time for other harvests.

"The University recognizes the natural and physical sciences as indispensable branches of education, and has long acted upon this opinion; but it would have science taught in a rational way, objects and instruments in hand—not from books merely, not through the memory chiefly, but by the seeing eye and the informing fingers. Some of the scientific scoffers at gerund grinding and nonsense verses might well look at home; the prevailing methods of teaching science, the world over, are, on the whole, less intelligent than the methods of teaching language. The University would have scientific studies in school and college and professional school develop and discipline those powers of the mind by which science has been created and is daily nourished—the powers of observation, the inductive faculty, the sober imagination, the sincere and proportionate judgment. A student in the elements gets no such training by studying even a good text-book, though he really master it, nor yet by sitting at the feet of the most admirable lecturer.

"If there be any subject which seems fixed and settled in its educational aspects, it is the mathematics; yet there is no department of the University which has been, during the last fifteen years, in such a state of vigorous experiment upon methods and appliances of teaching as the mathematical department. It would be well if the primary schools had as much faith in the possibility of improving their way of teaching multiplication.

"The important place which history, and mental, moral, and political philosophy, should hold in any broad scheme of education is recognized of all; but none know so well how crude are the prevailing methods of teaching these subjects as those who teach them best. They can not be taught from books alone; but must be vivified and illustrated by teachers of active, comprehensive, and judicial mind. To learn by rote a list of dates is not to study history. Mr. Emerson says that history is biography. In a deep sense this is true. Certainly the best way to impart the facts of history to the young is through the quick interest they take in the lives of the men and women who fill great historical scenes or epitomize epochs. From the centers so established, their interest may be spread over great areas. For the young especially, it is better to enter with intense sympathy into the great moments of history, than to stretch a thin attention through its weary centuries.

"Philosophical subjects should never be taught with authority. They are not established sciences; they are full of disputed matters, and open questions, and bottomless speculations. It is not the function of the teacher to settle philosophical and political controversies for the pupil, or even to recommend to him any one set of opinions as better than another. Exposition, not imposition, of opinions is the professor's part. The student should be made acquainted with all sides of these controversies, with the salient points of each system; he should be shown what is still in force of institutions or philosophies mainly outgrown, and what is new in those now in vogue. The very word education is a standing protest against dogmatic teaching. The notion that education consists in the authoritative inculcation of what the teacher deems true may be logical and appropriate in a convent, or a seminary for priests, but it is intolerable in universities and public schools, from primary to professional. The worthy fruit of academic culture is an open mind, trained to careful thinking, instructed in methods of philosophic investigation, acquainted in a general way with the accumulated thought of past generations, and penetrated with humility. It is thus that the University in our day serves Christ and the church."—President Charles W. Eliot, Harvard University, 1869. In S. E. Morison, *The Development of Harvard University* (Cambridge: Harvard University Press, 1930), pp. lx, lxiii. Also in *School and Society*, March 22, 1924.

"Every town in Connecticut has the right to establish a high school that desires to do it. In a few towns we have admirable high schools. Those in Hartford and Norwich rank high. There are other high schools, but they are restricted to our larger cities and towns. What we need there is a school for a region, to which boys from villages may come as well as from the cities. It is to small towns and villages that we shall have to direct attention; for something must be done for those young men in the manufacturing villages who are trained in our popular schools to go forward. It is clearly a question whether we had better have a few strong high schools, or to diffuse them all over the State? Another point is, that State supervision and local exertion should go together. If alone, we are likely to have what we do not want; but combined, State control and local interests, with the watchfulness of parties, will secure a system that cannot fail to exalt the people."—Professor D. C. Gilman, Yale University, 1871. Addresses delivered in reference to Free High Schools before the legislature of New Jersey, March 1, 1871. Typescript copy in the library of the University of North Carolina.

"I believe with Dr. McCosh that we should, in some way, make education compulsory. How that is to be effected may be left now out of consideration; but we shall be able to take counsel together and devise means to carry out the object. It is with me a settled opinion that either indirectly or directly, every child of this State should be forced into attending school; and no person should be permitted to go to the polls who could not read and write. . . .

"The Board of Education have proposed, and the Governor concurs, that the schools should be free. There are fifteen hundred schools in the State, seven hundred of which are free; and it seems to me that it would be a great thing to make them all free. (Cheers) If you will do this, you will never be afraid to look a Jerseyman, who is a true patriot, in the face. When this is done, a great desire for knowledge will spring up in the minds of the rising generation, and wise legislators will meet the wants as they come."—President W. H. Campbell, Rutgers University, 1871. Addresses delivered in reference to Free High Schools before the legislature of New Jersey, March 1, 1871. Typescript copy in the library of the University of North Carolina.

"At the moment there is nothing which seems to me so important, in this region, and indeed in the entire land, as the promotion of good secondary schools, preparatory to the universities . . . every large town should have an efficient academy or high school; and men of wealth can do no greater service to the public than by liberally encouraging, in their various places of abode, the advanced instruction of the young."—President Daniel Coit Gilman, The Johns Hopkins University, 1876. *Inaugural Address* (Baltimore: John Murphy and Company, 1876), p. 59.

"As regards our system of instruction at large in the public schools, it seems to me that more instruction should be given in general history, especially through political biography and in the history of our own country."—President Andrew D. White, Cornell University, 1878. "Political Education," *Report of Commissions to the Paris Universal Exposition, 1878*, p. 371.

"But it is urged that the supporting of these schools will be virtually taxing one part of the community to benefit another. The answer is at hand. The whole community receives the project by a highly-educated people being trained. The High

Schools should be so located and furnished that all have access to them, the poor as well as the rich, and the rich as well as the poor. . . . But then it is said that we are rearing too many educated men. I simply deny that this is so."—President James McCosh, Princeton University, 1880. *Proceedings of the National Education Association, 1880.*

"Among all this great multitude of educational institutions, not one seems to have made education the subject of investigation, or to have regarded instruction in the theory or practice of education as a part of its business. . . . No body of professional men is in position to exert a more powerful influence upon the destinies of the race than that of educators; and yet no body of men are left more completely to accident for the attainment of the qualifications which may properly fit them for the discharge of their important functions. . . .

"The educational system of the country will, however, never be what it ought to be until education is made a profession, . . . and such a state of things cannot be possible until instrumentalities exist for regularly training men to this profession. It appears to the undersigned that the time has come when Columbia College may very properly make an attempt to supply the serious defect in the educational system of our country which has here been indicated. A department embracing the history, theory, and practice of education, . . . would bring the College more directly, and to more effective purpose, into contact with the outside world than almost any other."—President F. A. P. Barnard, Columbia College, 1881. *Report for 1880-1881.* Quoted in *The Rise of A University*, Vol. I, ed. William F. Russell (New York: Columbia University Press, 1937), pp. 289, 293, 294.

"We need, then, secondary schools of high rank, with courses of study extending about midway up the average college course, as the foundation for the genuine university."—President W. W. Folwell, The University of Minnesota, 1884. *Education*, January, 1884.

"The secondary school, then, I hold, should not be a mere isolated nomad, an educational island. It should be in quite definite relations to other institutions of the same and of higher rank.

"It should not be a mere servant of the colleges. It should be a coördinate part of a definitely organized system, with a voice in important questions of mutual interest. Teachers in such schools should have academic recognition as of a high grade of dignity. Perhaps if these more intimate relations between the preparatory school and the college should be formed, there would be fewer instances of the startling drop which students sometimes experience now, when they pass from the hands of the skillful and learned teacher of the fitting school into those of the callow college tutor.

"These are mere outline suggestions. But I am convinced that when the American Federation of Colleges and Secondary Schools is formed, it will be found that the colleges are enormously strengthened, fitting schools are lifted and energized, and that no boy or girl will be kept out of college because at some time he has unconsciously shunted on a side track that leads away from anywhere. It will be found that in union there is strength."—President H. P. Judson, The University of Chicago, 1894. "The Relation of the Secondary School to the College," *Williams College Centennial Anniversary, 1793-1893*. Cambridge, Massachusetts, 1894.

"To secure unquestioned recognition a secondary school should have at least three things:

"1. Well arranged courses of study, the last four years of which are devoted chiefly to Latin, Greek, French, German, English, history, algebra, geometry, and science.

"2. A sufficient number of well-trained teachers.

"3. Sufficient equipment, consisting of a library, suitable rooms, and a laboratory or laboratories.

"In many places music, drawing, manual training, bookkeeping, gymnastics, etc., are added. These are desirable additions, but provision for proper instruction in the nine subjects mentioned above is enough to establish a valid claim to the title of secondary school. A number of questions may reasonably be asked as to these essentials.

"1. Is it necessary that the courses be always four years long? May they not be six or three years long? I would answer yes to both questions. Some private or church fitting schools give courses six years long, but they generally take boys at about ten years of age and give some studies of elementary grade. On the other hand some fairly good high schools have courses only three years long, but in such cases until proof of excellence is furnished the presumption is always against them.

"2. Is it essential that both Latin and Greek should be taught? May not one or even both of them be left out? And may not modern languages be omitted? Is it absolutely necessary to teach science? Some schools of respectable quality do not teach Greek. A few of unquestionable merit omit both Latin and Greek. Many of them omit modern languages and some teach no science at all. But the question how much may be omitted without sacrifice of title is like the question how many limbs may be removed from a man without loss of life. Most of our universities in their lists of approved schools include some that have courses only three years long, and many that teach no Greek and many again that leave out modern languages; but most of these schools are struggling forward and will in a few years repair their temporary defects. With hundreds of high schools and academies that meet fully the essentials as stated above, and with a constant tendency towards this standard on the part of even the defective, I dare not set the definition lower. Chicago alone has fourteen high schools that more than meet the terms of the definition, and they have enrolled over 8,000 pupils. For sufficient reason, we all know how to make exceptions to any rule or definition.

"Many of our secondary schools teach political economy, and in the elementary grades civil government has become a characteristic. I would that in both subjects the instruction could be so broadened as to include something of social ethics. In my opinion it is highly important to teach carefully the duties of life that arise from its greater relations—such duties as come from the relations of parent and child, husband and wife, neighbor and neighbor, citizen and municipality, citizen and state, corporation and general public, etc. . . .

"As a result of personal experience let me plead for a larger use in our secondary schools of the library and laboratory, and for a wider reading of the masterpieces of English and American literature, with a minimum of talk on the part of the instructor. In my opinion the best teacher of literature is one whose head and heart are full of the subject and whose mouth is prone to silence. There is a tendency to launch small portions of literature upon a stream of teachers' talk. In the presence of the masterpieces of our literature the wisest and best of us should let our words be few. If facts about science be the aim, a text-book with a few experiments at the lecture counter far excels the laboratory, but the laboratory cultivates habits of mind that in the range of studies are of greater importance than any number of scientific facts. A library in charge of a librarian should be recognized as an essential part in every secondary school. The librarian should do nothing but keep the books and help the pupils in their investigations. The library is the laboratory and the librarian the laboratory assistant for work in language, literature and history."—President R. H. Jesse, The University of Missouri, 1896. "What Constitutes a College and What a Secondary School," *The School Review*, May, 1896.

"I personally believe that the course of study which is best for the fortunate children whose education is to be prolonged beyond the age of eighteen years of age, is also the best for those children whose education is, unfortunately, to stop at eighteen. I do not believe there is the least distinction between the best thing for one set of children, and the best thing for another set. I believe the great sin in our public high schools is that they give an inferior course of instruction to those children whose education is to be the shortest. But, accepting the statement that there should be nothing taught in the secondary schools which is not placed there in their own interest, I must protest against the proposition that it is more important for the secondary school to connect itself with the elementary school than with the higher institutions. I believe that to be an absolutely fatal error, just exactly as I think it is a fatal error in the individual if he does not look up, and not down—if he does not seek his inspiration from above himself. Can any proposition be plainer than that in a school we must always look upward? Shall we not follow Emerson's advice and hitch our wagon to a star, and not to a bowlder by the roadside that has not moved for millions of years. Practically, what has been the source of improvements in education, here in the United States, for the last two generations? It is fifty years since Agassiz landed here. Where did laboratory teaching begin? Who brought into this country the method of studying zoölogy by observation and experiment? Louis Agassiz. Who did the same service for botany? Asa Gray, whose honorable name has been already mentioned here this morning. From what institutions have come the superior methods of teaching Latin and Greek within the last twenty-five years? (1872-1897). Those languages have been taught in American secondary schools ever since the Boston Latin School and the Roxbury Latin School were founded in the seventeenth century; but where did the improved methods come from? From the colleges, and the colleges only. Who started the method of reading at sight? Who produced books designed to encourage it? The classical department at Harvard College. Where are you who teach geometry, getting today the inspiration for the right mode of teaching it? Geometry is one of the oldest and most important subjects of human instruction; but who introduced that method of teaching geometry which requires something more than the committal to memory of a series of propositions—which demands that the pupil learn to originate or invent something himself? The mathematical and physical departments of Harvard University, taken together. Who have been most active, most energetic, most hopefully successful in developing the teaching of history in the United

States? The college professors. Who have written the best books for teaching history? The college graduates. You cannot mention a subject of instruction in the secondary schools in which the inspiration to better teaching has not come out of the universities in this country and in Europe. I submit, then, that it is for us to hold firmly to the conviction that the way to improve the secondary schools of the United States is to cling closely to the colleges and universities, and to multiply the points of contact between schools and colleges. And I will add that the way to improve the elementary schools is to associate them closely with the secondary schools, and to correlate, at every point where it is possible to, the work of those two departments. By and by we shall find out that all these distinctions between grades in education are in the highest degree artificial; and there should be but one aim, one method, and one system throughout the entire course of education."—President Charles W. Eliot, Harvard University, 1897. "Secondary School and College," *Educational Review*, May, 1897.

"I go on to speak definitely of the effect which the high school, viewed as the school of the community, is actually producing upon the higher education. The effect is distinctly manifest in these three points:

"It is introducing a new and valuable constituency into our colleges and universities. . . .

"The two active causes which send students to college are opportunity and incentive. Opportunity represents those who could not otherwise go. Incentive represents those who would not otherwise go. The high school, as the school of the community, stands in an increasing degree for both opportunity and incentive. It is distributing these active causes over a wider and wider area. It is putting them at work in all localities, avoiding waste, and ensuring contact.

"In some cases the high school acts as an incentive simply by taking the place of some other incentive. Those who are reached in this way I do not reckon among the new constituency. The new constituency consists of those to whom the high school stands for opportunity, and the only opportunity. Our colleges are becoming, therefore, through the agency of the high school, more and more representative of the entire population. They have always been democratic: they are now becoming thoroughly representative. Through the gateway of the locality the sons of every race, and religion and occupation, find the natural path to the college. . . .

"A second effect produced by the high school, the school of the community, has been the broadening of the scope of the higher education—at least the college curriculum. The old-time relation of the college to the secondary school was that of an accepted domination. The secondary school was assumed to exist not only for the college, but to perpetuate the traditional academic system. What the college said ought to be taught, was taught, and without question. The subject matter of the new education found its way into the college partly from above, through the investigations carried on in the universities, and partly from below, through the growing demands of the high schools which could not ignore the educational conditions out of which they were born. . . .

"And the last result of the expansion of the high school has been a corresponding widening of the door of entrance, at least at Harvard. The new system of admission to Harvard virtually makes allowance for all subjects which are well taught in the high schools. It has always been the contention of President Eliot—I think it a just contention—that no courses can be framed for our high schools, which may be supposed to fit for 'life,' which can on the whole do that work so well, as the very courses which fit for college; and further that it is unfair to introduce short and disconnected courses, which must throw a scholar off the line, or bring him to a pause, provided he afterward wishes to take a college course. . . .

"A third possible effect of the high school upon the higher education is to be deprecated. I refer to the tendency to place the graduates of the high school at once under professional training. The high school has been so far advanced that it meets the requirements of some professional schools. But if the graduate of the high school can be admitted to the professional school, it by no means follows that he can afford to take the privilege. The professional school may care only for technical qualifications. The man himself has other interests at stake. He has before him the privilege of being an educated man, as well as of being a technically trained man. The question is not, can he satisfy his profession, but can he satisfy himself, and those larger requirements of society which are not bounded by one's profession or business. I know the reply—'One cannot afford the time; the process is too long. The high school delivers to the college at nineteen, the college to the professional at twenty-three, the professional school into the world at twenty-six, or later if one is to be a specialist. That is more time than one can afford.' With privilege of making an exception, I must deny the premise. As Horace Greeley replied to the man who demanded a job of him, on the ground that he must live—'that' said Mr. Greeley, 'remains to be proven'."—President W. J. Tucker, Dartmouth College, 1898. "The Relation of the High School to the Higher Education," *Education*, June, 1898.

"The fact that it is head of the public-school system gives the state university opportunities that have to be acquired by private colleges. Moreover this fact justifies state institutions in expending money to widen the circle of their conscious influence, whereas private institutions would naturally hesitate to encounter the outlay. For a liberal outlay of money, be it understood, is indispensable. Perhaps this paper would be most useful, if, without discussing further the general proposition, I point out some ways in which state universities may best exercise conscious influence upon the schools below them.

"In the first place, in justice to secondary education, the university should not maintain a preparatory department. It is idle to quibble on this subject. A university that maintains a preparatory department does deep wrong to every secondary school in its commonwealth. The best thing it can do for itself and for the commonwealth is to strangle its preparatory department. . . .

"In popular estimation the highest evidence of success is a large enrollment. It takes some courage therefore to abolish preparatory courses and to demand for admission to every department a high-school diploma. If this be done suddenly, the inevitable result will be a large reduction in enrollment. Numbers of students that apply for admission must be sent back home. These malcontents spread dissatisfaction in their respective neighborhoods, which brings great peril to the institution. No wise man would in a year abolish preparatory courses and require for admission to every department of the university a high school diploma. This would be courting disaster. But there is no reason why within a space of ten years any university may not abolish its preparatory courses and so raise the standards in every department, that at the end of the decade good high-school training shall be necessary for admission. . . .

"The whole system of public instruction should be articulated. Naturally the university should approach first the high schools. These, when articulated with the university, become agents for them. Every high school should sustain to the elementary schools about it a relation similar to that which the university sustains to the high schools. This proposition will not be disputed. It may be profitable perhaps to examine the various ways of articulating the high schools with the state universities. . . .

"What authority should the state university have over the high schools? In my opinion it should have none. In New York the Board of Regents exercises considerable control over all secondary education. In Minnesota the Board of Education, consisting of three persons, largely controls the public high school. The chairman of this board is President Northrop. The high-school teachers are not allowed in New York to grade the papers of the students applying for graduation. This is done through the board. Now to my mind this necessarily implies distrust of the schools and exaltation of that very questionable thing known as examinations. The teachers of the high schools are trusted to instruct the pupils but not to examine them. If they are competent to do that which is greater, should they not be held competent to do that which is less? In Missouri the University has no control whatever over secondary schools, public or private. We should regard the acquisition of such power as a serious obstacle to our work. We have now the privilege of visiting these schools, of helping them, advising them, of quarrelling with them in gentlemanly manner, and of loving them sincerely. We have the privilege of spending thousands of dollars per annum in promoting their interests, chiefly through the agency of the examiner and the summer school. This is sufficient for our purpose. More would be a hindrance."—President R. H. Jesse, The University of Missouri, 1900. "The Influence of the State University on the Public School," *School Review*, October, 1900.

"So long as no university existed, in the strict meaning of the word, all institutions of higher learning belonged to the same class; nor was the line drawn between these institutions and institutions of a lower class, known as academies and preparatory schools. But since in these last years institutions having the real character of universities have been established, it is inevitable that these in time will differentiate themselves from the college, and the college will in time differentiate itself from the academy."—President William Rainey Harper, The University of Chicago, 1902. "The Trend of University and College Education in the United States," *North American Review*, April, 1902.

"That every boy, on reaching the age of twelve or thirteen, should receive an education of the same type, seems to me, to say the least, a very doubtful proposition. I think that there are some boys with whom it is desirable that the technical education should follow the primary education just as speedily as possible; boys with whom the stimulus of earning a living is the one educational force which can be made very effective. To say that we should meet the needs of these boys if we only had a varied secondary education arranged for their several aptitudes seems to me really an evasion of the point. If you so extend the meaning of secondary education as to include bricklaying, you can appeal to some boys who are interested in bricklaying and in nothing else; but you have so widened the term 'secondary education' as to make it little more than an unmeaning symbol."—President Arthur T. Hadley, Yale University, 1902. *School Review*, December, 1902.

"From certain approved tendencies in the high-school education of today we may, in some degree, forecast the high-school education of the future. It is plain, to begin with, that broadening of the horizon of human knowledge will still further widen the scope of the high school. With the greater attention to the individuality of students characteristic of all educational advance, this means still greater range of elasticity in courses of study, with still further diminution of prescribed work. It will clearly appear that there is no reason why a group of young men and women of the same age should take the same studies, or that, even in secondary instruction, there is any one subject which is for all persons and at all times fundamental to mental development."—President David Starr Jordan, Leland Stanford Junior University, 1904. *The Educational Review*, September, 1904.

"The higher education of any country depends upon the lower. Consequently it is a matter of great satisfaction to observe that during the last half century public schools have been introduced in every state of the union, and that the education of the people in primary and secondary schools is everywhere provided for. The great problem what to do for the Negro race still exercises the minds of wise and thoughtful people."—President Daniel Coit Gilman, The Johns Hopkins University, 1906. "Remembrances," *The Launching of A University* (New York: Dodd, Mead and Company, 1906), p. 154.

"The real grievance of the secondary schools is not at all as it is usually stated to be; it is quite different and very real. What is needed is adequate provision by which students who have completed any serious curriculum in a secondary school may go on to more advanced study of something for which their school training has fitted them. This is quite a different thing from saying that any study which the secondary school chooses to introduce should be counted as the equivalent of any other in estimating the qualifications of candidates for admission to college. Most of the students who wish to go to college on terms of their own making do not really wish to go to college at all; they wish to go to some kind of institution that will give them serious systematic and scientific training of a kind that will lead them to gain mastery over the elements of a given vocation. Such students do not want a college education; they want vocational training, and it goes without saying that the education system of the country ought to make provision for them."—President Nicholas Murray Butler, Columbia University, 1911. *Annual Report of the President, Columbia University, 1910-11*, p. 52.

"It seems to me that the great problem which confronts preparatory schools as well as the colleges today is to make the work seem real and worth while to the student, and after making the work seem worth while, to see that it is done in a way that gives the student thorough training. American students today do not approach the classroom in the right spirit, and far too many of them endeavor to select easy courses and to slide through. I doubt whether we can return to the old drill method of twenty or thirty years ago. I believe our present problem is to select subjects which are worthwhile and real, and which will function somewhere in the life of the student and then to give it to them in a way which will demand thorough preparation and first-class drill on their part."—President R. M. Hughes, Miami University, 1915. "Plea for Thoroughness," *Journal of Education*, September, 1915.

"It is quite easy to point out changes that might be made in secondary school. It is not so easy, however, to justify them and show they are necessary and possible.

"Outside of New England and to an increasing degree in New

England, college preparation occurs in publicly supported high schools. These high schools must minister to the needs of the community that supports them. Any particular emphasis laid upon a special course because it prepares for college is unfair to the great mass of students who do not expect to enter a higher institution of learning.

"The greatest change needed is one that will better adjust college requirements to high school needs. College education is, after all, only more education. The high school should in all its courses, give enough academic knowledge to make it possible for a student who completes the high school course to profit by more education in some college or university. Institutions of higher learning need to go further than they have in adjusting their work to the preparation that the high school gives. It should be as easy to pass from the high school to college as it is to pass from the grammar school to the high school.

"What is needed most in college work is the ability to study and the alertness of mind that comes from proper high school training. It is probable that most secondary schools could improve their product by requiring harder work from their pupils, and particularly by giving them more definite instructions in methods of study."—President R. J. Aley, The University of Maine, 1915. "Adjust College Requirements," *Journal of Education*, September, 1915.

"It is best not to use the words preparatory school at all or get into the habit of thinking what the use of that term implies. The secondary school should not be merely a preparatory school, but should stand upon its own feet and do the work appropriate to the age of its students and to the environment in which they live.

"In many ways and from many points of view, secondary school training has mightily improved in the last generation. This is particularly true of the high schools, which are public high schools. This improvement, however, has been accompanied by certain weaknesses which are perhaps due to the rapid development of secondary education and to the period of educational transition through which we have been passing. One cannot help noticing the waste of time and the waste of energy in secondary education that are due to attempting to cover too many subjects and to gain a little knowledge about many things instead of centering attention upon a few important subjects and gaining the discipline and knowledge which come from something approaching mastery of them. . . .

"College admission examinations show that secondary school teaching in the modern European languages is painfully inefficient. A boy or girl of high school age ought to be taught four things: to observe, to record, to compare, and to express. The secondary school graduate who comes to college having learned to do these four things fairly well, will find no difficulty in meeting the most rigorous demands of a college course.

"In regard to the present insistent interest in vocational training, it may be said that the earlier a pupil is turned toward a specific vocation, the more likely he is to remain a mediocrity in it as well. The chances of success are far greater for the pupil who can postpone somewhat his preparation for a particular vocation and can acquire adequate knowledge and adequate discipline with which to pursue it."—President Nicholas Murray Butler, Columbia University, 1915. "Teach Four Things," *Journal of Education*, September 16, 1915.

"There is one important educational enterprise in which I trust I may be successful in arousing the interest of the entire state; that of promoting the more effective training of teachers for rural schools. The next generation of men and women of Montana will be made up largely of those who will come from the farms of the state. To provide for the farm boys and girls of the present the soundest and broadest common-school education is a solemn responsibility which may not be shirked."—Chancellor E. C. Elliott, The University of Montana, 1916. *School and Society*, June, 1916.

"To confer, as we do, the diploma in school or college, solely for an accumulation of credits for courses, inevitably means disregard of the correlation of the knowledge acquired and neglect of the result of the whole education on the mind of the pupil. He need not have pursued any subject long enough to learn it, but may have made up the required number of credits out of heterogeneous fragments; his store of knowledge may resemble an intellectual junk shop—largely perishable at that. In the cards actually sent in by applicants for admission to college, the elements that go to make up the high school course include, in addition to commercial courses, credits for such subjects as the following: spelling, public-speaking, debating, glee club, orchestra, band, declamation, elocution, expression, dramatic art, physical training, gymnastics and football. Good in themselves, they are but by-products or extra curriculum activities rather than a proper integral part of a sound secondary education. In one case that I saw, the high school record consisted, besides four years of English, of a couple of years Spanish; some algebra; a little plane geometry; one year each of American history, general science, chemistry, commercial arithmetic and bookkeeping; a year and a half manual training, glee club running through three years; and one year of 'quartette.' That is, of course, an extreme case, but the same defect occurs in a lesser degree in many school records. In the colleges some sort of order exists, no doubt, at the present time—less, so far as I can gather, in the public schools."—President A. Lawrence Lowell, Harvard University, 1920. At the inauguration of President Harry W. Chase, of the University of North Carolina, 1920. *The State University and the New South* (Chapel Hill, N. C., 1920), pp. 27, 28.

"The state university is going to find a place in the hearts of the people of the state and it is going to find a place among the public school people when it starts out to render some service and to have some connections with them."—President M. G. Neale, The University of Idaho, 1934. *Transactions and Proceedings of the National Association of State Universities, 1934.*

In the South

"Normal schools [he said] have been brought into some disrepute among the better class of educators. Too many of them attempt a task at once useless and impossible. They try to teach methods to people who know nothing else. They undertake to fit uneducated people to give instruction to others.

"Good methods are of immense value to any teacher; but brains and knowledge are of more importance still. The blind cannot lead the blind, even when a lamp is furnished to guide their feet. Mere methods resemble a system of dry aqueducts and empty conduits which irrigate nothing. It is only when fullness of knowledge like a fountain of living water pours and pulsates through them that the desert blossoms as a garden and bud and fruit crown the verdure. . . ."—President W. P. Johnston, Louisiana State University, *ca.* 1881. Quoted in W. L. Fleming, *Louisiana State University, 1860-1896* (Baton Rouge: Louisiana State University Press, 1936), p. 402.

"The limit of culture in public schools has not been reached until the ability of the community to pay for such improvement and expansion has been carried to its utmost. Universal education is the only secure basis for any commonwealth to rest on that is controlled by universal suffrage."—President George T. Winston, The University of Texas, 1896. *Proceedings of the Association of Colleges and Preparatory Schools of the Southern States, 1896*, pp. 11-12.

"To the honor of the South be it said, that the southern states are not avoiding, but are inviting, discussion of this most urgent question, the establishment of a well-defined system of secondary schools throughout the southern states. What ten years ago required courage to broach, is now being agitated by our southern educators and our ablest writers."—President Jerome H. Raymond, The University of West Virginia, 1899. "Secondary Schools—The Need of the South," *North Carolina Journal of Education*, February, 1899, p. 21.

"No two schools can be made alike in all details, nor is such uniformity desirable; but it is the hope of the Committee that what has been given will serve as an aid for the reconstruction and enrichment of many school programs."—Chancellor James H. Kirkland, Vanderbilt University, 1899. "Report of the Committee on Program of Studies for Preparatory Schools," *Proceedings of the Association of Colleges and Preparatory Schools of the Southern States*, 1899, p. 23.

"It is tolerably evident, to the observant and interested teacher, that, for many years to come, the preparation of pupils for college, in our state at least must be done largely by the graded schools, or not done at all. . . . All that the colleges would have a right to ask, or would be disposed to ask, in the way of fitting for their courses, would naturally be within the scope of any high school curriculum worthy of the name. . . . All that is needed is a correct understanding and appreciation of the situation, and a reasonable willingness to accommodate ourselves to it. . . . The matter of foremost necessity is to induce the colleges to take the first step; the schools will not need to be persuaded to follow."—President F. C. Woodward, South Carolina College, 1899. "The Correlation of Colleges and Preparatory Schools," *Proceedings of the Association of Colleges and Preparatory Schools of the Southern States, 1899*, pp. 56, 63.

"A four months primary school for the children of North Carolina is a pitiful and inadequate ideal. . . . Our ideal should be an eight months school, aided by as generous a general tax as possible, and supplemented by local taxation."—President Edwin A. Alderman, The University of North Carolina, 1899. "Four Things To Do," *North Carolina Journal of Education*, November, 1899.

"Now, as to the specific modes in which a university can be useful to the schools. The first is the supplying of trained, efficient teachers. Of course you will admit this, and many may think the matter simple and easy and that all universities do this. 'What else are they for except to grind out teachers,'. . .

Yes, let the machine grind out teachers, but let them be good teachers, broad and strong, prepared in the branches which they are expected to teach and with some training in pedagogical methods. These men will do much, if filled with the university spirit, to impart breadth and vigor to the schools. New and improved methods and a general intellectual inspiration will be thus transmitted from the large centers of learning and will permeate the state. The omnipresence of university students in the French and German schools has much to do with their excellence and with their progressive spirit. The first aid to the schools from the university, then, is a careful selection of the teachers and a due preparation of them for their work.

"A second important method of building up the schools is by occasional examination or inspection of them by the university officials. This is not always practicable in the strictest sense with our mixed system of public and private schools. In some of the newer states the practice has been introduced with success. If managed with tact and wisdom it can only be beneficial to both parties. . . .

"In the third place, the university can be of great assistance to the schools by counsel and guidance. This may be shown in the matter of advice as to the entrance examinations. Circulars of information concerning these should be frequently distributed among the schools; due notice of increased requirements given; special and typical examinations published. Often special directions as to how students may be prepared for these examinations are helpful. . . .

"Again occasional conferences of the school teachers with one another, and with the professors of the university, develop a mutual helpfulness and esteem. Questions which might produce friction are more easily settled, misunderstandings are straightened out, and each learns to respect in the other whatever there is in his character of the true ministry of service.

"I cannot close without touching upon that very important question which has produced much friction between schools and colleges, namely, the admission of immature and unprepared men into the university to the detriment of the schools. In the first place, only a complete system of schools equalized as to standard and character of instruction can insure a class entering the university without conditions. Such a system does not exist in a single southern state. . . .

"Many excellent schools carry their students well beyond the entrance requirements of the university. For this they deserve all praise and every encouragement, and for such work their students should receive credit on examination. But I doubt whether the schoolmen realize that the university is between the upper and the nether stone, and there is much danger of its courses being seriously ground down. While the preparatory schools are developing and extending their courses and making every effort to retain their students a year or so longer, the professional schools are prolonging their courses, and so necessitating a shortening of the academic course or the absorption of too large a proportion of the span of life in the preparation for entering upon its work. If the schools keep the young man until he is eighteen, and the college takes four more years, and the professional school four more, then he will not be ready to start upon his work until he is twenty-six. Few can afford to wait so long, and the proposition is seriously and openly made in Chicago, New York, and elsewhere to cut the college course down two years. I only mention this matter to show that unselfish consideration for one another and coöperation with one another is necessary for all who are concerned in the training of the youth of the land for the high duties of citizenship."—President F. P. Venable, The University of North Carolina, 1900. "The Relation of the University to the Preparatory Schools," *Proceedings of the Southern Education Association, 1900*, pp. 71-74.

"The ground upon which public education rests is not that of charity, in any form. . . . It is, however, based on the facts that property is created and enhanced by legislation; that legislation is in turn stimulated, supported, and encouraged by intelligence; that intelligence, to be effective, must be universal;

that public education directed and supported in whole or in part by taxation, is the only available means of cultivating universal intelligence. . . . The state educates, therefore, not as a favor or in discharge of any obligation to the individual, but for its own protection and perpetuity, an educated citizenship being essential."—President James K. Powers, The University of Alabama, 1901. "Presidential Address," *Proceedings of the Association of Colleges and Preparatory Schools of the Southern States, 1901*, pp. 7, 8.

"The children of the Southern States have a right to as good training as the children of the other states in this wonderful democracy. Local taxation is the historic method by which advanced communities have secured for their children a nine months' school taught by a trained teacher in a good schoolhouse."—President Edwin A. Alderman, Tulane University, 1902. "The Child and the State," *Proceedings of the Fifth Conference for Education in the South, 1902*, p. 62.

"In the Southwestern field our great purpose has been to arouse an irresistable public opinion for the establishment and maintenance of a system of schools adequate for the needs of a free people. . . . The first achievement of this public opinion will be the appropriation of sufficient money for such schools. This money may be obtained by state appropriation, by local taxation and community effort, and by parish and county boards."—President Edwin A. Alderman, Tulane University, 1903. "The Southwestern Field," *Annals of the American Academy of Political and Social Science*, XXII (1903), 287.

"Looking at the situation in the South, what do we find? No well articulated system of education—universities, colleges, and high schools all competing for the same grade of student. . . . The first thing to be done is to complete the work of this association—to make a hard and fast line between the high school and the college so that there shall be no overlapping here."—President R. E. Blackwell, Randolph-Macon College, 1910.

"Necessity for Conservation of Educational Energy in the South," *Proceedings of the Association of Colleges and Preparatory Schools of the Southern States, 1910*, p. 39.

"The task immediately before us is the development of a reasonable system of certification. . . . Our requirements for admission need further amendment in the near future."—Chancellor James H. Kirkland, Vanderbilt University, 1912. "The Past and Future Work of the Southern Association," *Proceedings of the Association of Colleges and Preparatory Schools of the Southern States, 1912*, pp. 45, 46.

"From an educational standpoint the most vital need of Arkansas today is an efficient system of rural schools—schools where teachers whose impulses throb with the life of the present train the children in such a way as really to prepare them to live and take their places in the society for which they are destined."—President John C. Futrall, The University of Arkansas, 1915. *University of Arkansas Bulletin*, February, 1915.

"There is pretty general agreement, however, that the high school studies should all be such as to command the pupil's real interest, and what we call vocational subjects awaken interest in many cases where disciplinary subjects, like mathematics, fail to find much response."—President W. G. Frost, Berea College, 1915. "Studies to Command Interest," *Journal of Education*, September, 1915.

"The modern preparatory school is a wonderfully fine institution so far as organization is concerned. It offers a wide range of subject matter, and employs, in theory, efficient instructors. The institution responds readily to the demand of the people, more so than does the college, or even the primary school.

"The high school has its handicaps just as the college does. To set up new ideas and put them into operation, requires a change in teachers in order to secure efficiency. The high school too often introduces a subject or a method without having a teacher who understands the idea. . . . In the effort to make public education more practical, we are handicapped with teachers who attempt to teach as they were taught. The public school, both elementary and high, is striving to become practical, to meet the real needs of the people.

"A sort of industrial work has been put into the schools; science has been made prominent; business education is being emphasized, and less and less emphasis is laid upon classical studies. There is too much scholasticism in the public schools, and too much in the colleges, but it cannot be suddenly reduced. There is too much education through talk and book, and too little in doing. These are criticisms."—President J. W. Cantrell, Oklahoma Agricultural and Mechanical College, 1915. "Make It Practical," *Journal of Education*, September, 1915.

The Education of Women

"Among the advantages which seem to be involved in the system . . . are the following:

"1. Economy of means and forces. . . . If separate establishments were attempted for ladies, affording the same advantages, the outlay in men and means would have to be duplicated; or, as would often happen, the force would have to be divided and the advantages as well.

"2. Convenience to the patrons of the school. It has been a matter of interest with us to note the number of cases in which a brother is accompanied or followed by a sister, or a sister by a brother.

"3. Another advantage we find in the wholesome incitements to study which the system affords.

"4. Again, the social culture which is incidental to the system is a matter of no small importance.

"5. Closely connected with this influence is the tendency to good order which we find in the system.

"6. Nor can it be reasonably doubted that the arrangement tends to good order and morality in the town outside of the schools.

"7. Another manifest advantage is in the relations of the

school to the community—a cordial feeling of good will and the advance of that antagonism between town and college which in general belongs to the history of universities and colleges. The absence of disorder in the school is the prime condition of this good feeling; but beyond this, the constitution of the school is so similar to that of the community that any conflict is unnatural. . . .

"8. It can hardly be doubted that young people educated under such condition are kept in harmony with society at large, and are prepared to appreciate the responsibilities of life, and to enter upon its work.

"These are among the disadvantages of the system which have forced themselves upon our attention. . . .

"1. Have young ladies the ability in mental vigor and bodily health to maintain a fair standing in the class with young men? . . .

"I answer, where there has been the same preparatory training, we find no difference in ability to maintain themselves in the recitation room. . . .

"A breaking down in health does not appear to be more frequent than with young men."—President James H. Fairchild, Oberlin College, 1868. *American Journal of Education*, January, 1868.

"The attitude of the University in the prevailing discussions touching the education and fit employments of women demands brief explanation. America is the natural arena for these debates; for here the female sex has a better past and a better present than elsewhere. Americans, as a rule, hate disabilities of all sorts, whether religious, political, or social. Equality between the sexes, without privilege or oppression on either side, is the happy custom of American homes. While this great discussion is going on, it is the duty of the University to maintain a cautious and expectant policy. The Corporation will not receive women as students into the College proper, nor into any school whose discipline requires residence near the school. The difficulties involved in a common residence of hundreds of young men and women of immature character and marriageable age are very grave. The necessary police regulations are exceedingly burdensome. The Corporation are not influenced to this decision, however, by any notions about the innate capacities of women. The world knows next to nothing about the natural mental capacities of the female sex."—President Charles W. Eliot, Harvard University, 1869. Inaugural Address, in S. E. Morison, *The Development of Harvard University* (Cambridge: Harvard University Press, 1930), p. lxx.

"If women had not been cheaper than men, they would not have replaced nine-tenths of the men in the American public schools. . . . The superiority of men to women, or of women to men, has nothing to do with the matter now at hand. That frequent changes of teachers should result from having nine-tenths of the teachers women is a necessary consequence of two stubborn facts: first, that women have not the physical endurance of men, and secondly, that the great majority of female teachers stop teaching at marriage, an event which does not stop a man's teaching. . . . It is quite unnecessary to this argument to undervalue the work of women in schools. . . . This protest is directed against the excessive employment of women, into which towns have been let from motives of false economy."—President Charles W. Eliot, Harvard University, 1875. *New England Journal of Education*, May 29, 1875.

"Whatever may be the fate of the present suggestion [to open Columbia College to women], the undersigned cannot permit himself to doubt that the time will yet come when the propriety and wisdom of this measure will be fully recognized; and, as he believes that Columbia College is destined in the coming centuries to become so comprehensive in the scope of her teaching as to be able to furnish to all inquirers after truth the instruction they may desire in whatever branch of human knowledge, he believes also that she will become so catholic in her liberality as to open widely her doors to all inquirers without distinction either of class or of sex."—President F. A. P. Barnard, Columbia College, 1879. *Report for 1878-79*, p. 68.

"Women graduates are doing their full part in winning a reputation for Michigan University, and are justifying the wisdom of the Regents who opened to them the opportunities for a thorough classical training."—President J. B. Angell, The University of Michigan, 1880. Quoted in *Education*, September, 1883.

"Without intending the slightest disparagement of the teaching in any of the certainly excellent colleges for women in the country at this time, it is certainly allowable to say of it that it cannot possibly compare with that which is given in those ancient seats of learning where, through a long series of years, have been gradually brought together all the appliances necessary to facilitate research or illustration in every department of knowledge, and where the teachers are men of celebrity universally recognized as authorities in the world of science or letters." —President F. A. P. Barnard, Columbia University, 1881. *Report for 1880-81*, p. 74.

"The coeducation problem. Build up the local high school till it shall be the homologue of the gymnasia of Germany, or lyceum of France, and let your daughters resort to it from the safe harbor of home, and this problem is more than half-solved at once."—President W. W. Folwell, The University of Minnesota, 1884. *Education*, January, 1884.

"Educate a man and you have educated only one person; educate a mother and you educate a whole family. . . . The children of an educated woman are never illiterate. Homes and primary schools are the chief forces of civilization and they are made by women and not by men. The proper training of women is the strategic point in the education of the race. . . . Money invested in the education of women yields better dividends than that invested in men. Woman is the priestess in humanity's temple and she presides at the fountain head of civilization."—President Charles D. McIver, Normal and Industrial Institute (later North Carolina College for Women), *ca.* 1890. Quoted in Charles W. Dabney, *Universal Education in the South* (Chapel Hill: The University of North Carolina Press, 1936), I, 202, 203.

"Woman's physical nature demands a difference in treatment as to hours of study; as to times of physical exercise and the character of such exercises, as to regularity and uniformity of tasks assigned.

"Undoubtedly true. But give to the plan of coeducation its legitimate development—place in professional chairs without distinction in salary representative men *and* women and these differences will be recognized and dangers will be averted. . . .

"If no good argument can be adduced against the policy of coeducation in colleges . . . and if it be agreed that under the present plan of organization young men and women may be educated together as well as in separate schools—then one strong plea may be made for coeducational colleges on the score of economy."—President J. L. Pickard (1878-87), The State University of Iowa, 1893. *Education*, January, 1893.

"Brothers and sisters grow up in the same home, boys and girls play together in the yards, attend the village school together, go to picnics together, attend the same Sunday schools, and are expected to be social companions after college days, and become man and wife for a lifetime association; then why should college training, the supreme part of education, be separate? There is no answer, except that the thing began in other days and should continue."—President John C. Kilgo, Trinity College (North Carolina), 1894. Quoted in Paul N. Garber, *John Carlisle Kilgo* (Durham: Duke University Press, 1937), p. 142.

"No peculiar relation of cause and effect can be detected existing between the two movements, but it is the fact that the rise of college education for women has been contemporaneous with the rise of the elective system of studies. They are both movements toward individuality and freedom. . . . It is the age, not the college, which is to be held responsible for the vast increase in the number of courses of study. . . . The two perils belonging to the elective system are haphazardness and narrowness. . . . But these objections have slight force when put by the side of the one comprehensive argument for the elective system—*the development of the individual herself.*"—President Charles Thwing, Western Reserve University, 1894. *The College Woman* (New York: The Baker and Taylor Company, 1894), pp. 41 f.

"The proposition to open Trinity to the women is cheered most enthusiastically by the women, and already applications are being made by our young women; all this shows the latent desire of our young women for equal advantages with their brothers in education. It marks a new era in our State and its future will vindicate the prophetic wisdom of Mr. Duke."—President John C. Kilgo, Trinity College (North Carolina), 1897. Quoted in Paul N. Garber, *John Carlisle Kilgo* (Durham: Duke University Press, 1937), p. 143.

"One whose mind is upon educational questions cannot much longer hesitate to deal frankly with the duty of educational institutions to womanhood. . . . Does not every established institution of learning, with all its facilities for uplifting humanity, owe a duty to woman as well as man? All the vain, hysterical debate about woman's sphere and woman's limitations has been answered in the hard logic of splendid fact. . . . Are we the children of light while they sit in darkness? . . . I believe that the university at the earliest time practicable should open its post-graduate courses to the women of the state. Then perhaps it might enter into the purpose of some good man or woman with a heart for good deeds to build such a foundation for women here as would give them equal facilities with their brothers and make also for the softening of our manners and the humanizing of our life."—President Edwin A. Alderman,

The University of North Carolina, 1897. *The University Record*, February, 1897.

"Co-education is a dead issue. The American people have settled the matter. . . . Why discuss the matter further?"—President Nicholas Murray Butler, Columbia University, 1902. *Journal of Education*, November 13, 1902.

"The most frequent probably of all criticisms was the hygienic one. Although it was a matter of prehistoric knowledge that women could work all day in the field, many learned persons predicted a speedy decline for the audacious young female who attempted to follow the same collegiate course as her brother. . . .

"To behold the campus dotted with couples, billing and cooing their way to an A.B. is a thing, it is said, to rejoice Venus or Pan rather than Minerva, and were it the frequent or necessary outcome of coeducation, the future of the system would certainly be in jeopardy. . . ."—Professor James R. Angell, The University of Chicago, 1902. *Popular Science Monthly*, November, 1902.

"Shall a girl receive a college education?. . . It must depend on the character of the girl. . . . The highest product of social evolution is the growth of the civilized home, the home that only a wise, cultivated and high-minded woman can make. . . . A generous education should be the birthright of every daughter as well as of every son. . . . Untrained cleverness is said to be the most striking characteristic of the American woman. Trained cleverness, a very much more charming thing, is characteristic of the American college woman. . . ."—President David Starr Jordan, Leland Stanford Junior University, 1902. *Popular Science Monthly*, December, 1902.

"In my opinion, separate colleges for men and for women are often good; still better, other things being equal, is the university for men with an annex for women; but best of all for each sex is the coeducational university, in which men and women, side by side where association is wise, and apart where separation is wise, acquire together and partly from each other that training of mind, morals, body and social habits which fits best for larger usefulness."—President R. H. Jesse, The University of Missouri, 1904. *Proceedings of the National Education Association, 1904.*

"It is now well established that higher education in this country reduces the rate of both marriage and offspring. . . . I think it established that mental strain in early womanhood is a cause of imperfect mammary function which is the first stage of the slow evolution of sterility. . . . A boy forced to see too much of girls is sure to lose something, either by excess or defect, from the raw material of his manhood.

"The higher education of women involves all the difficulties of that of men, with many new problems of its own. The girls' colleges think it wisest to train for self-support, and hold that if marriage comes it can best take care of itself. I urge the precise reverse."—President G. Stanley Hall, Clark University, 1904. *Proceedings of the National Education Association, 1904.*

"As it seems to be by divine ordination that the sexes are compelled to grow up together, I think that in the West at least we shall continue to believe that they may be properly educated together, under such reasonable regulations as good sense will suggest."—President James B. Angell, The University of Michigan, 1904. *Proceedings of the National Education Association, 1904.*

"The weakness in the program generally offered by women's colleges is that it follows closely or even slavishly that usual at colleges for men, and so fails to meet the peculiar needs that many college women feel."—President Nicholas Murray Butler, Columbia University, 1904. *Report for 1903-04.* Quoted in *The Rise of A University*, Vol. II, ed. Edward C. Elliott (New York: Columbia University Press, 1937), p. 189.

"The high grade, thoroughly equipped colleges for women, established at great expense during the past two or three decades, have more applicants knocking at their doors than they can accommodate. This is a demonstration of dissatisfaction with the coeducational experiment."—President John F. Goucher, Baltimore Woman's College, 1904. *Papers and Addresses of the Association of Colleges and Preparatory Schools of the Southern States, 1904.*

"It is needless to say before this audience that none of the evils and few of the difficulties which were suggested against coeducation in advance of its trial, have been confirmed by experience. . . .

"The natural segregation of the sexes in subjects which should be attractive to both, is an undoubted educational tendency . . . believing as I do that coeducation gives satisfactory scholastic results for both sexes; I am in favor of taking such steps as are necessary to maintain coeducation in full vigor in the colleges of liberal arts."—President Charles R. Van Hise, The University of Wisconsin, 1907. Address in Boston, November 6, 1907, *Educational Review*, December, 1907.

"There is, however, one grave peril which must be averted from women's education at all hazards. Most of the universities of the west and many eastern universities, like Cornell, Columbia and Pennsylvania, are boring through their academic college course at a hundred places with professional courses. In many colleges everything that is desirable for a human being to learn to do counts towards a bachelor's degree—ladder work in the gymnasium (why not going upstairs?), swimming in the tank (why not one's morning bath?), cataloging in the library (why not one's letter home?)"—President M. Carey Thomas, Bryn Mawr College, 1908. *Educational Review*, December, 1908.

"Co-education is the most simple economical method, and has advantages both in attainment and extension over separate colleges. . . . The sentiment which insists in separate colleges for women, either regards their claims as inferior to those of men, or of so distinct a character as to admit of inferior endowment."—President John Bascom (1874-1887), The University of Wisconsin, 1908. *Educational Review*, December, 1908.

"The University as a whole is proud of Barnard College and of the admirable provision which it makes for the college education of women. The standards of admission and of graduation are identical with those of Columbia College; the program of studies is as rich and as satisfactory as the financial condition of the corporation will permit; the officers of instruction are accomplished and devoted. When these facts are clearly stated and recognized, it can hardly be doubted that the friends of the collegiate education of women will give without delay to Barnard College that new support which it must have unless it is to fall back steadily in educational effectiveness. The making of bricks without straw cannot go on indefinitely."—President Nicholas Murray Butler, Columbia University, 1910. *Report for 1909-10*. Quoted in *The Rise of A University*, Vol. II, ed. Edward C. Elliott (New York: Columbia University Press, 1937), p. 190.

"The very presence of the opposite sex has a restraining influence, preventing the expression of coarse and unrefined thoughts. . . . To object to co-education on the score of morals sounds like an echo from the far-off past. . . ."—President Thomas D. Boyd, Louisiana State University, 1910. Speech at the Semi-Centennial of Louisiana State University, 1910. Quoted in Marcus W. Wilkerson, *Thomas Duckett Boyd: The Story of a Southern Educator* (Baton Rouge: Louisiana State University Press, 1935), p. 277.

"The college must help a man or a woman to master the art of making a good living—justifying existence by productive labor in God's good world of things; and it must help a man or a woman to master the art of living a complete life—justifying existence in God's great world of ideas and ideals. In neither of these aspects of education has Southern opinion given sufficient emphasis to the education of women. Generally speaking, the public is not concerned about the higher education of women, except for those who mean to teach. The colleges themselves, therefore have, perhaps, not felt able to apply themselves with the high seriousness that the task demanded. . . .

"We have said with some unction that 'woman's place is in the home'—which is at once both a wise, beautiful, and also a very stupid thing to say, unless we realize the fact that the home, and the office, and the store, and the farm are an organic union in the economy of living. The college for women needs to take intelligent account of woman's relation to this great business, and it needs to help her interpret it in terms of large and liberal efficiency. Otherwise it fails."—President Edward K. Graham, The University of North Carolina, 1916. "Greetings from the State Colleges," at the inauguration of President Charles E. Brewer, Meredith College, Raleigh, North Carolina, 1916. In *Education and Citizenship and Other Papers* (New York: G. P. Putnam's Sons, 1919 [also University of North Carolina Press]), pp. 193, 194.

"In the Annual Report for 1879 President Barnard convulsed the educational world of that day by strongly advocating the admission of women as undergraduates in Columbia College. . . .

"In the Annual Reports for 1880, 1881, and 1882, President Barnard returned to the subject of the higher education of women and discussed it from every point of view with great cogency and with illustrations drawn from the educational experience of various lands.

"When President Barnard brought forward this highly contentious proposal, he was not a young and radical educational reformer, but a ripe scholar and highly seasoned educational administrator who had reached his seventieth year. . . .

"As a result of this proposal, and the violent controversy which ensued, a collegiate course for women was established in 1883, and a college for women bearing President Barnard's name came into existence in 1889 and was almost at once completely incorporated in the educational system of Columbia." —President Nicholas Murray Butler, Columbia University, 1918. *Report for 1917-18.* Quoted in *The Rise of A University*, Vol.

II, ed. Edward C. Elliott (New York: Columbia University Press, 1937), pp. 190, 191.

"One of our strongest traditions has been the emphasis upon democracy and simplicity. These ideals are closely related. It is difficult to conceive of one unaccompanied, at least in some degree, by the other. At the very outset, our insistence upon the democratic ideal led to the adoption of an advanced position with regard to the admission of women upon equal terms with men, resulting in the honorable distinction of our being the first college in New England to carry our democracy beyond the barriers of sex. Those first women students were brave indeed! Their presence was grudgingly allowed and often attended with ridicule and open antagonism. To the natural conservatism of New England, co-education in those days seemed like a strange exotic transplanted from the progressive prairies of the West. It is no mean accomplishment to have been among the protagonists of the modern feminist movement which is really a part of that larger drift in the direction of democracy that is coincident with the growth of the American republic among the nations. This fundamental feeling for democracy so characteristic of our history has surmounted other barriers besides that of sex. The color line has never been drawn in this institution and no one has ever found our doors shut in his face because of race or creed."—President Clifton Daggett Gray, Bates College, 1920. *Bates College Bulletin* (Lewiston, Maine), December 1, 1920.

"Many believe that the new found liberty which women have achieved but not fully understood has lowered the tone of our women's colleges both in manners and in morals."—President Emeritus C. A. Richmond, Union College, 1934. *Bulletin of the Association of American Colleges*, December, 1934, p. 468.

"At the time the land grant colleges were being established over the country the leaders in North Carolina did not see fit to combine the land grant college with the State University, and they were equally opposed to committing the State University to co-education or coördinate education at the time when higher education of women was getting well under way in this State. I am not criticizing our leadership for the course it pursued in any of these critical periods in the history of higher education. Indeed there is a good deal to say for education in the smaller units. At any rate, these decisions for which no one of us here has any responsibility have apparently put out of the picture a large educational center such as those developed through making other choices in states like Michigan, Wisconsin, Minnesota, and a good many others in the middle and far west."—President William P. Few, Duke University, March, 1939. Address before the North Carolina Education Association, Raleigh, March 17, 1939. Published in part in the Raleigh *News and Observer*, March 18, 1939.

The Education of the Negro

"The labor unit of the South is still the Negro, . . . and the industrial development of the South demands that the Negro be either improved or gotten rid of. The problem is not political, but purely industrial. With the South it is one of development; with the Negro, of existence. It must be solved, and solved aright. The mistakes of reconstruction must be corrected. The North and South, government and philanthropy, education and religion, all forces, domestic, social, and industrial, must combine to make the Negro a better workman. . . .

For this generation and many yet to come there is need of radical change in Negro education. His colleges of law, of medicine, of theology, and of literature, art, and science should be turned into schools of industrial training. Hampton Institute and Tuskegee should be duplicated in every Southern State—if possible in every congressional district. The visionary ideals of Wendell Phillips and Frederick Douglass should give place to the practical work of General Armstrong and Booker Washington."—President George T. Winston, The North Carolina College of Agriculture and Mechanic Arts, 1900. *Report, United States Commissioner of Education, 1900-1901*, I, 509.

"Nothing will bring the races together again but industrial skill and efficiency on the part of the negro. His education should look to this end. The leaders of the race should turn their energies and ambitions in this direction. The entire system of negro public education should be industrial. The negro must first be taught to earn a decent living; afterwards will come independence and self-reliance, and finally culture, learning, and refinement. . . . The foremost leaders of the negro race, both in slavery and since, have been mulattoes. The two really great men produced by the race in the United States, one the great anti-slavery agitator, the other the great apostle of industrial education, are the sons of white fathers, each possessing in a high degree the characteristics of the white race. . . ."—President George T. Winston, The North Carolina College of Agricultural and Mechanic Arts, 1901. "Industrial Training in Relation to the Negro Problem," *Proceedings of the Fourth Conference for Education in the South, Winston-Salem, 1901*, pp. 105, 106, 107.

"The most encouraging thing about public education in the South is the noble self-sacrificing way in which the southern people have given of their limited resources for the education of their recent slaves. That they will continue to do for the black man all that their means will permit, I firmly believe. These attacks upon the negro school fund, these proposals to give him for his schools only what he pays in himself, come from short-sighted people who fail to recognize the basal principle underlying all public education, namely, the duty of *all the people* to educate *all the people*. . . . We cannot longer take the risks of multitudes of ignorant voters controlled by a few wicked demagogues. . . . Many of our southern states make a similar mistake in trying to enforce in the schools of the black districts courses of study laid down for the whites. . . . Let us adapt our instruction to the needs of the people, and above all things, let us give them that industrial training which will prepare them to be self-supporting citizens."—President Charles W. Dabney, The University of Tennessee, 1901. "The Public School Problem in the South," *Proceedings of the Fourth Conference for Education in the South, Winston-Salem, 1901*, pp. 61, 62.

"The day of emotionalism and passion on the subject of negro education has passed. The negro race is a child race, backward in training and inferior in type to the race which surrounds it. The problem is to apply to this backward child race, slowly reaching up after the essentials of modern civilization, the agencies which will enable it to achieve real freedom and real usefulness. Freedom is an achievement, not a legacy."—President Edwin A. Alderman, Tulane University, 1902. "The Child and the State," *Proceedings of the Fifth Conference for Education in the South, 1902*, p. 59.

"All men, whatever may be their rank or their vocation, must come to take a sober view of the negro problem, if it must be called a problem. It must not be left to the demagogue, to the mob, to political intrigues, to the negro-hater among white men, or to the white-man-hater among the negroes. The issues are the issues of a human life and cannot be settled by passionate men of any race or section. . . .

"If the negro problem is not settled according to the eternal laws of righteousness, the negro will not be the only sufferer; he will not be the greatest sufferer; if it is settled in righteousness, he will not be the only one helped. . . .

"To whom should this race look for better help and more sympathetic help than to the colleges of the South? It is not the business of the college to take up the excited feelings of the street and nurse them into stronger forms of passion."—President John C. Kilgo, Trinity College (North Carolina), 1903. *The South Atlantic Quarterly*, October, 1903, pp. 383, 384, 385.

"The duty of the South to negro education, whatever we may find that duty to be, is a duty to the children and grandchildren of the Confederate negro; and this phase ought to include not only the faithful body-servant in war, but the old black mammy and Uncle Remus who were objects of so much affection in every Southern household. . . . There is no surer way in which a member of that race (white) can exhibit his unworthiness of the blood in his veins than to entertain an apprehension that the negro can so overcome racial characteristics and the advantage of a start of at least two thousand years as to endanger the supremacy of that race. In contradiction of the apprehension referred to, I would say that the only thing the South cannot afford in its relation to the negro race, is injustice. . . .

"The policy of separate schools will, of course, be maintained; and it is gratifying that this is not only the settled purpose of the whites, but that intelligent negroes are coming to see that any blending of the races would be between the higher types of their people and the lower types of the white race, and that coeducation of the races or any other intermingling is not to be desired from the point of view of the best interests of the negro race."—President W. B. Hill, University of Georgia, 1903. "Negro Education in the South," *Proceedings of the Sixth Conference for Education in the South, 1903*, pp. 207, 208, 210, 211, 212.

"One great problem of the future will be to determine what racial differentiation in the mode of education should be made for the negro race in view of his racial peculiarities and his social condition and family life. . . . Undoubtedly more of moral and parental training of various kinds may help to a successful solution of the problem as to what educational facilities are most helpful to the negro race in Mississippi."—President Robert B. Fulton, The University of Mississippi, 1903. "Educational Progress in Mississippi," *Proceedings of the Sixth Conference for Education in the South, Richmond, Virginia, 1903*, p. 109.

"The races are now segregated, and are seeking to advance separately along parallel lines. Hence the school is the main agency for training the negro in thrift, in the care of the home, in respect for law, and in moral initiative."—President Samuel C. Mitchell, The University of South Carolina, 1907. "The Task of the Neighborhood," *Proceedings of the Tenth Conference for Education in the South, 1907*, pp. 16, 17.

"The negro cooks our food, nurses our children, washes our

clothes, tends our homes, and in self-defense, if not from a spirit of altruism and patriotism, it develops upon us, the dominant race, to see to it that he is taught how to live intelligently, morally, and hygienically. He must be trained for his environment, and his education must be industrial, technical and moral, rather than literary, professional and cultural. . . . We may not go into his schools and instruct his children; but, without doing great violence to custom or tradition, might we not train the teachers—who are to conduct his schools?"—President John W. Abercrombie, The University of Alabama, 1911. "Southern Education," *Proceedings and Addresses of the Twenty-Second Annual Meeting, Southern Educational Association, 1911*, pp. 46, 47.

The Effect of the World War

"I presume we are impressed at the time with the necessity for military training, and there is a great wave of enthusiasm for it now. But I cannot help feeling that after the European war is over and we see that no one of the parties over there is coming over to gobble us up, a great deal of the enthusiasm for military courses will die away; and in the meantime I share the feeling that we are in danger of making preparation to give military training and military education on a scale so large that when the enthusiasm has died away a great many institutions will be left with white elephants on their hands."—President David Kinley, The University of Illinois, 1916. *Journal of Proceedings of the Association of American Universities, 1916.*

"I would far rather see national defense intrusted, in so far as its officers are concerned, to a considerable body of men whose primary interests are in civic life, and who look upon military duty as an emergency, a departure from normal life, rather than see it intrusted to a body of men whose primary interests are military or professional."—President George Comstock, The University of Wisconsin, 1916. *Journal of Proceedings of the Association of American Universities, 1916.*

"I think it is our duty, not only in state universities, but in the others, to train men for leadership in national defense, as well as for leadership in other connections."—President A. Ross Hill, The University of Missouri, 1916. *Journal of Proceedings of the Association of American Universities, 1916.*

"Is it our duty to coöperate if we can? I think it is . . . there is a unanimity of opinion that as long as we have colleges they should prepare for citizenship . . . one very important element in training for citizenship is preparation to defend the country in an emergency."—President Arthur T. Hadley, Yale University, 1916. *Journal of Proceedings of the Association of American Universities, 1916.*

"This is not the time to discuss what caused the present crisis, but the time to recognize that it is here and consider how to meet it. . . . It is a struggle of democracy against autocracy. It is a struggle that, for the first time in the history of nations, has brought about the recognition of education as a national resource."—President R. J. Aley, The University of Maine, 1917. "Obligations and Opportunities of the Schools During the War," *Proceedings of the National Education Association, 1917*, p. 162.

"As I walked down Fifth Avenue today and saw more Stars and Stripes than ever decorated the city on the most festal days, I felt and you feel that there is only one subject uppermost in our minds as American citizens, and that is loyalty. And in loyalty, Lafayette is not behind her brothers. True to their name, true to the immortal example of the great marquis, the men of Lafayette of this generation as of former generations have already given expression of their loyalty, their readiness to serve their country and the cause of freedom."—President J. H. MacCracken, Lafayette College, 1917. "The College and the Shadow of War," *College and Commonwealth* (New York: The Century Company, 1920), p. 121.

"We of the colleges, than whom there are none more ardent lovers of liberty, welcome the Student's Army Training Corps, because it is based on the principle of mutual coöperation between the school and the army, and because we believe we shall thus advance liberty in the world. Like the perfect courser admired of Lafayette it is quite conceivable that should the colleges of America perceive the whip, they too would throw down their rider.

"We welcome you then to both academic and military training. For the first time, a college president may properly begin as Vergil began his Aeneid: 'Arma virumque cano. . . .' "—President J. H. MacCracken, Lafayette College, 1918. *College and Commonwealth* (New York: The Century Company, 1920), pp. 82, 83.

"We mean to say here today, as our fathers said—and as the wholesome heroic heart of men will always say—that there are certain rights of liberty and life inalienable for men everywhere; and that whenever the vital growth of these rights is menaced we will be quick to defend them as a heritage more precious than life itself.

"We are happy today as we accept the sword of defense of these ancient and eternal principles; and more for the opportunity of a wider and deeper interpretation of them, that makes our present cause the equal cause of the liberal brotherhood of all good men everywhere, and makes the cause of our country the common cause of a free mankind.

"Is it fanciful to think that the heroes of freedom, whose stories we have studied here—of Thermopylae, of Runnymede, of Bunker Hill and the rest—give to us, in the beauty of this quiet spot, their benediction, as we take from their hands the torch of the eternal task, and 'carry on' to a new and greater victory?

"The spirit of this campus, the spirit of our State and our country, the spirit of the world today, assure to us the continuing courage and complete devotion that will bring to a glorious fulfillment the noblest adventure that ever called to the aspiring spirit of youth."—President Edward K. Graham, The University of North Carolina, 1918. Address on being inducted into the S. A. T. C., October 1, 1918. *Education and Citizenship and Other Papers* (New York: G. P. Putnam's Sons, 1919 [also University of North Carolina Press]), pp. 190, 191.

"I think the war is likely also, and this goes almost without saying, to stimulate our interest in applied science. Everybody sees how much engineering and the applied sciences have contributed to this war. . . .

"I am not without hope that even the humanities with us will gain as a result of the war. We have been dominated too exclusively for the last generation by the German point of view. . . .

"I should like to see military training and physical training combined, and I should like to see the combination required of all students for four years for about five hours a week. . . ." —President J. G. Schurman, Cornell University, 1918. *Journal of Proceedings of the Association of American Universities, 1918.*

"Two great changes in the popular estimate of education have, however, been brought by the war. In the first place, every intelligent person now knows that Germany has proved past all peradventure that an educational system may be exploited to mold the fundamental political and social ideals of a whole nation. . . .

"But, in the second place, the war has exhibited to an extent previously unrealized by the average man the extent to which the machinery of our civilization rests upon the foundations of applied science. . . ."—Dean James R. Angell, The University of Chicago, 1918. *Journal of Proceedings of the Association of American Universities, 1918.*

"In common with many other types of public service institutions, the universities have come into close relations with the national government as an incident to the organization of the nation for war. In some cases this relationship has brought about changes that can only be described as revolutionary, but it is not at all certain that many of them are not beneficial and worthy of continuance in some form. For instance, the war has brought back to the American people, and in some degree to the schools and colleges, the spirit of discipline which had been almost lost."—President Nicholas Murray Butler, Columbia University, 1918. *Report for 1917-18*, p. 6.

"We have been forced to grasp the grim fact that, when poison gas and shrapnel take the place of sweetness and light, the chief end of men who would glorify God is to kill Germans—and no explanatory footnotes required."—President Edward K. Graham, The University of North Carolina, 1918. A commencement address prepared, but undelivered, on account of illness for The Johns Hopkins University, June, 1918. *The Johns Hopkins University Circular*, July, 1918.

"This is the first commencement season in three years in which there is any indication that American colleges have resumed their normal life. Graduating classes throughout the country still show in their diminishing numbers the effects of our participation in the terrible conflict to which we had determined to give our last full measure of devotion. In an hour of imminent and deadly peril the nation looked to the colleges for those who should lead the new national army to victory. They did not seek in vain. Dormitories were turned into barracks and contribution was exacted from every course in the curriculum for the all-dominating purpose of the winning of the war. Professors and instructors by the hundreds left their classes and entered government service. There will never be a more glorious chapter in our history than the one entitled 'American Colleges and the Great War'."—President Clifton Daggett Gray, Bates College, 1920. *Bates College Bulletin* (Lewiston, Maine), December 1, 1920.

"It is true that we are in more confusion than usual. The mixing up of the war was confusing in itself, and it has been followed by a tangle of governmental, economic, and other relations of individuals and nations in extent beyond anything that the world has ever seen. The war, too, emphasized the power of force to control human action. It hastened the age of the modern petty tyrant, the gangster, and the racketeer. Strangely enough, while filled with human courage of the high-

22

est sort, it has left us supine under lawlessness."—President R. L. Wilbur, Leland Stanford Junior University, 1933. Commencement Address, *Stanford Horizons*, Stanford University: Stanford University Press, 1936.

Adult Education

"The education of youth is suffering from over-organization, from over-administration, and from hysterical over-emphasis. The continuing education of the adult, on the other hand, is suffering from lack of organization, from imperfect administration, and from no emphasis at all."—President Nicholas Murray Butler, Columbia University, 1924. *Report for 1923-1924*, p. 26.

"The movement for adult education is both an invitation and a warning. It is an invitation to remember that much remains to be done when school and college days are over, and it is a warning that much that school and college have attempted to do has not been well or competently done."—President Nicholas Murray Butler, Columbia University, 1930. *Report for 1929-1930*, p. 31.

"The older generation see with some clarity how life has been changed in their lifetime. . . . And so tens and hundreds of thousands of them are going to school.

"We have been interested at Minnesota in trying to find out why the older group is in school. . . . Roughly speaking, three fourths of them assign one or the other of two reasons: 'I expect it will help me to advance in my work,' or 'It will prepare me for a different job.' . . . The dominant motive is economic and personal. . . .

"At any rate it seems clear that we shall not be ready to draw final conclusions with regard to many of the simplest questions about the movement for adult education until we understand better the dominant philosophic and industrial trends of our times and until we know vastly more about the groups seeking opportunities for continued education in some form."—President Lotus D. Coffman, The University of Minnesota, 1930. In *Adult Education in Action*, ed. Mary L. Ely (New York: American Association for Adult Education, 1936), pp. 334, 335.

"The adult education movement is forcing recognition of the value and importance of continuing the learning process indefinitely.

"Among the far-seeing leaders of the movement in the United States, adult education is recognized not as a substitute for inadequate schooling in youth but rather as an educational opportunity superior to that offered in youth, because the learner is motivated by the honest desire to know and to enrich his experience and because he brings to his study relevant daily experience, and consequently the new knowledge 'takes root firmly, strikes deep, and feeds upon what the day's life brings it. . . .'

"Just as adult education programs, in order to survive, must have meaning and interest to those for whom they are designed, so the college program must have a similar significance if the aim is that of education for life and a lifelong education."—President Robert D. Leigh, Bennington College, 1930. In *Adult Education in Action*, ed. Mary L. Ely (New York: American Association for Adult Education, 1936), pp. 42, 43.

"There must be some agency that can bring the art spirit into the life of the adult, and it seems to be that agency is the college. It is true that colleges ordinarily deal with young undergraduates. Nevertheless, here is a great group of adult persons who need direction and who have, I am sure, an interest in using the fine arts as a means of satisfaction. If the colleges throw open their doors to adults and teach them by unacademic methods the history of art, art appreciation, its theory and practice, these colleges will develop a wider interest in adult education. . . ."—President Frank L. McVey, The University of Kentucky, 1930. In *Adult Education in Action*, ed. Mary L. Ely (New York: American Association for Adult Education, 1936), p. 384.

"The larger aspect of adult education, as I see it, has two

objectives. First, it must try to reach the individual at a time when his curve of possible growth and accomplishment is still rising and give him new power and ambition. If adult education functions as it should, there ought to be, fifty years from now, a noticeably greater number of persons whose curves of ability will still be rising at forty.

"The second objective of adult education should be the preservation of open-mindedness, of plastic sympathies, of elastic temper to a much later period than is now customary with the great mass of mankind."—President Nicholas Murray Butler, Columbia University, 1931. "To Keep Our Minds Open," in *Adult Education in Action*, ed. Mary L. Ely (New York: The American Association for Adult Education, 1936), pp. 7, 8.

"The developing movement of adult education interests me primarily because it is so much less hampered by vested interests and traditions than are other branches of education, and because it can therefore attack *de novo* some of the fundamental problems of education. . . .

"The most important point at which the concept of social education as a planned attempt to help men create, comprehend, and control their social order can be carried on is, I believe, in the field of adult education. In this relatively virgin field there is magnificent opportunity for us to turn away from the ground plan, the patterns, and formulas that dominate our departmentalized colleges and universities and to move forward to the creation of new educational patterns in both content and procedure. It is the challenge to that enterprise that, to me, is the most thrilling aspect of the whole adult education movement."—President Glenn Frank, The University of Wisconsin, 1935. In *Adult Education in Action*, ed. Mary L. Ely (New York: American Association for Adult Education, 1936), pp. 440, 442.

"If anyone has a right to occasional spasms of pessimism it is the adult educator. He has set out with the bravest expectations of bringing back to school the masses of adults whose behavior is crying proof of educational needs. By dint of ceaseless appeals he has succeeded in getting some small fraction of the masses into his classrooms. They seem pleased; but one drops out because his friends have organized a bridge tournament; another because the class hour hurries him intolerably with his dinner; a third because it is simpler to buy a book—which he seldom does—and read up—which he virtually never does. There is indeed a core of the faithful, but if one were to submit a test at the end of the course how many would show understanding? The public school teacher has his own difficulties, but the compulsory attendance law assures at least the physical presence of the pupils. The adult student is a volunteer, and a short-termer at that. Like the militia of our Revolutionary War, he may betake himself to his home on the eve of an engagement that promised success.

"No wonder the adult educator is occasionally discouraged. He is discouraged more often than he is willing to admit. . . .

"Before we can wisely make up our minds as to the utility and the practicability of systematic adult education we must consider carefully whether the formal educational system, from the kindergarten through the college, really equips one adequately for life in the modern state. . . .

"Perhaps the adult does not want to be educated, and we certainly can't apply compulsion to him. But perhaps the fault lies rather with the adult educator than with the public that needs education. The adult educator needs to stop regarding himself as a mere auxiliary in our grand army of education. He has a distinctive job of surpassing importance. He does not yet know how to proceed most effectively with this job. He has not the means of applying even the methods he believes would work. He is battered back and forth between trial and error like a punching bag. Probably he will not live to see the results of his effort. If he has faith he needs no visible results, for he knows that results better than he could specify are written in the skies."—Director Alvin Johnson, New School for Social

Research, 1935. In *Adult Education in Action*, ed. Mary L. Ely (New York: American Association for Adult Education, 1936), pp. 455, 458.

"Adult education is soundly based on the certainty that one may learn as long as he lives. Can the State bear the cost? To date all forms of public education have cost only two and a half per cent of the national income. This cost must be weighed against the drain of unemployment, of delinquency, and of crime."—Chancellor Ernest H. Lindley, The University of Kansas, 1937. In *Educating for Democracy: A Symposium* (Yellow Springs, Ohio: The Antioch Press, 1937), p. 20.

"Up to the present time postgraduate programs have at their best been principally concerned with professional training. The true educator will not fail to be dissatisfied with this situation. As one has remarked, a man 'is to be educated not because he is to make shoes, nails, and pins but because he is a man.' And 'the college, appealing to the mental part, is yet to train every part. It is doing its full duty only when it causes man to regulate appetite, to crush passions, to guide desires, to quicken affections, to prevent wrong, and to stimulate right choices.' While this has been more or less recognized as the aim of undergraduate teaching, it has not been pursued at all effectively as an important objective of adult education. A proper program of instruction beyond the college years will embrace both professional and cultural training, and will be as carefully prepared as undergraduate curricula."—President A. G. Ruthven, The University of Michigan, 1937. "The Role of the State University in American Higher Education," *Proceedings and Addresses at the Inauguration of Edmund Ezra Day, Fifth President of Cornell University* (Ithaca, 1937), pp. 23, 24.

"The most powerful instrument ever placed in the hands of man in his struggle for emancipation was literacy,—a mastery of reading and writing. Only by the intelligent use of this instrument can the masses of the population share in the benefits of a liberal democracy. In no other way can they come into full enjoyment of science, of art, of culture, of all the advantages of civilization. But man's longing for a better world may be thwarted by an inadequate or incompetent education.

"Literacy is the instrument through which democracy is achieved, but literacy alone will not promote or insure democracy. Misused it may become debased into the propaganda of demagogues or of a self-seeking press and radio. . . ."—President Lotus D. Coffman, The University of Minnesota, 1938. From President Lotus D. Coffman's biennial report on The University of Minnesota, written shortly before his death in September, 1938. Quoted in *Journal of Adult Education*, January, 1939, p. 17.

"The courses offered and the various opportunities afforded for 'adult education' prove that the educational process may no longer be regarded as terminated by the award of a degree but should be continued as long as life itself."—President F. C. Ferry, Hamilton College, 1934. *Bulletin of The Association of American Colleges*, December, 1934, p. 467.

"Most of us think of the boundaries of our respective states as the limits of the university campus. An effort is being made through our institutions to promote a comprehensive program of adult education as a means of satisfying the intellectual hungers of our people."—President W. B. Bizzell, University of Oklahoma, 1934. *Transactions and Proceedings of the National Association of State Universities, 1934.*

"Books are the medium through which the greater part of adult education must be carried on. I am not forgetting the importance of education in music and in art, in the crafts and the purely vocational subjects. But in other fields what we are doing, in the long run, is to lead people up to books in the hope that with the aid of them they will proceed to educate themselves. Consequently, books and the reading of books will always remain a very important part of adult education."—President William A. Neilson, Smith College, 1938. *Journal of Adult Education*, June, 1938, p. 229.

Federal Relations

"Let us cling fast to the genuine American method—the old Massachusetts method—in the matter of public instruction. The essential features of that system are local taxes for universal elementary education voted by the citizens themselves, local elective boards to spend the money raised by taxation and control the schools, and for the higher grades of instruction permanent endowments administered by incorporated bodies of trustees. This is the American voluntary system, in sharp contrast with the military, despotic organization of public instruction which prevails in Prussia and most other states of continental Europe. Both systems have peculiar advantages, the crowning advantage of the American method being that it breeds freemen. Our ancestors well understood the principle that, to make a people free and self-reliant, it is necessary to let them take care of themselves, even if they do not take quite as good care of themselves as some superior power might.

"And now, finally, let us ask what should make a university at the capital of the United States, established and supported by the general government, more national than any other American university? It might be larger and richer than any other, and it might not be; but certainly it could not have a monopoly of patriotism or of catholicity, or of literary or scientific enthusiasm. . . . As American life grows more various and richer in sentiment, passion, thought, and accumulated experience, American literature will become richer and more abounding, and in that better day let us hope that there will be found several universities in America, though by no means one in each state, as free, liberal, rich, national and glorious as the warmest advocate of a single, crowning university at the national capital could imagine his desired institution to become."—President Charles W. Eliot, Harvard University, 1873. "National University," *Proceedings of the National Education Association, 1873*, pp. 119, 120.

"While I hail with joy supplementary private gifts when not

used as fetters, I maintain that there can be no system more unrepublican than that by which a nation or a State, in consideration of a few hundreds of thousands of dollars, delivers over its system of advanced instruction, to be controlled and limited by the dogmas and whimsies of living donors or dead testators. In more than one nation, dead hands stretching out from graves closed generations gone, have laid with deadly chill upon institutions for advanced instruction during centuries. . . .

"Of all State treasures, the genius and talents of citizens are the most precious. That arch Bohemian, Sala, said that in no country is there so much genius and talent 'lying around loose' as in America. Now, it is just this talent and genius which, as all history shows, private capacity and the law of supply and demand will not develop.

"But I am met here, first by an undue extension of the *Laissez Faire* argument. It is said that the best policy is to leave the building up of such institutions entirely to private hands; that such a plan educates the people to give, makes them self-reliant.

"The latest form of this argument was put forth in the National Association of Teachers, last year, at Elmira, in a speech by President Eliot, of Harvard.

"Now, I do not yet take up the question of a single National University, at the National Capital, but when the distinguished President of Harvard College condemns by implication, as in the speech to which I have referred, all public provision for advanced instruction, whether by Nation or State, we all have the right to stand amazed. At its very beginning, the University over which he presides had aid from the State in which it stands, and it has not been slow to accept public aid at various periods since. In these latter days, its greatest glory, its Museum of Natural Science, is largely the result of constant applications to the Legislature of Massachusetts. The whole country has rejoiced that the State of Massachusetts has had the practical good sense thus to grant funds to carry on the great work of Professor Agassiz at Harvard, and they rejoiced also when the liberality of the State stimulated a noble growth of private liberality.

"But this is not all. So far as the public has learned, there stands in the annals of that University no record of any rejection of favors even from the National Government. The benefits accruing to that institution from the Coast Survey are well known, and when rich spoils came to it from the dredging expedition of the Hassler—a national ship—I remember no Spartan voice raised to repel them. . . .

"Grant that Harvard can now dispense with public aid (although her recent history looks so little like it) it does not at all follow that the other institutions of the country can dispense with it. Close under the shadow of the great palaces and warehouses of a metropolitan city that institution, to the joy of us all, is the recipient of splendid gifts from princely merchants and scholars. But how few of our colleges have the advantage of being near so great an accumulation of capital. . . .

"*Is it necessary that public provision be withheld in order that private persons may give, and that public spirit may thus be cultivated?* Even if it be so, I fail to see force in the argument. As well might President Eliot argue against any public provision for policemen, in order that individuals may toughen their muscles in fighting ruffians; or against any public provision for prisons, in order that individuals may sharpen their minds in outwitting thieves. The history of the private gifts for education crystallized about the various public gifts, and especially about that of 1862, shows that well-directed public bounty, like that of the general government in 1862, stimulates private bounty. It shows that Americans will give where they see something well-established to which it seems worth while to give. 'To him that hath shall be given' is the rule for advanced education."—President Andrew D. White, Cornell University, 1874. *Proceedings of the National Education Association, 1874*, pp. 63, 68, 69.

"Wherever government supports universities, there endowments fail, or are procured with difficulty, and the public spirit which prompts gifts for education languishes. This effect has been produced in all our Western States which support State universities."—President Charles W. Eliot, Harvard University,

1894. Letter from President Charles W. Eliot to President C. E. Taylor. Quoted in C. E. Taylor, *How Far Should a State Undertake to Educate?* (Raleigh: Edwards & Broughton, 1894), p. 16.

"My proposition is very simple: that the federal government shall grant to each state in the Union a sum of money equal to one dollar per annum per head of its population for the support of elementary and secondary education, that is, for the common schools; and that this money shall be expended for the purpose of strengthening what, for lack of a better term, we may call 'practical' education, that is, in agriculture, the mechanic arts, the trades, domestic science, commerce and business, etc.

"This would represent a contribution from the federal treasury toward the support of elementary and secondary education of approximately one hundred million dollars a year—less than the amount given to the building of a navy, far less than the amount given to general military purposes, a sum so small as compared with the total expense of such an educational system as this that many people would think it could hardly be effective in a large way."—President E. J. James, The University of Illinois, 1911. *Transactions and Proceedings of the National Association of State Universities, 1911.*

"It is now proposed to bureaucratize and to bring into uniformity the educational system of the whole United States, while making the most solemn assurance that nothing of the kind is intended. The glory and the success of education in the United States are due to its freedom, to its unevennesses, to its reflection of the needs and ambitions and capacities of local communities, and to its being kept in close and constant touch with the people themselves. There is not money enough in the United States, even if every dollar of it were expended on education, to produce by federal authority or through what is naively called coöperation between the federal government and the several states, educational results that would be at all comparable with those that have already been reached under the free and natural system that has grown up among us. If tax-supported education be first encouraged and inspected, and then little by little completely controlled, by central authority, European experience shows precisely what will happen. . . . For Americans now to accept oversight and direction of their tax-supported schools and colleges from Washington would mean that they had failed to learn one of the plainest and most weighty lessons of the war. It is true that education is a national problem and a national responsibility; it is also true that it has been characteristic of the American people to solve their most difficult national problems and to bear their heaviest national responsibilities through their own action in the field of liberty rather than through the agency of organized government. Once more to tap the federal treasury under the guise of aiding the states, and once more to establish an army of bureaucrats in Washington and another army of inspectors roaming at large throughout the land, will not only fail to accomplish any permanent improvement in the education of our people, but it will assist in effecting so great a revolution in our American form of government as one day to endanger its perpetuity. . . ."—President Nicholas Murray Butler, Columbia University, 1921. *Report for 1920-21*. Quoted in *The Rise of A University*, Vol. II, ed. Edward C. Elliott (New York: Columbia University Press, 1937), pp. 66, 67.

"Any program which attempts to deal adequately with the educational problems of the adult and adolescent population will be enormously expensive because of the absolute necessity of expanding and diversifying educational opportunity to meet the needs of the present day.

"The condition of our most important municipalities gives us little hope that they will be able to advance any such program. In this situation we can only follow the example of banks, railroads, insurance companies, farmers, the oil business, and industry generally and look to the federal government for aid. However, it is not by the route of distributing federal funds on a per capita basis without regard to need and without regard to merit that we must defend ourselves against bureaucracy.

The only protection against government, visible or invisible, is in the professional tradition. The history of educational institutions from the monasteries to the German universities shows that it is not the issue of private or public funds, private or public control that determines their independence. It is the strength of the professional tradition. . . ."—President Robert M. Hutchins, The University of Chicago, 1934. "Teacher, School and National Life," *Journal of the National Education Association*, October, 1934.

"No matter how much aid we may get from the Federal Government, or how much funds we may get from our own state, the most important thing, of course, is the preservation of the intellectual liberty of our respective institutions, and there are a good many indications that it is being jeopardized in some respects, not merely by some influences that flow directly from the Federal program but by partisan politics in some of our states, and by the influences which various pressure groups are bringing to bear upon our respective institutions."—President Lotus D. Coffman, The University of Minnesota, 1934. *Transactions and Proceedings of the National Association of State Universities, 1934*, p. 119.

"In the light of these facts, I therefore assert that the Congress not only has the right, but also . . . by precedent, by settled legislative policy and by the very social principles underlying our government is under definite obligations to assist in seeing that 'the means of education shall forever be encouraged.' . . .

"The case in favor of federal aid to public schools is nowhere put more cogently as far as I know than in an address by Dr. Zook, until recently U. S. Commissioner of Education, published recently in *School and Society*. With the main points of his contention I heartily agree. That agreement in no way decreases the force of any of the implications which are here pointed out."—President R. A. Kent, The University of Louisville, 1934. *School and Society*, September 15, 1934.

"During the winter, the Connecticut Legislature considered a bill which would require an oath of allegiance by all college teachers, including those in privately controlled institutions; fortunately, the bill was not passed. In this respect I believe Connecticut is wiser than her sister states to the west and north, each of which passed such a bill. There are many evidences of threatened state and federal supervision of private colleges."—President James L. McConaughy, Wesleyan University, 1935. "The Annual Report of the President," *The Wesleyan University Bulletin*, October, 1935.

"It is evident that there is no necessity for federal financial assistance to the schools under normal conditions as no state, even in prosperous times, has ever expended more than a trifling proportion of its resources on its schools."—President John J. Tigert, The University of Florida, 1937. "The Real Peril of Federal Subsidies," *Nation's Schools*, July, 1934.

"Economic trends these days are in substantial measure of governmental making. I think it is quite evident that it is possible to build a public opinion that will put government money in large amounts behind research activities in the universities. The question then will be: Under what conditions, on what terms, with what freedom, can the universities proceed with research if the funds come from public sources? Upon the whole, the experience at Ithaca seems to be reassuring on that side, but I have to confess that our situation, as you can see, is in some respects unusual."—President Edmund E. Day, Cornell University, 1937. *The Journal of Proceedings and Addresses of the Association of American Universities* (Chicago: The University of Chicago Press, 1937), pp. 88, 89.

"At this moment the federal government is studying the question of federal aid for scientific and scholarly research, how much it should undertake itself and to what extent it should assist scholarly research conducted by other agencies. Speaking for my own field and my own field only, that of the social sciences, I should view the entrance of the federal government into social science research on a comprehensive scale with grave doubts. The history of federal grants demonstrates that with grants from political sources goes the demand for control, and with control goes regimentation. . . .

"I don't like the thought that the country should begin to look to the federal government as a source of research funds for social scientists."—President H. W. Dodds, Princeton University, 1937. *The Journal of Proceedings and Addresses of the Association of American Universities* (Chicago : The University of Chicago Press, 1937), p. 83.

"While our association includes institutions under public control as well as those privately endowed, our friends in the state universities would, I think, unanimously regret anything which could harm the independent college. If the Federal Government embarks upon a large program of subsidies in which the state-supported institution is in an unduly preferred position, the private college will face a most severe threat to its continued existence. . . . Whether federal subsidy for higher education is desirable or not, and whether Congress is likely to vote it or not, is not so much the question for us as, 'If there are subsidies, shall the privately endowed institutions be excluded?'. . . We should, however, I think, be concerned if this large group of colleges, educating half our American college students at no direct public expense by taxation, were excluded from any such aid."—President J. L. McConaughy, Wesleyan University, 1938. *School and Society*, January 29, 1938.

"Federal aid to education became a historic part of the American system before even the adoption of the Constitution, has been continued in a long succession of congressional grants to the States for agricultural, vocational, and higher education, and will be a further fulfillment of the great American tradition of federal aid to the States for roads, agriculture, health, research, higher education, and social security. Failure to provide federal aid now for the elementary and secondary schools is a failure of the American system to follow through for the most basic of all our American institutions. It is a failure to carry forward the democratic idea of more equal educational opportunity for all American children. Equal educational opportunity of the children who are to be citizens of both the States and the nation is the main responsibility of our constitutional republic of States and people. . . .

"With democracy in retreat in many parts of the world may America give a lift to the democratic hopes of the forgotten millions in all parts of the world with a new declaration for equitable and democratic federal aid to public education under State control in the American way for the fairer chance and more equal opportunity of all the children in all the States."
—President Frank P. Graham, The University of North Carolina, 1938. "Federal Aid to Education." Mimeographed copy of radio address over Columbia Broadcasting System, Washington, D. C., May 7, 1938.

"Recognizing the importance of education in public policy and the obligation of government to provide basic training for citizenship and for primary economic competence, we register, nevertheless, our objection to the inclusion of junior colleges and teacher training institutions, agencies of higher education, in the pending proposal for federal aid to education.

"The bills as now drawn fail to define the exact sphere of education wherein the federal government would aid in the establishment of junior colleges, whether in the field of vocational or liberal arts training and we must disaffirm so vague and undefined a venture.

"More importantly, we believe the field of higher education should be kept entirely free from federal supervision or standardization, free for experimentation and the maintenance of the peculiar tradition or allegiances which give to particular institutions much of their validity. We believe that the discrimination in financial assistance which these provisions would create would seriously jeopardize the continuation of the privately administered college and thus imperil the existing dual system of our public and private control. We discern in the pending proposal tendencies or possibilities which, like the proverbial entering wedge, may open the way to greatly increased expenditures on the one hand or to subtler dominations of intellectual energy by centralized authorities. The fact that other pressure groups are imposing on government largess is no reason for our educational fraternity to do likewise."—Statement by the Association of American Colleges, 1939. Committee on Public Relations, President Francis P. Gaines, Washington and Lee University, Chairman, Association of American Colleges, 1939. Typescript copy in the library of the University of North Carolina.

"I hope that all the money overflowing at Washington won't overflow before some of it overflows to us for education."—President William P. Few, Duke University, 1939. Address before The North Carolina Education Association in Raleigh, March 17, 1939, Raleigh *News and Observer*, March 18, 1939.

"The issue of the Federal support for education is one of the most important, and one of the most contentious, of our day. It has been before the people in definite form since last February, when the President transmitted to Congress the report of his Advisory Committee on Education. . . .

"The real issue before the people is neither Federal control nor denominational support. The real issue is whether we mean what we say when we talk about equality of opportunity. Beside this great question the specters of regimentation of our children and of financing a foreign potentate with American dollars seem fantastic and remote. They seem, indeed, the creation of frenzied imaginations working overtime to concoct some reasons for opposing proposals against which no good reasons can be found. I believe that we shall someday look back on the report of the President's committee as the most important in the history of American education since the Northwest Ordinance, which, 150 years ago, declared that 'religion, morality and knowledge being necessary to good government and the happiness of mankind, schools and the means of education shall forever be encouraged'."—President Robert M. Hutchins, The University of Chicago, 1939. "Uncle Sam's Children," *The Saturday Evening Post*, January 28, 1939, pp. 23, 79.

GENTLEMEN OF THE GRADUATING CLASS

"We are in search for quality, not size; of human relationships and of sound human feeling, not mere efficient mechanical organization; and of the building of character and the increase of human satisfactions, rather than the multiplication of information or the wider diffusion of sterile intelligence. The university is now built, and in the next generation is to justify the hopes and ambitions of the builders. . . ."—President Nicholas Murray Butler, Columbia University, 1921. Commencement Address, *The New York Times*, June 2, 1921.

"To the wise mariner there are three things by which he steers his craft—the chart, the compass and the light of a guiding star. Your chart is the body of knowledge you have acquired, the compass is the unerring pointing of a disciplined and well ordered mind; but there must also be in your lives some constant star in the heavens above, some divine light upon human affairs, upon which you can steadfastly fix your gaze and lay your course. . . ."—President J. G. Hibben, Princeton University, 1921. Baccalaureate Address, *The New York Times*, June 20, 1921.

"What we need now is not more organization or more machinery, but more thought; personal thought, clear, far-reaching and profound, as unbiassed and illumined, and, not least, as widespread among our people as possible, for in the multitude of the wise is the welfare of the world; and where shall we look for this multitude if not among those upon whom has been lavished the best educational opportunities that our country can produce, the graduates of our colleges? . . ."—President A. Lawrence Lowell, Harvard University, 1921. Baccalaureate Address, *The New York Times*, June 20, 1921.

"Not always immediately, but ultimately, mankind is led by

those whose thinking is clear, conscientious and generous, and never in its history has the world been more in need of such thinking than it is now. . . ."—President A. Lawrence Lowell, Harvard University, 1922. Baccalaureate Address, *The New York Times*, June 19, 1922.

"Most important and most difficult of all for the educated man to meet are the demands of sheer character. The college graduate is naturally expected to possess all the basic virtues and to have them rather more highly developed than less favored youth. . . ."—President James R. Angell, Yale University, 1922. Baccalaureate Address, *The New York Times*, June 19, 1922.

"Many of you will be called to public duty in the State and Nation. Answer the call. The relative inferiority of American public officials in intellectual background and horizon, as well as in equipment for the positions which they occupy, is due, in part, to the fact that we regard politics as a profession, rather than a service; in part, to the fact that fit men so often stand aloof; and, in part, to the irrelevant considerations which control appointment to office. What a spectacle does any session of Congress or General Assembly present of self-seeking, partisanship, delays, bartering, buncombe, and all-round incompetence. I do not say that there are no men of intelligence and character in the public service. There are many. I am charging you to increase the number."—President William Louis Poteat, Wake Forest College, 1922. Baccalaureate Address to the Class of 1922, in *Youth and Culture* (Wake Forest: Wake Forest College Press, 1938), p. 120.

"There are comparatively few men and women alive in the world, although there are hundreds of millions of living human beings. . . . The insulated life is the selfish, the self-centered, the narrow, and sooner or later, the embittered life."—President Nicholas Murray Butler, Columbia University, 1930. Commencement Address, *The New York Times*, June 4, 1930.

"The world needs real men, men of courage, both moral and physical. Evil and injustice are not inert, much less dead. They stalk abroad in social life, in politics, in business. If men like you will not do battle with them, who should? . . ."—President James R. Angell, Yale University, 1930. Baccalaureate Sermon, *The New York Times*, June 16, 1930.

"There is a very pressing problem that every one sooner or later must meet and should attempt to solve. That is the origin of religious conviction, whether that conviction be theistical or atheistical. . . ."—President J. G. Hibben, Princeton University, 1930. Baccalaureate Address, *The New York Times*, June 16, 1930.

"My plea today is that you should take away from this campus a willingness, sometimes, to be a radical, to go beyond the crowd, to be a discoverer, to champion lost causes, and to try to reform the many wrongs in the world that we of the older generation have made. . . ."—President James L. McConaughy, Wesleyan University, 1930. Baccalaureate Address, *The New York Times*, June 16, 1930.

"Why is that progress in which we take such pride so uncertain, and indeed so inconsequent, in meeting not only the hopes but the needs of so many human beings? Where are we to look for the cause and the cure of that distress which is so widespread in the world, for which poverty is only one name?"—President Nicholas Murray Butler, Columbia University, 1931. Baccalaureate Address, *The New York Times*, June 3, 1931.

"But in general, wisdom does not appear to have increased. . . . Wisdom, both of statesmen and individuals, is closely associated with a sense of responsibility for one's actions; and the more remote the effects considered the greater the wisdom is likely to be. . . ."—President A. Lawrence Lowell, Harvard University, 1931. Baccalaureate Address, *The New York Times*, June 15, 1931.

"Wesleyan has tried to teach you self-education. You can

fool others, but not yourself. You know best whether your word is good, whether your efforts tally with your opportunities. You should be your own severest judge. . . ."—President James L. McConaughy, Wesleyan University, 1931. Baccalaureate Address, *The New York Times*, June 15, 1931.

"I believe that the critical period has passed and that the decade into which we have entered must be a period of reconstruction of the ideas we live by."—President J. G. Hibben, Princeton University, 1931. Baccalaureate Address, *The New York Times*, June 15, 1931.

"I am asking whether you and your generation can summon faith to believe that by patience and firmness and the exercise of intelligence, together with a decent national generosity, men can be brought to recognize the utter futility of war as a method of justly or effectively composing international differences."—President James R. Angell, Yale University, 1932. Baccalaureate Address, *The New York Times*, June 20, 1932.

"The text of my sermon may be regarded as a significant commentary upon the marked contrast between the period of temporary prosperity which we as a nation experienced and the consequent period of depression in which we find ourselves today. The gain has been turned tragically to loss.

"My chief concern today is that the young men who are about to leave us may realize the importance of a right attitude toward the conditions of our world of today. . . ."—President J. G. Hibben, Princeton University, 1932. Baccalaureate Address, *The New York Times*, June 20, 1932.

"As you go forth into the busy mart of the world strive to be sure that everything you do accords with the rights, and contributes directly or indirectly to the well-being of your fellowmen; and you will live on a high moral plane. . . ."—President A. Lawrence Lowell, Harvard University, 1932. Baccalaureate Address, *The New York Times*, June 20, 1932.

"When selfish personal concern comes always and everywhere

to the first place, and when the public weal lags always in the background, those traits of the politician which we so constantly deplore not only manifest themselves but flourish."—President Nicholas Murray Butler, Columbia University, 1932. Commencement Address, *The New York Times*, June 2, 1932.

"Certainly the generation to which I belong has made a horrible mess of things and we pass on shamefacedly to yours the task of rescuing humanity from its woes, hoping that from our grotesque and pathetic blunders you may learn wisdom and live."—President James R. Angell, Yale University, 1933. Baccalaureate Address, *The New York Times*, June 19, 1933.

"There is still too much astrology in business, too much buncombe in politics, too much superstition in daily life, too much exaggerated and perverted emotional life. Our proudest boast often is that we have had and do have *real* men. . . .

"I have confidence that in such groups as this leaving Stanford and hundreds of other institutions we have a new type of youth, looking on life with great idealism and courage, and with more ability and willingness to face realities than most of those who have gone before. . . ."—President R. L. Wilbur, Leland Stanford Junior University, 1933. Commencement Address, *Stanford Horizons*. Stanford University: Stanford University Press, 1936.

"Above all, let us bear in mind that a good citizen's first duty—mark you, by no means his only duty—but his first duty to the public is to preserve untarnished his own moral integrity." —President A. Lawrence Lowell, Harvard University, 1933. Baccalaureate Address, *The New York Times*, June 19, 1933.

"What was wise and best for us yesterday will quite probably not be best for us tomorrow. The man who tries to make a different world may be unpopular, but he will be meeting the issue of the hour."—President James L. McConaughy, Wesleyan University, 1933. Baccalaureate Address, *The New York Times*, June 19, 1933.

"Until a condition can be brought about in which money is looked upon and treated as the symbol which it is and not as a commodity men can never shake themselves free from the shackles of what they have so long described as the 'money power'."—President Nicholas Murray Butler, Columbia University, 1933. Commencement Address, *The New York Times*, June 7, 1933.

"What government does is almost certain to be done less well than what liberty does, and the reason is quite simple. In the field of liberty the choice of the doer is by a process of natural selection based on fitness. In the field of government the choice of the doer is too often based on importunity tempered by political availability."—President Nicholas Murray Butler, Columbia University, 1934. Commencement Address, *The New York Times*, June 6, 1934.

"All alumni are dangerous. They see their Alma Mater through a rosy haze that gets thicker with the years. They do not know what the college was really like. They do not want to know what it is like now. They want to imagine that it is like what they think it was like in their time. Therefore they oppose all change. If changes are made without their approval, they are resentful. Since no useful change could ever be made with their approval, few useful changes have been made in higher education."—President Robert M. Hutchins, The University of Chicago, 1934. Commencement Address at Oberlin College, *No Friendly Voice*. Chicago: The University of Chicago Press, 1936.

"It is my personal belief . . . that only to the extent that individuals are successful in their moral struggle will society become happier and the world a better place in which to live." —President James B. Conant, Harvard University, 1934. Baccalaureate Address, *The New York Times*, June 18, 1934.

"Wherefore, in your catalogue of morals, give important place to the virtue of tolerance. To love thy neighbor as thyself is still one of the two commandments on which hang all the law and prophets."—President H. W. Dodds, Princeton University, 1934. Baccalaureate Address, *The New York Times*, June 18, 1934.

"Nothing is more depressing than to remark the astonishing number who give absolutely no suggestion of intelligent acquaintance with anything outside the range of business and sport. . . . I would wish for you that you may never have dulled the keen edge of appetite for high spiritual adventure. . . ."—President James R. Angell, Yale University, 1934. Baccalaureate Address, *The New York Times*, June 20, 1934.

"So I am worried about your morals. This University will not have done its whole duty to the nation if you give way before the current of contemporary life. Believe me, you are closer to the truth now than you ever will be again. Do not let 'practical' men tell you that you should surrender your ideals because they are impractical. Do not be reconciled to dishonesty, indecency, and brutality because gentlemanly ways have been discovered of being dishonest, indecent, and brutal. As time passes, resist the corruption that must come with it. Take your stand now before time has corrupted you. Before you know it, it will be too late. Courage, temperance, liberality, honor, justice, wisdom, reason, and understanding—these are still the virtues. In the intellectual virtues this University has tried to train you. The life you have led here should have helped you toward the rest. If come what may you hold them fast, you will do honor to yourselves and to the University, and you will serve your country."—President Robert M. Hutchins, The University of Chicago, 1935. Commencement Address, *No Friendly Voice*. Chicago: The University of Chicago Press, 1936.

WHAT DO THEY SAY? — A SUMMARY

The history of education in the United States has spoken with many tongues. It has spoken through constitutional provisions for schools, through charters for higher educational institutions, and through statutory educational legislation. It has spoken through court decisions, such as those given in the Dartmouth College Case, the Kalamazoo Case, the Oregon Case, the Berea College Case, and the more recent Missouri Case.[1] The history of education has spoken through administrative regulations, official reports, and statistics. It has spoken through proceedings of educational conventions, resolutions of state and national educational associations, educational journals, and other publications. In recent years also it has spoken, if now and then a bit feebly, through many high sounding phrases of a wonderfully made pedagogical literature.

American educational history has also spoken, and continues to speak, through statements of college and university presidents. What these leaders in higher education in the United States say constitutes an important chapter in the history of education in this country. For the story of education in the United States in the past and now, as in other periods and places, seems unfailingly to show that education reflects conditions about it.

The annual reports of presidents, whether formal or informal, are in a measure somewhat intimate documents, intended primarily for trustees and, if published beyond this body, for the

[1] For a discussion of "the more significant of the records of the Judicial experience" of colleges and universities in the United States, see E. C. Elliott and M. M. Chambers, *The Colleges and the Courts* (New York: The Carnegie Foundation for the Advancement of Teaching, 1936).

supporting constituency. In these documents generally appear reports of the state of the institution and a statement of its educational and fiscal needs. Sometimes a president may use his annual report to discuss his philosophy of education and to give his views on many other things, as he often does in his inaugural address. President Barnard's reports at Columbia for nearly twenty-five years have been described by James E. Russell, former Dean of Teachers College, of that university, as "unexcelled in the literature of American education. No current problem escaped Barnard's attention and every problem that he discussed was thereafter the easier of solution, because of his comprehensive view and convincing argument." The reports of President Butler, of Columbia, are among the most distinguished educational documents ever written by a college or university president.

In the preceding pages are set out some of the views which college and university presidents have expressed during the past seventy-five years. For the most part the quotations selected from the inaugural addresses, reports, and occasional papers and speeches speak for themselves, if sometimes a trifle vaguely and now and then in "languages of great ductility."

It has been said that there is "nothing new except what is forgotten." This is not to suggest that college and university presidents do not ever reveal originality in their pronouncements. Some of them may. But it does appear that many of them make statements which have already been made by presidents. Nevertheless, an attempt at a brief summary and perhaps interpretation of at least the apparent trends in presidential statements made during the period covered by this study may here be in order.

The Presidency

In the main the colleges are well officered, said President Francis Wayland, of Brown University, in 1842, when he gave other important views on the collegiate educational system of the United States. The same assertion could have been made with considerable accuracy at other times since Wayland's and could be made today. Dean James O. Murray, of Princeton, was apparently correct when, in 1888, at the inauguration of President Patton, of that institution, he said that college presidents had "been men of noble mark." Most of them have been such men. But the wise Charles W. Eliot, in his inaugural at Harvard in 1869, had warned that administrative officers should not undertake to do everything themselves. And the failure of some of them to take this advice has now and then brought into question the statement of Dean Murray.

Criticism at this point is implied in the statements of college presidents about college presidents and the college presidency. Many of these have been anonymous. Why are these frank discussions of the college presidency so cautiously made? Do college presidents really mean what they publicly say? Is there significance in the suggestion, reported to have been made at the inauguration of Chancellor Charles Wesley Flint, of Syracuse University, in 1922, that college presidents should form a society in which they could discuss their problems "behind closed doors" and "give vent to their feelings in stronger words than would be wise or diplomatic in public"?

How college presidents have acquired the reputation for being "prevaricators" is not altogether clear. Perhaps the best statement available on the point is that made by President Harper. He noted that "A superficial observer will find much to substantiate the very common accusation that the college president is professionally a prevaricator." He also noted that the president who succeeded now and then in concealing his "real thought concerning this man or that subject is politely called a diplomat. Is it diplomacy or is it lying?" President Harper asked. The story which President H. W. Dodds, of Princeton, told at the inauguration of President William A. Eddy of Hobart and William Smith Colleges, in 1936, is also in point. A new college president expressed to an experienced college president the belief that his first year would be the most difficult. This was not the experience of the seasoned veteran: "My third year was the hardest. It was in that year that the faculty found out that I was a liar." President Dodds was inclined to discount the story and said: "A good executive would not have let the faculty find it out."

President Harper pointed out in his discussion that the college president is after all "an ordinary man." But he gave two common maxims for the regulation of the work of the chief university officer: "One should never himself do what he can in anyway find someone else to do." And, "The president should never do today what by any possible means he can postpone until tomorrow." He warned against premature action as "the source of many more mistakes than procrastination."

Whatever his reputation for veracity may be, the president is potentially the most influential person connected with higher education. Competition has placed upon him such a heavy and "harrowing burden," that his position has become almost an impossibility. Conflicting pressures on a multitude of hideous matters, from alumni, trustees, students, faculties, and supporting constituencies and the so-called "public," may at times make him appear to be all things to all men. The college presidency is a job which has never been adequately analyzed, as one college president has recently said. Being a professor or a dean, he says, is a help in becoming a president, and so is training as a public speaker, but as "for the rest—it seems to depend on chance." He does not indicate whether the gift of tongues is much more worth while for the prospective president or for the cause of education, although some observers know that such a gift seems to favor the president. Another college president has recently said that "the actual selection of presidents is a sadly hit and miss affair. The wonder is that so many good men are chosen." He noted that the selection was often made on such considerations as "personal friendship, nepotism, party or religious politics, or propagandized campaigns for election."[2]

---

[2] A recent study disclosed that fewer than a third of seventy new presidents had the Ph.D. degree and the A.B. was the only degree held by seventeen of them. Seventeen were Phi Beta Kappas, but ten had "honorary" membership in that society. The names of only thirty-one appeared in *Who's Who in America* when they

Few college presidents seem to fit the Earl of Beaconsfield's description of Gladstone: "A sophisticated rhetorician, inebriated with the exuberance of his own verbosity, and gifted with an egotistical imagination that can at all times command an interminable and inconsistent series of arguments to malign an opponent and to glorify himself." Not American college and university presidents. For they are, taken by and large, among the politest of the population. Their politeness and generousness of spirit appear not only in their inaugurals but elsewhere.

Inaugurals.—The inaugural addresses of college and university presidents seem to run to a few fixed patterns. The styles of these academic statements do not greatly change, nor do these addresses often exhibit exciting originality. In general, inaugurals may very properly be described as "fireside chats" with the academic and supporting household. But two characteristics of this type of presidential statement are obvious.

It may be perfectly natural for college presidents to applaud those "giants who have labored here," those who "subdued kingdoms of difficulty, wrought righteousness where evil contested every foot of the way, . . . and put to flight the armies of the opposition." Ancient academic custom not only permits but encourages college and university presidents to recount and pay tribute to the achievements of those who have gone before. Generally, presidents applaud those whose burdens they pick up; usually, of course, they pick up these burdens reluctantly, and always with humility and contrite hearts. And graciously do they express their personal and institutional loyalties.

Here and there an exception to the ancient custom may be found. President Charles W. Eliot at Harvard in 1869 got through his inaugural of one and three-quarters hours without naming any of his predecessors except President James Walker (1853-1860).[3] President Lowell, forty years later, began his in-

became presidents.—See James L. McConaughy, "The College President," *Educational Forum*, May, 1938.

[3] On the preparation of his inaugural address, Eliot had the advice of "George J. Brush and Daniel Coit Gilman of Yale, meeting him discreetly on neutral ground

augural by quoting Aristotle, and he referred briefly to only one predecessor, Mr. Eliot.[4] Most college presidents, however, call the roll of past presidents and the muster of the sons.[5]

Any one who is even slightly acquainted with the history of higher education in the United States knows that not all colleges and universities in this country have always been singularly blessed with as great and good presidents as their successors proclaim. True, few of the heads of American colleges and universities have resembled the first head of Harvard, Nathaniel Eaton, who had placed in him by the community and the institution's supporting constituency more trust than was justified. Eaton must have been a mean person—he beat his assistant brutally "with a walnut-tree cudgel, 'big enough to have killed a horse',"—and thus set a bad example in higher educational administration. But the record shows that in the past midgets have often sat in the seats of the academic mighty. And it shows that in some of the seventeen hundred colleges and universities of this country now, midgets may be sitting in such seats. But if one may judge by the inaugural addresses of college and university presidents, no American college or university has ever been afflicted with an unworthy or unsuccessful president. According to the statements of incoming presidents all of their predecessors have been paragons of perfection. And according to the addresses of guest presidents, speaking at the inaugurations of new presidents, one would never suspect that keen competition still exists among the institutions of the higher learning.

Money! Money!! Money!!! The other most striking characteristic of inaugural addresses needs little further comment. College and university presidents generally ask for money. True, not all of them directly pass the plate or the hat at inaugura-

at Springfield."—S. E. Morison, *Three Centuries of Harvard* (Cambridge: Harvard University Press, 1936), p. 329.

[4] S. E. Morison, *The Development of Harvard University* (Cambridge: Harvard University Press, 1930), p. lxxix.

[5] At the conclusion of a very lengthy inaugural by the president of a state university in the South a few years ago, a keenly observing lady and great admirer of the new president telegraphed a mutual friend in another state: "—rang the bell so long that he broke the rope."

tions. But most of them do so indirectly. Those who resist in their maiden speeches the temptation to ask for funds seem soon to get to that responsibility in their reports and speeches to alumni and their supporting constituencies, as may be seen in Section IV, on "Finance." Apparently the fiscal problem of higher education is a persistent one; and in this problem are reflected competition among the colleges and pressures upon and fears among the presidents.

Most presidents say that alma mater needs more money. Some say that the ingratitude of her children is breaking her heart and that she is fast failing under the strain. "If there is danger of America being absorbed in money getting for its own sake," said President John Henry MacCracken, of Lafayette College, in 1916, "there is also danger that college presidents may catch the same disease." President Francis Wayland, of Brown University, had warned against this tendency in 1842 and so had President W. W. Folwell, of the University of Minnesota, in his inaugural address in 1869. But most presidents have seemed to agree with President Charles W. Eliot, of Harvard, who said in his inaugural in 1869: "An institution like this College is getting decrepit when it sits down contentedly on its mortgages. . . . It should be always pushing after more professorships, better professors, more lands and buildings, and better apparatus."

The Purposes of Higher Education

When James Walker was inaugurated president of Harvard in 1853 he said that "next to religion, there is no subject on which there is so much cant as education." In 1864, when F. A. P. Barnard took over Columbia College, he said that the fundamental principles of a truly liberal education were stated by Aristotle, Seneca, and Quintilian—more clearly stated, he thought, than by "those of the most judicious thinkers of modern times." He also said that there was little that was settled and much that was uncertain about higher education.

In statements on the aims of higher education many presidents have been loquacious and discursive and appear as ductile on this subject as on some other subjects. Presidents of small denominational colleges naturally discuss and applaud Christian education as the aim of the higher learning. Presidents of small and sometimes large institutions that began and continued for a time under denominational inspiration and support, but later came to refer to themselves as independent while still admitting, perhaps, tenuous denominational control, are careful not to go back on the faith of the founding fathers. It is but natural also that presidents of state universities should talk and write considerably about the service of higher education to the commonwealth.

Mental and religious discipline was the primary purpose of higher education for many decades. This was the purpose when Barnard took over at Columbia in 1864. It was the purpose when Eliot took over at Harvard five years later. But, "Our new President," wrote Dr. Oliver Wendell Holmes in 1870, "has turned the whole University over like a flapjack. There never was such a bouleversement. . . ." The radical alteration of classical prescriptions for the Harvard degree showed that the aim of education, at least in the minds of the young Chemist-President and those whom he could persuade to his view, had now changed. Other colleges and then secondary schools fell in line—showing the imitativeness of higher education—and soon college students from Maine to California could nibble all over the catalogues.[6]

This theory of education held sway until, about three decades ago, college presidents and others discovered that some of the promises of the elective system were unfulfilled. The aims of higher education seemed to have become more and more vague. Soon the swing away from freedom of election to a measure of prescription showed also a shift in the aim or aims of higher

[6] "It is a hard saying, but Mr. Eliot, more than any other man, is responsible for the greatest educational crime of the century against American youth—depriving him of his classical heritage."—S. E. Morison, *Three Centuries of Harvard* (Cambrdge: Harvard University Press, 1936), pp. 389, 390.

education. College presidents began to ask, at least by implication, did not college students need acquaintance with "a common intellectual world" and opportunities to develop more social intelligence? Experimentation with the college curriculum was widely made, general and required courses in the social and the natural sciences were introduced, and there has been a tendency also to introduce such courses in the humanities. These practices and tendencies seem to show that higher educational leaders have not been so clear in recent years, nor are they now so clear, about the aims of education as they were a century or even seventy-five years ago. Confusion of aims—which run all the way from the "intellectualism" of President Robert M. Hutchins, of the University of Chicago, to the "holoism" of President W. H. Cowley, of Hamilton College—is a conspicuous fact of higher education, as of education at other levels in the United States.[7]

President Francis Wayland, of Brown University, wrote in 1842 that the purpose of higher education was not to "give away a modicum of Greek and Latin and Geometry to every one who chooses to ask for it, but to foster and cultivate the highest talent of the nation, and raise the intellectual character of the whole, by throwing the brightest light of science in the path of those whom nature has qualified to lead." This was substantially what Thomas Jefferson had said more than sixty years earlier and in some measure what President James B. Conant has said in the past few years.

The Weaknesses of Higher Education

Probably nothing in social history so reveals the aims of education as do criticisms of education. Purposes of education, at least in the minds of the critics, are implied in their criticisms.

---

[7] One comparatively recent writer has listed 1,581 social purposes of English; another has listed more than 300 aims of arithmetic in the first six grades. If confusion in educational aims reflects confusion in life aims, the American people—and American educational leaders—are befuddled. See H. L. Caswell and D. S. Campbell, *Curriculum Development* (New York: American Book Company, 1935), p. 119.

This principle in educational history finds illustration all the way from Aristophanes—who disliked the Sophists, praised the earlier manners of the Athenians when discipline prevailed and when there was "no babbling in the schools"; and Aristotle who poked fun at Hippodamus, town-planner and lecturer-at-large, because the latter favored the extension of education beyond the campus—to Hutchins, who thinks that the higher learning has no place for courses for beauticians or barbers.

President Philip Lindsley, of the University of Nashville, in 1837 pointed out some weaknesses of higher education. President Francis Wayland, of Brown University, said in 1842 that higher education in the United States "required material modification," and President James Walker, of Harvard, was very critical of the higher learning in 1853. President F. A. P. Barnard, of Columbia, in 1864 urged a return to "first principles." These criticisms appear throughout the entire history of higher education in this country. They may be heard and read nowadays as they were heard and read in this country in the seventeenth, the eighteenth, and the nineteenth centuries.

Since the onset of the depression, higher education has been severely criticized by college and university presidents. Some of them question whether the colleges are equipping their undergraduates so that "in after life they will be able to understand the world not in terms of the intellect alone but in terms of human emotions and human relations." They seem to agree also, that college graduates do not stay educated, because the colleges fail to educate them. The trouble, they seem to think, is not that alumni are dumb to begin with but become so in the process of the years. "This fatty degeneration of too many alumni goes back to a vice not yet eradicated from our college system." Undergraduates must submit to "forced feeding," and when their supervised diet stops, their education also stops, leaving them not self-supporting intellectually and culturally. It is charged that colleges give students bad habits of intellectual dependence which has seemed to increase with their years. Other criticisms relate to the absence of any "spiritual core" in the curriculum and the neglect of the humanities. A student may be graduated from a so-called college of arts without having "taken a single course in any of the arts, and be so ignorant of philosophy that he cannot tell you the difference in a problem in ethics and a hole in the ground." Apparently the interest of undergraduates in letters is keen, but it pertains mainly to sweaters. They may have learned all about advertising, but they whine when they lose in the stock market. As a group, American college alumni possess almost "no common ideal which differentiates them as a class from the rest of the population." So some of the higher educational leaders say.

The test of education, according to the presidents generally, is the "ability to deal with the unexpected, to meet disaster, and still get something out of life." In these criticisms the presidents exhibit little originality. When the promises of education appear to be unfulfilled, college and university presidents, as others, tend to criticize their own creations, to look upon their work and see that it is not good. It should be noted, however, that business men and publicists also complain of the deficiencies of education, and this fashion of criticism extends to higher educational leadership.

In his inaugural address in 1909, President A. Lawrence Lowell, of Harvard, said that "if we can increase the intellectual ambition of college students, the whole face of our country would be changed." The following year, President W. P. Few, of Trinity College (North Carolina), said that the increasing "importance that secondary concerns hold in the thoughts of undergraduates is more and more tending to obscure the true ends of a college course." These criticisms of the lack of intellectual interests among college students are old and typical.

Competition and Coöperation.—In competition and the need for coöperation, which have often been pointed to as weaknesses of higher education, appear presidential fears and hopes. The criticism is not new. It reaches back to President Josiah Quincy, who, in his inaugural at Harvard in 1829, warned higher educational institutions against yielding to temporary excitement and desire for popularity "in the hope of increasing their numbers." President F. A. P. Barnard, of the University of Mississippi, noted in 1856 that religious denominations divided "our people." The criticism of competition occupies a recent report of President Walter A. Jessup, of The Carnegie Foundation for the Advancement of Teaching, who was president of a great state university for eighteen years.[8] The criticism extends all the way from President Eliot, who opposed in the 1870's the proposal to establish a national university, to the latest opponents of federal aid to education. And the fear which Eliot reflected is not unlike that which is nowadays reflected when federal appropriations pour through the Works Progress Administration for buildings in higher educational institutions.[9]

It should be noted also that in almost every state, especially in earlier days, the efforts of denominational colleges to prevent legislative appropriations to state universities reflected the fiscal fears of college presidents.[10] The threat of taxation has been particularly disturbing. The veto of the governor of Connecticut alone kept Yale's athletic fields off the tax rolls. Many presidents are today "keenly worried" about the possibility of taxation on their endowments or properties. "We who are Protestants," wrote the author of "Prexy" in *Harper's Monthly Magazine* for January, 1938, "feel that the main hope we have of remaining tax free rests with our Catholic brethren; they do not wish to pay taxes on their collegiate property either, and bishops usually have more influence than presidents with governors and legislatures."

Competitive pressures have appeared in the discussions of the

---

[8] "College Competition and the Student," in the *Thirty-Second Annual Report*, The Carnegie Foundation for the Advancement of Teaching (New York, 1937), pp. 3-11.

[9] Eighty per cent of the colleges established in this country before 1860 died. Competition was among the causes of their suicides. See D. G. Tewksbury, *The Founding of American Colleges and Universities Before 1860* (New York: Bureau of Publications, Teachers College, Columbia University, 1932).

[10] For this contest in one state, see L. L. Gobbel, *Church-State Relations in Education in North Carolina Since 1776* (Durham, N. C.: Duke University Press, 1938), Chapters III and IV.

comparative merits of small and large institutions. In 1922 the department of public information of Columbia University announced that with more than 32,000 students it was "believed to be the largest institution in the world." The office of the president of the University of California promptly challenged the claim of Morningside Heights by claiming more than 43,000 students.[11] Institutional loyalties also may be seen in press releases on the number of alumni whose names appear in *Who's Who in America*, *American Men of Science*, and other books of biographical reference.

Organization and Administration

Apparently, most of the presidents see the college of arts as the heart of higher education. In the main, presidential definitions of a liberal education seem somewhat vague. But it is also apparent that the college is regarded as peculiar to American higher education. The college of arts is looked upon as "a school of culture," whose aim must be cultural rather than vocational. Some presidents also believe that the achievements of the liberal arts college should in the future surpass the achievements of its long past, if it can survive vocational competition, as may be seen from "Changes in Two Decades," the concluding part of Section IV.

Curriculum.—Statements concerning the curriculum throw light on the purposes of higher education, discussed in Section II above. The American College is a native institution in the sense that it is a European institution transplanted to this country in the seventeenth century. It soon became an accepted part of life in this country and is still taken for granted. Real changes in its way of life have come slowly. In aims and policies the colleges were very similar down to the middle of the nineteenth century—similar in the programs of study, in materials and methods, with a curriculum prescribed and fixed for all students without regard to their needs or abilities. Electives

[11] See "The Greatest on Earth," editorial in *The New York Times*, March 12, 1922.

were not widely known until Charles W. Eliot became president of Harvard. Until that time the classics dominated the curriculum and the college subjects were ends in themselves. The elective system gained widely under the influence of Harvard and Eliot.

Most of the writings of college presidents before 1869 dealt with the fixed curriculum and the doctrine of mental discipline, which was as fashionable in education as was that of original sin in theology. The religious and social philosophy that emerged in New England was long a powerful influence in determining college work from one end of the land to the other.[12] After 1869, as noted in the introduction to Section IV, the classics began to yield to the natural sciences, and more recently presidents have emphasized the importance of the social sciences and the need for giving students "social intelligence." The secular change that came in the latter part of the past century, the development of powerful business enterprises, the work of the psychological laboratory and the doctrine of individual differences, and other forces have been reflected in presidential statements concerning the materials of collegiate instruction.

Student Relations.—The kind of student college presidents see clearly reflects their philosophy of education. The findings of psychology and other influences have changed the views of presidents at this point. In the old days the energies of presidents and faculties were absorbed in making and enforcing rules. The colleges were patriarchal institutions, the life of the student was regimented, and each hour was covered by a rule. Presidents prayed in chapel "with one eye open" for trouble-makers. Discipline was difficult, parents were very troublesome, and in some of the smaller colleges a few students and a few "tuition fees might be the margin of financial solvency." And before the days of extra-curricular activities, mischief-making was about the only outlet for college youth who bore such a heavy burden of original sin. Theology, which made old-time college students

[12] Forty per cent of the college presidents in this country before 1860 were born in New England.

imps of the devil, made the tasks of presidents very different from their tasks today, even if modern psychology tends to make college students chemical episodes.

It appears, however, that college presidents are nowadays, more than in the past, raising searching questions about their students, are more concerned than formerly for their physical, mental, and spiritual welfare, are freer to encourage some student self-government, are coming more and more to look upon students as human beings, to respect their personalities, and to show concern about the product of their colleges. They seem to know better than formerly that the college is judged by its graduates, whether it is small or large, liberal or vocational, independent or state-supported, Christian or "pagan." This point of view is fortunate for American society.

The expanding work of colleges and universities has increased the interest of presidents in administrative machinery. The index to *The Later Years of Columbia College*, excerpts from the reports of President F. A. P. Barnard from 1864 to 1889, edited by Dean William F. Russell, of Teachers College, Columbia University, does not contain the word "administration." The index to a companion volume, *The University in Action*,[13] excerpts from the annual reports of President Nicholas Murray Butler from 1902 to 1935, edited by President Edward C. Elliott, of Purdue University, contains more than a score of references to various phases of higher educational administration, for which nearly fifty pages of the book are used.

It seems clear that emphasis upon the mechanics of organization and administration has become one of the most conspicuous features of higher education in the United States in recent years. The immense expansion of the activities of the higher learning and the extension of an ideal of democracy which seeks to educate everybody "from the gutter to the university" help to explain the immense administrative machine. The influence of big business also appears at this point—the colleges apparently have imitated the methods employed by captains of industry.

[13] Both volumes published by the Columbia University Press, 1937.

Here, again, the imitative character of education is evident. The mechanical practices of the factory and the counting house have come more and more to be those of the colleges. There is hope, however, that President Butler's quotation of the cynical definition of educational administration may impress itself upon presidents and deans: educational administration is "the doing excellently of things that should not be done at all."

Athletics.—Apparently there has been a larger presidential wordage on this than on almost any other single subject on which presidents have spoken and written. It has been dealt with in many thousands of words "by the best orators of the intercollegiate world." Intercollegiate football has attracted so much attention that it has come to be called "Dementia Americana."

President Eliot did not discuss athletics in his inaugural in 1869, but President Lowell, forty years later, got to the subject of "the overshadowing interest in athletic games," in the fourth paragraph of his inaugural, which was about half the length of Eliot's. President Barnard, of Columbia, and President Eliot, of Harvard, were the first to draw their blades on this dragon. Barnard, as early as 1888, believed that there should be "an absolute prohibition of intercollegiate games altogether." President Eliot deplored the unhealthy conditions in intercollegiate football, and by 1903 was pointing out numerous evils which have persisted in this sport until the present. Professionalism, gate receipts, expensive coaches, training tables, the purchase of players in the annual market, casuistry and hairsplitting, lack of faith among the colleges, the steady and subtle increase in dishonesty, covert methods employed by college officials, alumni, and trustees, and other alleged evils have been charged and counter-charged. Throughout the lengthy discussion of the most popular collegiate sport in the United States, college and university presidents have charged each other with hypocrisies and deceit. President G. Stanley Hall, of Clark University, in 1910 said that college and high school authorities and athletic committees had been "pedagogically both stupid and wasteful" in dealing with athletics.

It appears that the athletic ideals of college and university presidents, expressed in their speeches and writings, differ markedly from the athletic practices of the institutions over which they preside. This condition seems to prevail the country over. Apparently in no phase of higher education is more suspicion exhibited by brother college and university presidents than in intercollegiate athletics.[14]

Finance.—As noted in Section I, "Money! Money!! Money!!!" the fiscal problems of higher education, as seen by presidents, seem old and persistent.

Faculty Relations

Apparently, presidents are generally aware of the professional and fiscal problems of their professors and research workers, and try to relieve these colleagues from unnecessary demands upon their time and energies and to provide them with good working conditions, reasonably adequate compensation and security. At least these are among the concerns of the leading presidents.

Academic Freedom.—Prior to the publication of Darwin's theories, college presidents in the United States did not often have to comment on or defend academic freedom. The issue of freedom of teaching did not arise acutely so long as the collegiate curriculum was formal and lacking in liveliness and serious differences of opinion about it were few if not almost impossible. True, the issues of slavery and abolition had vexed the governing authorities of some educational institutions, with academic freedom not always carrying the right to advocate the abolition

---

[14] A remark by President Francis Wayland, of Brown University, seems to be in point here. Professor Alexis Caswell, of that institution, once had some difficulty with a student whose angry parent complained to President Wayland that Caswell had called the lad a liar. President Wayland said to the indignant father: "Dr. Caswell is universally known to be a man of imperturbable good nature. He never told your son he was a liar. He did tell your son that he found great difficulty in believing what he said."

of slavery.[15] Three members of the faculty of Western Reserve College were forced to resign because of their views on abolition. Professor B. S. Hedrick, of the University of North Carolina, was dismissed from that institution in 1856 because he favored Frémont for President of the United States, and President David L. Swain did not stand up for the professor. Gag rules were applied against anti-slavery societies at Miami University in Ohio, at Illinois College, Kenyon College in Ohio, and Phillips Exeter Academy. Henry P. Tappan was dismissed from New York University along with seven other men, but the charge was that of signing a statement of lack of confidence in the administration. Tappan was later dismissed from the presidency of the University of Michigan, where he was accused of Prussianizing education in that state. President E. Benjamin Andrews of Brown University in the late 1890's left that institution because of his views on the free coinage of silver. Twenty-five of his colleagues protested to the Brown Corporation and asserted that "The life blood of a University is not money, but freedom." A general memorial to the Corporation was signed by some college presidents including President Gilman, of the Johns Hopkins University, and President Eliot of Harvard.

Presidents of small denominational colleges have not often pronounced upon the subject. It has been discussed more fully by presidents of state and large independent universities. Freedom of teaching they generally endorse, but they urge on the other hand academic obligation on the members of the faculty

---

[15] It appears that the center of intellectual (or emotional) gravity has shifted, during the past several centuries, from theology, then to politics, then to science (versus theology), and then to economics, or theories of economics, centers in which are to be found the most deep-seated interests of human beings. Socrates, who died in 399 B.C., was the first victim in the issue of freedom of teaching. In this country Henry Dunster was the first victim. When this head of Harvard went antipaedobaptist in 1654 his neighborhood was as dismayed as Cambridge would be today if President Conant should invite Hitler or Stalin to come to Harvard, give the commencement address, and receive an honorary degree. Dunster could have remained president of Harvard if he had remained quiet on controversial issues. Professor Samuel E. Morison, the official historian of Harvard, describes Dunster as "one of the greatest" of a long line of the presidents of that institution.

who, when they speak or write, do so not alone in their own name—what they say or write has meaning in part because of the prestige of the college or university to which they belong. The presidents would doubtless all question the acrid statement that: "academic freedom means freedom to say what you think without thinking what you say." In the main, presidential pronouncements on academic freedom make clear the reciprocal nature of the academic obligation. If a professor grossly violates his part of the obligation he may not be dismissed, but his position can be declared vacant. This method has often been resorted to by authorities governing higher education. Presidents say that when they wish their institutions to work for the good of their supporting constituencies, "we are bound to consider their characteristics and not arouse their prejudices unnecessarily, else they won't let us work for them."

Research.—President Cornelius Conway Felton, of Harvard, said in his inaugural in 1860 that it was the "duty of professors to add to the literature and science of their respective departments" and that the university failing to do so failed "in an essential portion of its proper business." Since 1876, when the Johns Hopkins University was opened, presidents of state and the larger independent universities have increasingly called attention to research—"that blessed word"—which is so often "used to reduce everyone to silence, acquiescence and appropriation," as President Nicholas Murray Butler, of Columbia University, said in his report for 1924-25.

Presidents generally think that research is important, but the heads of the small and denominational colleges rarely discuss it. They tend to emphasize teaching. Presidents of universities, especially the larger institutions, say that the spirit of inquiry distinguishes "the true university" and should be encouraged and supported. But even the most energetic advocates of research among these presidents say that in many instances "research is research in name only," that much of it is of little value, and that capacity for genuine research is rare among men and women. President Butler has stated that between 75 and 90 per cent "of what is called research" is not research and that "not many persons in any one generation are capable of real research." In recent years there has been increasing criticism of the vocational atmosphere of the Ph.D. degree, which is now in mass production.[16] The effect which the highly vocationalized system of graduate work in the United States may have on the teaching of undergraduates seems to be causing some of the presidents concern. This problem has caused considerable discussion of methods of teaching. On the value of the lecture method there is division of opinion among the presidents, who have written and spoken far more on athletics, however, than on the improvement of instruction or the welfare of students. Research, on the proper pronunciation of which there is not agreement, does seem to lend itself to loquacity and discursiveness. Not all presidents have been productive scholars. Those who have had a flair for research have been irked by administration—as was President David Starr Jordan, of Leland Stanford Junior University, who is reported to have complained that every time he learned the name of a student he forgot the name of a fish.

Obligations to Society

Judged by what they say, the presidents reveal awareness of the difficult problems and opportunities in the society of which their institutions are parts. For colleges are not isolated phenomena but in reality are important parts of the society in which they move and live and have their being. They tend to reflect rather faithfully the conditions about them. Many of the presidents seem to take interest in the public questions of the day, but the ideals and standards of judgment of higher educational leaders are often those that are found in society at large,[17] al-

[16] About three thousand Ph.D's. annually. Professor William James, of Harvard, as early as 1903 protested against "the Ph.D. Octopus," in an article under that title in the *Harvard Monthly* for March of that year. This article was reprinted in the *Educational Review* for February, 1918. Notwithstanding its large facilities for research, the United States ranks fourth in Nobel Awards, although its relative position has greatly improved during the past decade.

[17] As noted elsewhere, it appears that presidents have talked and written more

though, as President A. Lawrence Lowell said in his inaugural address at Harvard in 1909, an important responsibility of higher education is "to counteract rather than copy the defects of the civilization today." But presidents are as other human beings, and the statements of some of them on some subjects lend emphasis to Mr. Dooley's remark that "th' Supreme Coort follows th' iliction returns."

The Lower Schools.—As early as 1842 President Francis Wayland, of Brown University, noted the obligation of the colleges and universities for "the intellectual cultivation of the community." It appears that most higher educational officers have all along recognized this obligation. Their concern, for example, for the improvement of the "lower schools" apparently has been very keen. Leaders in the East and West early lent their efforts to stimulate interest in the development of secondary schools, especially after the decision in the Kalamazoo Case in 1874, which established the right of the state or local community to levy taxes for the support of public high schools. College and university presidents were quick to see the increased demand among the people for the upward extension of public education. When, after the turn of the century, interest in public high schools gained in the Southern States, where private academies had so long flourished, higher educational officers in that section of the country used arguments similar to those which college presidents had earlier used in the East and West.

The Education of Women.—The position of the presidents of colleges for men on the higher education of women may be seen in the quotations under this section. President F. A. P. Barnard, of Columbia, was among its earliest and most vigorous supporters. In general, public opinion, long aided by theology, opposed such an opportunity, and courageous were the few pres-

about athletics than any other subject. Charles R. Foster, Jr., in his *Editorial Treatment of Education in the American Press* (Cambridge: Harvard University Press, 1938), shows that "King Football" ranked in the high frequency of editorial comment in twenty-five carefully selected and representative newspapers of the United States, next to the vague general value of education, which had first place. The study covered the period of 1930-1935.

idents who stood up for the women. When, about 1900, the cause won wide enough public approval the issue was pronounced dead, and nowadays it does not occupy the attention of presidents in their speeches and reports.

The Education of the Negro.—Here, again, is an example of the slow growth of favorable opinion on a vexed question. As the Southern people got further and further away from the Civil War (or "War Between the States") and the tragedy of reconstruction, and as race prejudice grew less intense and bitter, educational leaders in the Southern States were able more safely and wisely to discuss the problem of the education of their brothers in black. The attitude of these leaders was much more wholesome after than before 1900. By that time the political status of the Negro had undergone radical changes, and the tendency to stir up the fires of racial antipathies was less strong than formerly.

This tendency did not disappear suddenly, of course. One of the most notable cases involving academic freedom in the South was that of Professor John Spencer Bassett, of Trinity College in North Carolina in 1903. A North Carolinian and a distinguished historian, Bassett published in October of that year an article in *The South Atlantic Quarterly*, in which he praised Booker T. Washington. In the same issue of the magazine appeared an article by President John C. Kilgo, of Trinity College, on "Our Duty to the Negro." This was the first issue of the *Quarterly* in which the race issue was discussed. Bassett's article caused a storm of protest, and demands for his resignation came from many people in high position and from most of the press of the state. Bassett resigned, but Kilgo and all the members of the faculty stood by; and when the trustees came to hear the case—and to vote eighteen to seven not to accept Bassett's resignation—Kilgo, who made a powerful plea for academic freedom, had in his pocket his own resignation and that of each member of his faculty, to be submitted if Bassett's resignation had been accepted. It is probable that a decade earlier the case would have turned out differently; and it is also highly probable that such an article today would pass without such cries of prejudice as the piece in 1903 drew from so many quarters.[18]

The World War.—The necessity for military training seems to have impressed most presidents after the outbreak of the World War, and particularly after the United States entered that conflict, as the quotations in Section VI indicate. Most of the presidents looked upon it as a duty to use their institutions in training for leadership in the national defense and to coöperate as fully as possible with the government. Preparation to defend the country was viewed as an important part in training for citizenship. The struggle was viewed as a contest between democracy and autocracy, and students were urged to serve their country in the cause of freedom. Generally, the Students' Army Training Corps was welcome. Some presidents viewed the emergency as an aid to the promotion of interest in applied science. The close relations of the colleges and universities with the national government were looked upon as "beneficial and worthy of continuance in some form."

Adult Education.—Interest in adult education, as an organized activity, did not begin to develop until about two decades ago. With the organization of the American Association for Adult Education, the publication of *The Journal of Adult Education* by that organization, and the publication of scientific evidence that adults can go on learning, college presidents, like others, began to discuss problems in this educational area. As early as 1924 President Nicholas Murray Butler, of Columbia University, said that adult education was suffering from "lack of organization, from imperfect administration, and from no emphasis at all." Later, however, higher educational leaders began to look more favorably upon adult education, "as both an invitation and a warning," as some of them had viewed "extension" services of higher education earlier. In recent years presidents of

[18] The position of educational leaders in some of the Southern States on the decision of the United States Supreme Court in the Missouri Case, decided in December, 1938, in the matter of professional and graduate work for Negroes, shows the change in attitude on a matter that has long vexed Southern educational leadership.

state universities have come to view "the boundaries of our respective states as the limits of the university campus."

Federal Relations.—The fears and hopes of competition and cooperation, noted in Section III, have been reflected among college presidents since 1856 when President Buchanan vetoed the bill sponsored by Representative Justin P. Morrill, of Vermont, to aid education in agriculture and the mechanic arts—the first real threat to the monopoly so long held by the private institutions. The bill signed by President Lincoln became the Morrill Act of 1862. But its operation and effect were feared by many college presidents, as many now fear the effect of federal aid to general education and the intrusion of the federal government into the educational jurisdiction of the states.

Commencement Addresses.—In the commencement addresses of college and university presidents is also reflected the temper of the times. As the World War approached, for example, and the United States finally made up its mind to enter it, the speeches and reports of presidents naturally swayed in the direction of war. One president said in a commencement address in 1918, that "when poison gas and shrapnel take the place of sweetness and light, the chief end of men who would glorify God is to kill Germans—and no explanatory footnotes required."

With the onset of the depression, commencement addresses differed markedly from those given in the fair weather days of the 1920's. If no real issue divides the people or no obvious emergency calls for timely utterances, full protest by commencement speakers against crime and corruption generally, and the monopoly of mediocrity in high places, is always good form; it lends itself admirably to ringing presidential periods. If there is threat to democracy, as in recent years and now, totalitarianism and authoritarianism come in for discussion and attack. Presidential oratory at commencement time seems likely to pass in the popular channel. Here, also, does higher education seem to reflect life about it.

What Do They Say?—It seems natural that college and university presidents should not needlessly offend public sentiment.

They do not generally do or say things or encourage the doing or saying of things that "may disturb the harmonious intercourse of those who support, and those who direct and govern" their institutions. But, it is doubtful if any "guild" in the United States is more likely to be misunderstood than the "guild" of college and university presidents, largely because they are forced to talk on so many subjects and now and then perhaps—contrary to the advice they would give their professors—on subjects which they are not always competent to discuss. This necessity tends to make some of them appear to be political "fence-sitters."

Resentment of interference by the many "partners" in higher education—which is one of the "main industries" of the United States—extends all the way from President Philip Lindsley, of the University of Nashville, with only a handful of boys, nearly a century ago, to "Neilson of Smith," with "two thousand daughters," only yesterday.[19] Lindsley said in a commencement address in 1848 that parents seemed to think that their sons were "high-minded, honorable, brave, generous, goodhearted young gentlemen" and the faculty "bigots, charlatans—without feeling, spirit, kindness, honesty, or common sense." In 1937 President Neilson was quoted in the press of New York City as saying that, looking back over two decades of the presidency of Smith College, faculty, students, trustees, and alumnae seemed to show improvement. Only parents did not progress, thus interfering with much that the college tried to do.

Many presidents have been and some are today the first citizens of their states or localities. Most of them seem to like their responsibilities, although now and then they may get discouraged. There may be point to the story of the two presidents who were discussing what they would do if they had opportunity to live their lives over. "I'd prefer the superintendency of an orphanage to a college presidency—no letters from parents," said

[19] President William Allan Neilson, of Smith College, who once recommended a "Be-Kind-to-College-Presidents Week."

one. "I'd prefer to be warden of a penitentiary—the alumni rarely return," said the other.

The influence of one man or one institution on broad educational policies, changes, or movements, is difficult to show, as President Frederick T. Keppel, of Carnegie Corporation of New York, has pointed out so well.[20] Reforms in education generally appear as the results of the combined labors of many people. Apparently, the educational influence of a college or university president cannot be separated from the work and influence of his associates. But most of the presidents generally appear true to conscience and commonwealth, some have been unafraid of their minds, and some have shown a quiet willingness to be forgotten. Yet, apparently, many of them say what they are expected to say by their supporting constituencies. When they insist on saying what they are not expected to say they are soon not allowed to say anything. To say that most of them keep their ears to the ground is no more a condemnation of college and university presidents than of publicists, bankers, realtors, legislative leaders or other public servants. Presidents, as other leaders, seem to believe with Falstaff that discretion is the better part of valor, and with St. Paul that the things which may be lawful are not always expedient.

---

[20] "President Lowell and His Influence," *The Atlantic Monthly*, June, 1933, pp. 753-763.

INDEX

INDEX